TWENTIETH CENTURY VIEWS

The aim of this series is to present the best in contemporary critical opinion on major authors, providing a twentieth century perspective on their changing status in an era of profound revaluation.

Maynard Mack, *Series Editor*
Yale University

ROBERT PENN WARREN

ROBERT PENN WARREN

A COLLECTION OF CRITICAL ESSAYS

Edited by
Richard Gray

Prentice-Hall, Inc. A SPECTRUM BOOK *Englewood Cliffs, N.J.*

Library of Congress Cataloging in Publication Data
Main entry under title:

Robert Penn Warren, a collection of critical essays.

(Twentieth century views) (A Spectrum Book)
Bibliography: p.
  1. Warren, Robert Penn, 1905-   — Criticism and
interpretation — Addresses, essays, lectures. I. Gray,
Richard J.
PS3545.A748Z86 1980   813'.5'2   79-23295
ISBN   0-13-781914-5 case.
ISBN   0-13-781906-4 pbk.

Editorial/production supervision by Betty Neville
Cover design by Stanley Wyatt
Manufacturing buyers: Cathie Lenard, Barbara A. Frick

10   9   8   7   6   5   4   3   2   1

PRENTICE-HALL INTERNATIONAL, INC. *(London)*
PRENTICE-HALL OF AUSTRALIA PTY. LIMITED *(Sydney)*
PRENTICE-HALL OF CANADA, LTD. *(Toronto)*
PRENTICE-HALL OF INDIA PRIVATE LIMITED *(New Delhi)*
PRENTICE-HALL OF JAPAN, INC. *(Tokyo)*
PRENTICE-HALL OF SOUTHEAST ASIA PTE. LTD. *(Singapore)*
WHITEHALL BOOKS LIMITED *(Wellington, New Zealand)*

Contents

Acknowledgments

Grateful acknowledgment is made to Random House, Inc., Harcourt Brace Jovanovich, Inc., Harvard University Press, and Martin Secker & Warburg Limited to quote from the copyrighted works of Robert Penn Warren.

The quotation from Malcolm Cowley, editor, *Writers at Work:* The Paris Review *Interviews* is used by kind permission of The Viking Press.

The excerpt on page 76 from Leslie A. Fiedler's *Love and Death in the American Novel* is reprinted with permission of Stein and Day Publishers. Copyright © 1966, 1960 by Leslie A. Fiedler.

ROBERT PENN WARREN

Introduction

by Richard Gray

I

Robert Penn Warren has yet to be given the recognition he deserves. Much has been written about him, and he has received his fair share of awards; yet despite this acclaim there seems to be a reluctance, in critical and academic circles and (to a lesser extent) among the public at large, to see him for what he is, a writer—not specifically a poet or a novelist, but a *writer*—of major stature. One reason for this is perhaps obvious: Warren is extremely difficult to categorize or pin down, because his achievement is so various. He is, after all, one of the founders of an international school of criticism, an eminent teacher, and a commentator on national affairs, as well as a poet, novelist, and poetic dramatist. Faced with this variety, with a man whose apparently inexhaustible energy has led him to produce important work in so many different fields, critics have been tempted either to ignore some of those fields or to suggest that his work as a whole is not of the first rank. As we are told only too often, ours is an age of specialization, when success seems to depend on certain deliberate acts of exclusion; and in such an age many people, perhaps invariably, find it difficult to believe that one man can do so much so consistently—and so well. Surely, as several unsympathetic commentators have suggested, the fact that Warren is a critic must have some kind of adverse effect upon his creative work. Does not his interest in public affairs, past and present, draw his attention away from the plight of the isolated individual consciousness and its search for what Warren once called "the unsleeping principle of delight"? And is not his commitment to the kind of historical specificity and social density that is the special preserve of the novel at odds with the notion, articulated in his later verse, that "all Time is a dream, and we're all one Flesh, at last"?

The only feasible response to these kinds of doubts and queries is simple. Warren, it must be insisted, is one of the few living American writers to whom the terms "man of letters" and "man of principle" can be applied without embarrassment—and without the related sense that there is something pejorative, some trace of criticism, implicit in those phrases. He believes in literature and the power of the word; to be more exact, he obviously feels that language can be used in different ways and in various fields of activity to investigate life, explore basic values, and finally discover what he has called in a recent essay, "the special fullness of the relation of a self to the world." While many contemporary novelists have turned from criticism of experience to analysis of their own art; while many poets have rejected the public world and attempted to create their own private space; and while many writers, generally, have been busy erecting fences between fiction and fact, ideas and events, the signifier and the signified, Warren has been attempting steadily to reassert the principle that a person's work is the expression of his or her entire consciousness. To quote from one of his discussions of the subject, his writing as a whole bears eloquent testimony to his belief that the "made thing," the written word, can at its best embody

> the experience of a self vis-à-vis the world, not merely as a subject, but as translated into the experience of form. The form represents uniqueness made available to others, but the strange fact is that the uniqueness is not to be exhausted. ... The "made thing," the "formed thing," stands as a perennial possibility of experience, available whenever we turn to it.[1]

The recognition of responsibility, an acceptance of human fallibility, and above all a realization that the personality is complex and finds—indeed creates—itself through a continuing relationship with others—these are the beliefs underlying all of his writing. They help to explain why Warren has tried so many different fields of endeavor: because, as he sees it, only in this way can every aspect of his identity and his place in the human fabric be articulated. And they help also to suggest why he has performed so consistently in each: because, to put it simply, he is concerned with essentially the same things (that is, with what the narrator of *A Place to Come To* calls "the kind of idea that touches life at the root") whatever he happens to be doing.

   Warren is capable, then, of astonishing depth in quite disparate fields; the principles he embraces actively encourage an interdisciplinary approach, since they lead him to view the individual disciplines as alternative routes to the same place—different ways of understanding what one of his poems terms "the human filth, the human hope." The differences are emphasized, certainly, since it is these that make for individual identity or particular aspects of an identity, but threading his various activities together is his habitual concern with man seen—to quote from his poetry again—"in the light of humanness, and under the shadow of God's closing hand." What emerges from this light and shadow, though? What, as Warren describes it in his work, is the nature of "human filth" and provides the sources of "human hope"? And how, in detail, does he find "a way by which the process of living can become Truth"—a means, that is, whereby the experiencing and documenting of facts can be metamorphosed into a dis-

---

[1]Robert Penn Warren, *Democracy and Poetry* (Cambridge, Mass.: Harvard University Press, 1975), p. 72.

covery of values? Obviously, these are difficult questions to answer; indeed, the only wholly satisfactory way of answering them is to look at the entire body of Warren's writing, since his ideas spring directly and rightly out of his imaginative engagement with the world and are, in a sense, inseparable from it. But it may be that the hint of an answer can be provided here. Some suggestion can perhaps be offered of the complex and frequently paradoxical themes that underpin all of his books—this being one means of mediating between those books and the reader.

II

It might be useful to begin a summary of some of Warren's more recurrent preoccupations with his own words. Consider, for example, the following two passages, one from his critical essays, the other from his recently re-written version of *Brother to Dragons:*

> Wisdom...is the recognition of...the necessity of living with the ever re-newing dilemma of idea as opposed to nature, morality to action...justice to material interests. Man must make his life somewhere in the dialectical process of these terms, and...achieve redemption...through an awareness of his condition that identifies him with the general human communion....[2]

> JEFFERSON: I think I know what you would say to me.
> One day I wrote to Adams,...
> ....
> I wrote, and said
> That the dream of the future is better than the
> dream of the past.
>
> Now could I find hope to find courage to say
> That without the fact of the past, no matter how terrible,
> We cannot dream the future?[3]

At basis, as both of these passages suggest, Warren believes in the reality of evil. An "adequate definition of terror" and of pain is necessary because, as Willie Stark argues in *All the King's Men,* man is "conceived in sin and born in corruption." Nobody can escape this fact; everyone must recognize and come to terms with it; and one of the best ways of recognizing it, clearly, is to dwell upon the past and foster the historical sense. "History," says Warren in one of his later poems, "is what you can't/ Resign from"; nor should you try, since what the "dream of the past" can help develop, above all, is a

---

[2]"'The Great Mirage': Conrad and *Nostromo*," in *Selected Essays* (New York: Pub. Random House, 1958), p. 54.

[3]The rewritten version of *Brother to Dragons: A Tale in Verse and Voices* is to be published by Random House in 1979. I wish to thank Mr. Warren for permitting me to see a copy of the typescript.

healthy awareness of human limits—a sense of the sheer "massiveness of experience" bearing down upon the human personality and drastically circumscribing its capacity for action. Looking at what has gone before, man can learn from his mistakes and also begin to understand the nature of that fallible human community to which, whether he likes it or not, he belongs.

That is not the entire story, however; as Warren indicates in the lines from *Brother to Dragons*, there is the dream of the future as well as the dream of the past. "Of the brute creation" man may be, but he is also, in potential at least, only "a little lower than the angels"; consequently, while he certainly requires an adequate definition of terror to remind him of his monstrous origins, he needs at the same time to find some way of "accommodating flesh to idea," so as "to be able to frame a definition of joy." It is not difficult to see that behind statements such as these (all culled from his poems and essays) lies the firm conviction that neither the actual nor the potential is an absolute; both are partners, however unwilling, in a kind of marriage, the offspring of which is truth. Values, according to Warren, are created by people out of the actual experience of living and, even as they develop, qualify and enrich that experience. The process is an essentially dialectical one; and there is no end to it and so no end to the growth and discovery of the self other than that offered to each of us individually by death.

By implication, at least, two very different kinds of people are being criticized here: the idealists, who, in the name of their ideals, reject or ignore actual experience; and those who are often referred to, significantly enough, as realists—the positivists, that is, the materialists and behaviorists who cling to the given facts and deny the human need for meaning. The first are perhaps the more familiar to Warren's readers, if only because they are the more noticeable, particularly in his fiction. Indeed, lovers of the abstract abound in Warren's work—from the fanatical John Brown, who "had no scruple at deception" because for him, "the end justified the means," to Cy Grinder in *Meet Me in the Green Glen*, who feels that he cannot marry the girl he loves until, by virtue of a process of rigorous preparation, he has become "an untarnished Adam walking the new earth." But, for all that, those who sacrifice moral principle to material interests are no less common and symptomatic of the writer's concerns and, in fact, include some of his finest creations: among them, Bogan Murdock in *At Heaven's Gate*, Willie Stark in *All the King's Men*, and Murray Guilfort in *Meet Me in the Green Glen*. Products of what Warren, in a famous phrase, once called "the terrible division of their age," they are no less hollow—without guiding principles and, therefore, no less deficient in their creator's eyes—than those who live in the ice cold world of ideas.

Having said this, though, two qualifications are immediately necessary.

Warren's beliefs commit him to specificity, or what Ezra Pound christened ideas in action. At the same time, he sees the world as continuous, the past engaged with the present, the public world interlocked with the private, so that each man or woman will find his or her own personal dilemmas repeated, written in a larger hand, in history. The qualifications imply a paradox of the kind familiar to us from Aristotle's *Poetics.* Warren insists in his books on the particularity of particular cases, for which the terms *idealist* and *materialist* can only act as crude equivalents; but he also argues for their potential universality, since, as he sees it, the growth of the individual self, for good or ill, is integrally related to and eventually imaged in the growth of society. As far as the second point is concerned, this means, among other things, that he can envision entire cultures taking refuge in abstractions or a mindless devotion to the world of objects and use just as so many of his characters do. This is one of the points he makes or, rather, it is one of the assumptions he builds upon in *The Legacy of the Civil War.* Here he suggests, not without reason, that the Old South sought refuge in a narrow legalism which conveniently protected it from the pressures toward change, whereas the North, convinced of the absolute rightness of its cause, simply tried to impose its ideals, its own notion of the "higher law," without acknowledging the presence of possible impediments. The South saw only the past, the "world's stew," and the consequent need for caution. The North perceived little besides the future, the glowing promise of which seemed to justify anything it might do. And the result of *this* terrible division was as fatal as the conflict described in *All the King's Men* between Willie Stark and Adam Stanton, and as poignant, in its own way, as the contrast offered in the poem "Two Studies in Idealism: Short Survey of American and Human History" between a Confederate veteran and a raw, young, Harvard-educated recruit.[4]

Warren's reading of history does not stop here, of course; there is, beyond this, his perception of the present state of things. And here he is, with whatever qualifications, pessimistic. Certainly, he does not discount the continuing possibility of *personal* fulfillment; it is, after all, the very existence of this possibility that irradiates his later poems. Nor does he deny that progress has been made in certain areas. This is particularly true of the area of race relations, where, as Warren sees it, there has been some attempt made to create a "context for possible solution" out of a simultaneous recognition of what should be and what can be done. But there is no getting away from the fact that, in Warren's view, as in that of so many contemporary artists, our world is given over to the forces of disorder. Fulfillment, the realization of the individual self, has been made that much more difficult because divorce and division are the signs of our times. There is little sense

[4]For a fuller discussion of this and related points, see the essay by William C. Havard included in this volume.

of the past left and therefore little sense of a significant future (since, as Jack Burden puts it in *All the King's Men*, "only out of the past can you make the future"); little feeling for the community and therefore hardly any aware- ness of personal identity (since, in the words of one minor character in *Flood*, "there is no you except in relation to all that unthinkableness the world is"). The problem is stated as baldly and brutally as it can be by one of the characters in Warren's most recent novel, *A Place to Come To:*

> We are...feeling the first pangs of modernity...the death of the self which has become placeless. We are to become enormously efficient and emotion- less mechanisms, that will know—if "know" is not too old-fashioned a word to use in this context—how to breed even more efficient and emotionless mechanisms.[5]

The person speaking here is one Stephan Mostoski, an *emigré* Polish Jew who fought against (and *against* is the operative word) both Russians and Germans during the Second World War. In effect, he has very particu- lar reasons for saying what he does. He has witnessed certain things and participated in events which have turned the concept of anonymity into a *belief* felt upon the pulses by him—and now, in a different way, by us. This leads us back to the second qualification it is always necessary to make when discussing Warren's ideas: that both his idealists and his materialists are placed firmly in experience, actual or imaginative, seen as thwarted in- dividuals rather than illustrations of a point. For example, among those who could be described as idealists are political fanatics like Professor Ball in *Night Rider* and Percival Skrogg in *World Enough and Time*, a reli- gious visionary like Ashby Wyndham in *At Heaven's Gate*, romantic dreamers like Adam Rosenzweig in *Wilderness*, and those driven by some purely erotic illusion such as Nick Pappy in *The Cave* and Leroy Lan- caster in *Meet Me in the Green Glen*. Alternatively, and more subtly, Warren's investigations of the idealistic impulse can include a character like Yasha Jones in *Flood*, who is not an idealist in the conventional—and rather limited—sense of the word at all. Jones, a film director, has retreated into what Warren calls at one point in the novel the "joy of abstraction" and into the protection from ordinary human relationships provided by his job in the Hollywood dream factory. He has, in a sense, stopped living, taking risks with other people, and turned himself into a permanent ob- server. This is also true, with a difference, of Brad Tolliver, the protagonist of the novel, and at least two of Warren's other protagonists, Jack Burden in *All the King's Men* and Jed Tewksbury in *A Place to Come To*. Unwilling or unable to participate fully in life, and feeling (as Yasha Jones does) out- side even their own experience, they find their particular refuge from the challenge of the real in a mask of cynicism, calculated indifference to the claims of others, and a "tough guy" version of self-mockery.

[5] *A Place to Come To* (London: Secker and Warburg, 1977), p. 348.

The feeling that Warren is allowing the idea to grow out of the situation rather than vice versa is also generally aroused by his portraits of those caught up in the muck and mire of things. Such characters can range from embodiments of pure appetite like the "Gran Boz" in *World Enough and Time*, through opportunists like Senator Tolliver in *Night Rider* and, less seriously, Miss Idell in *Band of Angels*, to philosophical nihilists such as the Emperor Tiberius in Warren's poem "Tiberius in Capri," who finds a justification for his own languid sensuality in the message the ocean sings to him:

> *All is nothing, nothing all.*

At this point, the betrayed dreamer and the materialist meet, yearning for each other, as Warren puts it in *All the King's Men*, because each is instinctively aware of his own futility and incompleteness. Not that such awareness is invariably just a matter of instinct: beyond this particular point, in a sense, lie the people who know only too clearly what they have lost by becoming a part of the "ruined world"—a group that includes the narrators of many of Warren's later poems. The speaker in "To a Little Girl, One Year Old, in a Ruined Fortress," for example, suffers painfully and quite self-consciously from his imprisonment within the naturalistic vision, feeling overwhelmed by the signs of decay around him while wishing, without much genuine hope, that he could participate in his daughter's joy. His sense of having fallen from some airier region of possibility is beautifully caught in the closing lines of an earlier poem, "Picnic Remembered," where Warren uses an image recurring throughout his work to describe lost innocence and vanished dreams:

> Or is the soul a hawk that, fled
> On glimmering wings past vision's path,
> Reflects the last gleam to us here
> Though sun is sunk and darkness near
> —Uncharted Truth's high heliograph?[6]

The lines from "Picnic Remembered" should provide a reminder that so far only Warren's exploration of the negative side of things has been considered. Truth, Warren implies here, may be difficult of access but it still exists, even if on the other side of the horizon; the hawk may have fled, but it could return. Most obviously, this is suggested in Warren's creative work by the presence of characters who provide what he has called "'models' of selfhood"—who seem to be complete with a completeness that springs (to borrow a phrase from *A Place to Come To*) from "their willed and full embracement of the process of their life in time." These include Willie Proudfit in *Night Rider*, who, as a result of a kind of mystical experience, comes to

[6]*Selected Poems: 1923-1975* (New York: Random House; London: Martin Secker & Warburg Limited, 1976), p. 311.

recognize his involvement in the human community; Mr. Calhoun in *At Heaven's Gate,* whose clumsiness is an outward and visible sign of his flawed humanity and humility; and Judge Irwin in *All the King's Men* together with Colonel Fort in *World Enough and Time,* two men of principle who try to do what good they can, in public and private life, while recognizing their essential limitations. There is also Mr. Starr, in *Band of Angels,* whose crimes against his daughter are inseparable from his affection for her; Aaron Blaustein in *Wilderness,* a rich family friend of the protagonist, who tells him, "the hardest thing to remember is that other men are men. ... But that is the only way you can be a man yourself"; and Blanding Cottshill, a small-town lawyer and farmer in *Flood,* who is convinced that "things are tied together" in some mysterious way, that "there's some spooky interpenetration of things." The trouble with such characters, of course, is that they can seem just a little too complete, too perfect in their very acceptance of their own imperfection. However dramatic the story of their past may be, they can sometimes sound just a little too much like models, convenient emblems of the Good Life, offering at best a measure of the distance the hero or heroine still has to travel.

The really effective counterbalance to Warren's vision of evil lies not here, in fact, in these rather allegorical figures, but in the struggle experienced by his protagonists, and in many of the poems by Warren himself, as they try to find a measure of fulfillment—some

> process whereby pain of the past in its pastness
> May be converted into the future tense
>
> Of joy.[7]

To use Warren's own critical terms, it is not the "'models' of selfhood" but the "adventure in selfhood," represented in the total dramatic structure of the poem or story, that offers us a really convincing sense of possibility. Two types of dramatic structure, two patterns that recur throughout Warren's writing, help, in particular, to illustrate this. In terms of their mythological origins, the two are ultimately inseparable, and when Warren uses them they often tend to merge into each other. They should perhaps be discussed separately here, however, since the relative degree of emphasis given to each does vary from work to work, and each carries with it its own separate configuration of imagery. According to one pattern, explored more fully by Robert Berner in his essay in this volume, the protagonist's journey toward fulfillment is charted principally in terms of his relationship to his father, or a father figure. The action begins with the hero unable to achieve a clear understanding of himself, and this is symbolized by his rejection of his father. The father rejected, disorder and a sense of inner

---

[7]"I Am Dreaming of a White Christmas: The Natural History of a Vision," in *Selected Poems,* p. 34.

division inevitably follow; and the hero, confused and placeless, may seek refuge in another father figure, someone who inevitably turns out to be hollow and fails his would-be disciple. Alternatively, he may try to escape into some patently unreal world, a false notion of peace. Whatever he does, though, he attains self-knowledge only when he returns to his father and the childhood home, because only in doing this does he achieve a reconciliation with his historical and spiritual roots and so discover what Warren, in his essay on *The Rime of the Ancient Mariner*, calls "the chain of love which binds human society and the universe." Seeing his father properly, probably for the first time, the hero begins to see himself; accepting and embracing him, warts and all, he begins to accept his own limitations and embrace the human community. At once a profoundly personal experience and a universal one, this pattern of return and rediscovery is memorably described in the closing section of "The Ballad of Billie Potts," where it is seen as something shared by all creation:

> The salmon heaves at the fall, and, wanderer, you
> Heave at the great fall of Time...
> ....
> Brother to pinion and the pious fin that cleave
> Their innocence of air and the disinfectant flood
> And wing and welter and weave
> The long compulsion and the circuit hope
> Back,
> And bear through that limitless and devouring fluidity
> The itch and humble promise which is home
>
> And the father waits for the son.[8]

Closely related to this vision of a place where the father waits for the son is Warren's own special version of the Fall and Redemption, the second pattern running through so much of his work. Of course, Warren is not a Christian. But he has absorbed many of the prevailing assumptions of Christianity. So it is not really surprising that he turns to the Bible and to religious myth quite frequently to supply him with an appropriate language. What he offers, in essence, is a *humanist* version of Christian legend comparable to, say, William Faulkner's in *A Fable;* and its basic outlines, at least as far as his notions of sin and salvation are concerned, can be summarized fairly quickly. Man, according to Warren, begins like Adam, enjoying a sense of oneness with the world. To quote from his essay "Knowledge and the Image of Man" (which offers the best single key to his use of this myth), man starts out with a "primal instinctive sense of unity." But then comes the Fall, an inevitable event which each individual must experience for himself, when man suddenly realizes that he is separate from his surroundings and "discovers the pain of self-criticism." He now takes upon

[8]*Selected Poems*, pp. 283-84.

himself the knowledge of Original Sin, which in Warren's terms means an awareness of dissociation and incompleteness. Redemption is possible, however, and it issues from the simple recognition that, with all his flaws and frailty, the individual is still vitally attached to his surroundings. By realizing that he is involved in an intimate, two-way relationship with the world, an "osmosis of being, which in the end does not deny, but affirms, his identity," man can, in effect, come back to his lost Eden, now admittedly altered by the passing of the seasons, and to the sense of communion and completeness it symbolizes. Or, as Warren puts it at the end of "Knowledge and the Image of Man":

> Man can return to his lost unity, and if that return is fitful and precarious, if the foliage and flower of the innocent garden are now somewhat browned by a late season, all is the more precious for the fact, for what is now achieved has been achieved by a growth of moral awareness.[9]

The figure of the garden or clearing — "browned by a late season," slightly unkempt or unruly perhaps, and yet not without a sense of serenity — recurs throughout Warren's work, and it brings together the two patterns of the Fall followed by Redemption and the return to the father. For it is at once the familiar home of Adam and the old homestead to which people like Billie Potts return — set, it may be, somewhere in western Kentucky. Quite apart from that, it also offers a reminder of that notion of equipoise, or the reconciliation of opposites, so vital to Warren's work, since it is neither completely savage nor utterly subdued. Just as the human personality, as Warren sees it, operates best in the space between fact and idea, public and private, past and future, so the various clearings he describes exist in a border territory between forest and town, the raw energies of the wilderness and the structures of civilization. They are not necessarily cultivated spots. For example, the place where the protagonist in *Audubon: A Vision* has his first mystical experience is, quite simply, an open space created by nature:

> October: and the bear,
> Daft in the honey-light, yawns.
>
> The bear's tongue, pink as a baby's, out-crisps to
>   the curled tip,
> It bleeds the black blood of the blueberry.
> ....
> Bemused, above the fume of ruined blueberries
> The last bee hums.

[9]"Knowledge and the Image of Man," *Sewanee Review,* 43 (Spring 1955), 187. Victor Strandberg's *The Poetic Vision of Robert Penn Warren* (Lexington: University Press of Kentucky, 1977), offers an excellent account of Warren's use of this myth in his poetry.

> The wings, like mica, glint
> In the sunlight.
> He leans on his gun. Thinks
> How thin is the membrane between himself and the world.[10]

They are always, though, as this passage suggests, both outer landscapes and inner ones; they are products partly of history and Warren's own experiences and partly of myth, his fictive powers.

III

So far this discussion has concentrated on generalities, the broader themes and ideas implicit in Warren's work rather than the individual works themselves. It is, however, the specific poem or story or play, or indeed the specific essay, that charges these ideas into life, and subjects his themes to the test of experience; and it would be wrong to conclude without some tangible recognition of this—without looking, in other words, however briefly and inadequately, at one particular text. One of the poems from Warren's most recently published collection, *Now and Then: Poems 1976-1978*, may serve here, since the volume as a whole shows how Warren has retained the ability to move quickly and almost imperceptibly between different levels of perception, and how also, acting on his belief that the discovery of the self is a continuing process, he has not ceased to develop and experiment. For example, the seventh poem in the book, "Red-Tail Hawk and Pyre of Youth," offers a fresh expedition into familiar territory, that of personal reminiscence about Warren's boyhood in Kentucky. Like all his writing, it grows out of his earlier works and is enriched by our knowledge of them, but it is also something new: it uses Warren's ideas and imaginative preoccupations, not in a programmatic way but as a series of living, still maneuverable possibilities.

"Red-Tail Hawk" opens with an evocative description of one particular day in the poet's boyhood, when he went climbing a neighboring mountain, taking his gun along. The characteristically "loose" line of Warren's later poetry is used with a consummate sense of drama here, to suggest both the boy's effort in climbing and his feelings of excitement and anticipation:

> Breath clamber-short, face sun-peeled, stones
> Loose like untruth underfoot, I
> Had just made the ridge crest, and there,
> Opening like joy...
> ....
> The sky...[11]

[10]*Selected Poems*, pp. 85-86.

[11]*Now and Then: Poems 1976-1978* (New York: Random House, 1978), pp. 17-21. I wish to thank Mr. Warren for permitting me to see the proofs of the book.

The awe implicit in that last, utterly simple phrase prepares us for the naïve wonder of the boy's reaction when suddenly a hawk appears in the vast expanse above him. At first, the narrator tells us,

> I did not know its name. Nor mine.

Like Adam before the Fall, he has no knowledge of either himself or the world and so no identity — at least, in the adult sense. However, his eyes, following the hawk's flight, are to lead him, a little unwillingly, into a new vision of reality, just as the hawk's eyes, returning his stare, are to haunt him in later years with a sense of shame and acute self-consciousness.

The new vision begins to come into being in the brief second section of the poem, when the boy raises his gun and shoots the hawk. He hardly seems to know what he is doing; what is significant about his behavior is in fact, that he responds instinctively. For, as Warren has said of an analogous moment, the killing of the albatross in *The Ancient Mariner,*

> The act re-enacts the Fall, and the Fall has two qualities important here: it is a condition of will, as Coleridge says, "out of time," and it is the result of no single human motive.[12]

The boy's action is a part of all human history, and with it both the circles of the hawk's flight and the closed circle of the child's world are broken. The line at this point seems to break down too, collapsing with apocalyptic effect upon the last word in the section:

> I pressed the cool, snubbed
> Trigger. Saw
> The circle
> Break.

After the event comes a deep sense of loss. The boy's first reaction, we are told, is to cuddle "the bloody/Body" and take it home, where he then attempts, with the help of needles and thread, to put it all back together again. This macabre attempt at resurrection, described in the third and fourth sections of the poem, is at once utterly understandable, the natural reaction of a child to the grim consequences of what he has done, and profoundly significant. For, like so many of Warren's protagonists, the boy is trying, in a sense, to deny the Fall, to recapture the innocence of that purer, ethereal self which the hawk somehow embodies. Warren's account of the process nicely captures these two levels and at the same time keeps a careful balance between a feeling of tragic pathos and a sense of the grotesque.

There is a sudden widening of horizons, a stretching out of time, in the next two sections, as the narrator moves from boyhood to adulthood. Time passed, he tells us, he eventually left the family home and the bedroom

---

[12]"A Poem of Pure Imagination: An Experiment in Reading," in *Selected Essays*, p. 227.

where he kept the shabby, tacked-together remains of the red-tail hawk; and yet, over the years, the bird would return in nightmares to haunt him, its eyes, in particular, reminding him that in its own way it had had its revenge. Then, in the seventh section, we return to a specific moment, this time in the more immediate past, when the narrator took the long circuit back to his father's house and discovered there, in the lumber room, what was left of the bird he had slain. As he presents himself at the moment of discovery, he seems a little battered, with "one eye long gone" like the poor, resurrected hawk: a piece of self-description which is at once accurate and apt, since, from his earliest poetry on, Warren has tended to associate knowledge of evil with images of monstrosity. Like Yeats, Warren possesses the magical ability to turn the actual into the legendary, a fact which becomes the more obvious when the narrator tells us what he then proceeded to do:

> And so made a pyre for
> The hawk that, though gasoline-doused and wing-dragging,
> Awaited, with what looked like pride,
> The match.

He gives the hawk a funeral pyre, using as fuel the other detritus of youth ("my first book of Milton,/ ...a book of poems friends and I had printed at college.../ The collection of sexual Japanese prints..."). But the fire which destroys can also create: in dreams, the narrator informs us, the hawk has returned to him,

> And always the rifle swings up, though with
> The weightlessness now of dream,
> The old .30-30 that knows
> How to bind us in air-blood and earth-blood together
> In our commensurate fate
> Whose name is a name beyond joy.

"All knowledge that is worth anything," according to Jack Burden, "is maybe paid for by blood"; and the blood shed by the hawk has proved that here. Addressing the hawk directly now, and moving swiftly from "I" through "you" to "us," the narrator reveals that he has learned one simple truth: that man and hawk, slayer and victim, earth and air are bound together in one life, an "osmosis of being." In effect, the poem has charted a passage from Fall to Redemption. A new unity of being has been discovered, as a result of suffering and self-criticism and sacrifice, and the discovery of this unity brings with it joy, a sense of meaning and exhilaration which is memorably caught in the tenth and last section of the poem:

> And I pray that in some last dream or delusion
> ....
> I'll again see the first small silvery swirl
> Spin outward and downward from sky-height

> To bring me the truth in blood-marriage of earth and air —
> And all will be as it was
> In that paradox of unjoyful joyousness,
> Till the dazzling moment when I, a last time, must flinch
> From the regally feathered gasoline flare
> Of youth's poor, angry, slapdash, and ignorant pyre.

The meaning of these last lines is perhaps obvious: Warren prays, finally, that his belief in the unity of being will be with him when he dies, so that he can see his life, now passed, as part of a significant pattern and his death, now imminent, as simply the conclusion to one chapter in the tale of time — a tale which is, to quote again from *Audubon: A Vision,* one of "deep delight." What is possibly less obvious, however, and so needs emphasizing here, is how carefully the poet has prepared for this final moment. The rhythm has been built up from the tentative, halting movement of the first section to the rolling thunder of the last. The imagery of hawk, circle, blood, fire, and dreams has been developed almost by stealth, accumulating further dimensions of meaning without ever losing its original specificity. The language, while remaining rooted in the colloquial, has acquired a peculiar resonance; one word is set in tension with another, and each phrase or line catches fire from its predecessor in a manner reminiscent of William Faulkner. And issuing out of all this, everything that Warren says at this moment seems to have been *won* from experience; his sense of jubilation strikes one as authentic and thoroughly, because dramatically, earned. Like all Warren's best work, in fact, the final section of "Red-Tail Hawk," and indeed the poem as a whole, is at once profoundly symbolic and convincingly realistic; or, to be more accurate, it makes the terms *symbolism* and *realism* seem what they are, starved and essentially inadequate. For the generalizations about values that Warren offers here have grown out of a careful documentation of the facts. The reconciliation of opposites that he is now arguing for is something that has been visibly there in his own creative meditations.

IV

"If poetry does anything for us, it reconciles…the self-divisive internecine malices which arise at the superficial level on which we conduct most of our living." This, from the conclusion to Warren's essay on *The Ancient Mariner,* offers another clue to his achievement in "Red-Tail Hawk" — or, for that matter, in books like *All the King's Men* or *Brother to Dragons:* he manages to reconcile the divisions, those vindictive dualisms that most people use most of the time to mediate between themselves and the world. In a sense, he is a writer who thrives on paradox, actively embracing and resolving what are conventionally supposed to be opposites: which is why one useful way of approaching him, and at least beginning to summarize his work, is simply to see him as paradoxical—in terms, that is, of the various oppositions that he manages, somehow, to resolve. For example, we could say, if we wished to, that Warren is at once the most worldly of writers—since he is an accomplished historian and social commentator who never fails to emphasize that "The world is real. It is there"—and the most *un*worldly, since so much of his writing has a philosophical bias, or a mystical dimension, and he is clearly not very interested in the commonplace pursuits of getting and spending. We could say, possibly, that, like William Carlos Williams or Ezra Pound, he is a great believer in the reality of reality. For things are as they are for him; they exist out there in the world beyond the self, complete, with their own essential properties, and irreducible. But we could also argue that, like W. B. Yeats, he believes in the reality of the imagination, because he is very much committed to the idea of a saving illusion, some dream or fiction discovered, not like Yeats's somewhere beyond our given environment, but here and now, in things and our relationship to them. We could say that he uses language in a strictly referential way, because so often he makes statements that we can cite almost as if they were proverbs. But we could also suggest, with as much assurance or lack of it, that he uses it in an emblematic, allegorical fashion, or in a symbolic manner, or, more obscurely, as if it were a kind of mathematics or music. Realist and symbolist, historian and visionary, pragmatist and mystic—Warren, like many major writers since the Romantic revolution, never loses his capacity to surprise us with another change of roles, it may be, a fresh argument or synthesis, or by throwing new light on a world that seemed to have grown stale with familiarity. And, then again, this quality, too, can generate its own opposite, for Warren can just as quickly turn around and write something so pure, so simple and to the point, that we must greet it with an immediate sense of recognition. Here is an example, from the closing section of *Audubon: A Vision:*

> Long ago, in Kentucky, I, a boy, stood
> By a dirt road, in first dark, and heard
> The great geese hoot northward.
>
> I could not see them, there being no moon
> And the stars sparse. I heard them.
>
> I did not know what was happening in my heart.[13]

"Modern art," Wallace Stevens remarked once, in one of his characteristically apocalyptic asides, "often seems to be an attempt to bridge the gap between fact and miracle." The facts in the case of Robert Penn Warren are, as this volume indicates, fairly numerous but still not impossible to sum-

[13]*Selected Poems*, p. 100.

marize. The miracle of his writing, however, is a different matter. In effect, his work is rather like that secret clearing, or place to come to, that he celebrates in so many of his poems and novels: something which is undeniably there, to be perceived, sensed, and enjoyed—but which exists, finally, beyond the reach of the mind and its explanations.

Experience Redeemed in Knowledge

by Cleanth Brooks

The poetry, the fiction, and even the critical essays of Robert Penn Warren form a highly unified and consistent body of work. But it would be impossible to reduce it, without distorting simplifications, to some thesis about human life. The work is not tailored to fit a thesis. In the best sense, it is inductive: it explores the human situation and tests against the fullness of human experience our various abstract statements about it. But Warren has his characteristic themes. He is constantly concerned with the meaning of the past and the need for one to accept the past if he is to live meaningfully in the present. In this concern there are resemblances to Faulkner, though Warren's treatment is his own. Again, there are resemblances to W. B. Yeats in Warren's almost obsessive concern to grasp the truth so that "all is redeemed/ In knowledge." Again, as with Yeats, there is a tough-minded insistence upon the facts, including the realistic and ugly facts— a fierce refusal to shield one's eyes from what is there.

This commitment to the truth, and the deep sense that the truth is rarely simple, account for Warren's sharp scrutiny of the claims of rationality. He never glorifies irrationality: he is not the poet of the dark subliminal urges or the novelist with a mystique to exploit. But he does subject the claims of twentieth-century man to the sternest testing and he is suspicious of the doctrine of progress and of the blandishments of utopianism.

Faulkner's effective, though perhaps unwitting and unconscious, belief in original sin constitutes a bulwark against this heresy. Yeats' vigilant and unflagging resistance to what he calls "Whiggery" consitutes a similar safeguard. One could argue that, in general, the artist's commitment to the concrete situation and his need to focus upon the dramatic exigencies of the human predicament make it easier for him to reject this form of abstraction. Dedication to his art, then, would not necessarily bring the artist to Christianity. It would be foolish to claim *that*. But dedication to his art may well protect the artist from some of the deceptions endemic to our time.

"Experience Redeemed in Knowledge." From Cleanth Brooks, *The Hidden God: Studies in Hemingway, Faulkner, Yeats, Eliot, and Warren* (New Haven: Yale University Press, 1963), pp. 98-111, 118-27. © 1963 by Cleanth Brooks. Reprinted by permission of Yale University Press.

On the positive side, dedication to his art will probably help him at least to *see* the problems of the human spirit to which Christianity—and any other serious philosophy—addresses itself.

The work in which Robert Penn Warren challenges most directly some of the liberal secular ideas of our time is his long poem *Brother to Dragons*, published in 1953. It is about Thomas Jefferson, or rather about Jefferson's nephews, Lilburn and Isham Lewis, the sons of Jefferson's sister, Lucy Jefferson Lewis. The Lewises removed from Virginia to western Kentucky. There, after the death of their mother and after their father, Dr. Charles Lewis, had returned to Virginia, the two young men, Lilburn and Isham, murdered one of their slaves. On the night of December 15, 1811, the night when the New Madrid earthquake shook the Mississippi Valley, Lilburn, having called the other slaves together into the meathouse to witness what he was going to do, butchered on the meatblock a slave named George. George's offense had been to break a water pitcher on his way back from the spring to which he had been sent to fetch fresh water.

After some months, hints of the crime leaked out. Lilburn and Isham were indicted for murder, but before they could be arrested and put in jail, Lilburn was dead. Apparently the brothers had planned to stand, each on one side of their mother's grave, and shoot each other. When the sheriff's posse came up, Lilburn had been shot and was dying. Isham was captured, but while awaiting trial, broke jail and disappeared—to turn up, of all places, at the battle of New Orleans in 1815, one of the two Americans killed in that engagement. This, at least, was the story that the Kentucky riflemen brought back with them from New Orleans. In any case, the indictment naming Isham bears under the date March 20, 1815, the docket: "Ordered that this suit abate by the death of the defendant."

It is a fantastic story, a terrible and blood-chilling story. It is, however, a true story, with the documents on record. Thomas Jefferson must have been aware of the depths of wanton cruelty to which his nephews had sunk, but nowhere among the Jefferson Papers is there any reference to it. It is hard to imagine what the great Virginian who thought so much of man's possibilities, who penned the Declaration of Independence with its confident claims for man, who knew and was sympathetic to the French eighteenth-century rationalists—it is difficult and exciting to try to imagine what Jefferson's reaction must have been. This is the task that Warren takes upon himself. To my mind his effort of imaginative reconstruction results in a great and moving poem. That has been also the opinion of some of the most discerning critical minds here and in Great Britain. But not of all, I should add. For a great many Americans, Jefferson comes close to being a sacred figure, and to dare to portray a Jefferson troubled and in doubt, a Jefferson embittered and cynical, even though only temporarily, was to lay profane hands upon the idol. In fairness to Warren's conception of Jefferson, I should say that *Brother to Dragons* is not written in any spirit of debunking. It is a great Jefferson who emerges at the end of Warren's poem, a Jefferson who has, in giving up his more callow hopes in man, actually strengthened his basic belief in man's potentialities. At the end of the poem Jefferson is a chastened though not a disillusioned man.

A book-length poem does not adequately reveal itself in brief quotations. If I confine myself to quotations of reasonable length, I can hope to do no more than suggest something of the flavor of the poem. The impassioned dialectic and the stages of the drama through which the action works to its final resolution must be taken on faith unless one has read the poem. Yet I do want to quote two or three excerpts. Here is the way in which Warren imagines Jefferson's hopes for man as he sat down to write the Declaration of Independence:

> We knew we were only men
> Caught in our errors and interests. But I, a man,
> Suddenly saw in every face, face after face,
> The bleared, the puffed, the lank, the lean, all,
> On all saw the brightness blaze, and I knew my own days,
> Times, hopes, books, horsemanship, the praise of peers,
> Delight, desire, and even my love, but straw
> Fit for the flame, and in that fierce combustion I—
> Why, I was dead, I was nothing, nothing but joy,
> And my heart cried out, "Oh, this is Man!"
>
> And thus my minotaur. There at the blind
> Blank labyrinthine turn of my personal time,
> I met the beast. . . .
> . . . But no beast then: the towering
> Definition, angelic, arrogant, abstract,
> Greaved in glory, thewed with light, the bright
> Brow tall as dawn. I could not see the eyes.
> So seized the pen, and in the upper room,
> With the excited consciousness that I was somehow
> Purged, rectified, and annealed, and my past annulled
> And fate confirmed, wrote. And the bell struck
> Far off in darkness, and the watch called out.
> Time came, we signed the document, went home.
> Slept, and I woke to the new self, and new doom.
> I had not seen the eyes of that bright apparition.
> I had been blind with light. That was my doom.
> I did not know its eyes were blind.

I would like to quote also the poet's own commentary on man seen against the background of nature—man who is not "adjusted" to nature and can never be adjusted—who must live in an agony of will, and who finally in his need projects upon nature itself the struggle with circumstance that engages his own heart. The scene is winter, as it descends upon the Lewis brothers after their mother's death and burial:

> And the year drove on. Winter. And from the Dakotas
> The wind veers, gathers itself in ice-glitter
> And star-gleam of dark, and finds the long sweep of the valley.
> A thousand miles and the fabulous river is ice in the starlight.
> The ice is a foot thick, and beneath, the water slides black like a dream,
> And in the interior of that unpulsing blackness and thrilled zero
> The big channel-cat sleeps with eye lidless, and the brute face
> Is the face of the last torturer, and the white belly
> Brushes the delicious and icy blackness of mud.
> But there is no sensation. How can there be
> Sensation when there is perfect adjustment? The blood
> Of the creature is but the temperature of the sustaining flow:
> The catfish is in the Mississippi and
> The Mississippi is in the catfish and
> Under the ice both are at one with God.
> Would that we were!

By the end of the poem Jefferson can accept the past with its violence and evil; he is willing to acknowledge the fact of his kinship with his black-browed butcher of a nephew, and he exults that

> ...nothing we had,
> Nothing we were,
> Is lost.
> *All is redeemed,*
> *In knowledge.*

Jefferson tells his sister that "without the fact of the past we cannot dream the future," and he remembers that he had once written to Adams, his old political rival and friend,

> To Adams, my ole enemy and friend, that gnarled greatness, long ago.
> I wrote to him, and said
> That the dream of the future is better than the dream of the past.
> Now I should hope to find the courage to say
> That the dream of the future is not
> Better than the fact of the past, no matter how terrible.
> For without the fact of the past we cannot dream the future.

The necessity for accepting the past is the dominant theme of what is probably the best known of Warren's novels, *All the King's Men.* The task of making sense of history is the specific problem of its hero. Jack Burden is a young man who is trying to write his dissertation for a Ph.D. in history. His chosen topic is the life of an ancestor of his who died during the Civil War. The papers and documents have come down through the family to Jack. He has all the facts about this ancestor, Cass Mastern, but somehow the facts do not make sense to him. Cass Mastern as a young man was sent away to school at Transylvania College in Kentucky. While he was there he seduced—or perhaps it may be more accurate to say he was seduced by—the wife of his friend, whose house he has frequently visited as a guest.

Later something occurred to make Mastern realize that his friend's death by gunshot was not the accident that the world had supposed. His friend had somehow learned of the betrayal and had shot himself. Cass Mastern in his remorse tries in various ways to expiate his sin. When the Civil War breaks out, he refuses a commission, marches in the ranks, never firing a shot himself but courting the bullet that he hopes will find him. Finally, in 1864, the bullet does find him, and he dies in hospital of the infected wound. Jack Burden knows the facts, and even possesses Mastern's carefully kept and intimate journal, but he cannot understand why Mastern did what he did. This is the way in which Jack, speaking of himself in the third person, was able to put the matter some years later:

> I have said that Jack Burden could not put down the facts about Cass Mastern's world because he did not know Cass Mastern. Jack Burden did not say definitely to himself why he did not know Cass Mastern. But I (who am what Jack Burden became) look back now, years later, and try to say why.
>
> Cass Mastern lived for a few years and in that time he learned that the world is all of one piece. He learned that the world is like an enormous spider web and if you touch it, however lightly, at any point, the vibration ripples to the remotest perimeter and the drowsy spider feels the tingle and is drowsy no more but springs out to fling the gossamer coils about you who have touched the web and then inject the black, numbing poison under your hide. It does not matter whether or not you meant to brush the web of things. Your happy foot or your gay wing may have brushed it ever so lightly, but what happens always happens and there is the spider, bearded black and with his great faceted eyes glittering like mirrors in the sun, or like God's eye, and the fangs dripping.
>
> But how could Jack Burden, being what he was, understand that?

What Jack Burden was then, and how he later became something different constitute the matter of the novel. The knowledge that Jack's earlier life and his years at the university failed to give him, he learns painfully as a cynical newspaper reporter, watching, among other things, the meteoric career of Willie Stark as Stark rises to dictatorial power in this southern state. Through much of the course of the novel Jack Burden is acting as Stark's man Friday, advising him, doing various jobs for him, and, among these, applying his talents for historical research to the past lives of the governor's political opponents. What he is able to dig up usually disposes of that particular opponent. And, Jack cannot help noticing, there is usually something to dig up—no matter what the subject's reputation for probity. Once, when Jack demurs that there can be nothing to find in the past of the respectable Judge Irwin, Willie Stark assures Jack that there is always something: "Man is conceived in sin and born in corruption and he passeth from the stink of the didie to the stench of the shroud. There is always something."

There is not time, and for my purposes there is no need, to treat in detail the involved plot of this rich, violent, even melodramatic novel. Warren's novels are written with a kind of Elizabethan gusto. Though the school of criticism with which he is sometimes associated is charged with being over-intellectual, formal, and even Alexandrian, Warren's own creative work, in its color and strident action, calls in question that oversimple account. Neither his poetry nor his fiction wears a prim and chilly formalism.

All the King's Men has been often described as a novel that depicts under a thin disguise the career of the late Huey P. Long. When the novel first appeared, a number of critics who should have known better disgraced themselves by their inability to make a distinction between the character of Willie Stark and that of the late senator from Louisiana. Certainly many things in the novel remind one of Louisiana under the Long regime; but this is a novel, not a biography, and finally—despite the importance of Willie Stark—the novel tells *Jack Burden's* story. The story of Willie Stark finally has its importance because of the way in which it affects the story of Jack. For as I said a few minutes ago, this novel is an account of how Jack Burden came to be a man capable of understanding the story of Cass Mastern—which means, of course, ultimately capable of understanding his own life and his relation to his parents, his friends, and the world.

Before Jack reaches this stage of knowledge, however, he has to be carried even further toward disillusionment and despair. For a time he comes to believe that man is a thing, a mere mechanism. He believes in what he calls "the Great Twitch." Men simply react to stimuli. Their actions are only more complicated versions of what happens when one runs an electric current through the severed legs of a frog. Given the stimulus, there is the automatic response.

The violence latent in the situation depicted in the novel finally comes to a head Willie Stark is shot and killed by the young doctor Adam Stanton, who is Jack's boyhood friend; and Stanton himself is cut down by a fusillade fired by Stark's bodyguard. Moreover, Jack not only observes the death of his friends, he finds himself directly involved in violence, for he learns that he has been the unwitting cause of the death of his own father. For a time, as Jack tells us, his belief in the Great Twitch was a comfort, for if there was no God but the Great Twitch, then no man had any responsibility for anything, and he was somehow absolved from having caused his father's death. But later Jack tells us

> he woke up one morning to discover that he did not believe in the Great Twitch any more. He did not believe in it because he had seen too many people live and die. He had seen Lucy Stark and Sugar-Boy and the Scholarly

Attorney and Sadie Burke and Anne Stanton live and the ways of their living had nothing to do with the Great Twitch. He had seen his father die. He had seen his friend Adam Stanton die. He had seen his friend Willie Stark die, and had heard him say with his last breath, "It might have been all different, Jack. You got to believe that."

He had seen his two friends, Willie Stark and Adam Stanton, live and die. Each had killed the other. Each had been the doom of the other. As a student of history, Jack Burden could see that Adam Stanton, whom he came to call the man of idea, and Willie Stark, whom he came to call the man of fact, were doomed to destroy each other, just as each was doomed to try to use the other and to yearn toward and try to become the other, because each was incomplete with the terrible division of their age. But at the same time [that] Jack Burden came to see that his friends had been doomed, he saw that though doomed they had nothing to do with any doom under the godhead of the Great Twitch. They were doomed, but they lived in the agony of will.

The sobered and chastened Jack Burden, in his new knowledge and sympathy, is now actually able to understand and accept the man whom he had been brought up to believe was his father but whom from boyhood he had secretly despised because he felt that he lacked force and manhood. Now, long divorced from Jack's mother, the supposed father has become something of a religious fanatic—in the cynical young newspaperman's eyes, at least—writing religious tracts and doing good works in the slums of the city. But as the novel closes, Jack has brought him home to live out under Jack's protection the few months remaining to him. Jack even helps him with some of his tracts, since the old man, too feeble to write, can still dictate. One of the passages he dictates claims Jack's special attention:

"The creation of man whom God in His foreknowledge knew doomed to sin was the awful index of God's omnipotence. For it would have been a thing of trifling and contemptible ease for Perfection to create mere perfection. To do so would, to speak truth, be not creation but extension. Separateness is identity and the only way for God to create, truly create, man was to make him separate from God Himself, and to be separate from God is to be sinful. The creation of evil is therefore the index of God's glory and His power. That had to *be* so that the creation of good might be the index of man's glory and power. But by God's help. By His help and in His wisdom."

He turned to me when he had spoken the last word, stared at me, and then said, "Did you put that down?"

"Yes," I replied.

Staring at me, he said with sudden violence, "It is true. I know it is true. Do you know it?"

I nodded my head and said yes. (I did so to keep his mind untroubled, but later I was not certain but that in my own way I did believe what he had said.)

The elder Mr. Burden's notion that man is "doomed to evil" veers toward the Manichaean heresy, but the truth that he is trying to render is evidently close to that to which Milton testified in *Paradise Lost*. Milton, of course, was careful to point out that man's fall was not *decreed* by God; yet God clearly did create the potentiality of evil as the necessary price to be paid for making man a free agent. Moreover, in His perfect foreknowledge, God knew that man would misuse his power to choose and that he would fall into sin. As God sums the doctrine up in Book III:

> I made [man] just and right,
> Sufficient to have stood, though free to fall.
> Such I created all th' Ethereal Powers
> And Spirits, both them who stood and them who faild;
> Freely they stood who stood, and fell who fell.
> Not free, what proof could they have givn sincere
> Of true allegiance, constant Faith or Love. ...

Mr. Burden would evidently gloss the last three lines as follows: man *not* created free to fall would be merely an extension of God—no true creation.

Warren touches upon the problem of evil in a number of his poems. A very brilliant treatment is given in the momentarily bewildering poem entitled "Dragon Country." The country in question is, as the allusions in the poem make plain, Warren's native Kentucky. But as the dedication of the poem ("To Jacob Boehme") hints, the country in question is a country of the mind in which men encounter not human forces merely but principalities and powers. There is no reason, of course, why the two countries should not be one and the same, and in the poem they do coalesce. Indeed the brilliance of the poem comes in large part from the sense of the earthy and commonplace—"fence rails...splintered," "Mules torn from trace chains," the salesman traveling over the Kentucky hills "for Swift, or Armour"—and from the tone, colloquial, racy, and dry with a countryman's wit—both of which elements contrast with the preternatural horrors that are recounted, and thus give substance and solidity to them.

The reader of the poem may still ask "But why Kentucky?" And the answer would have to be: Kentucky, or any other Southern state. For the poem reflects the Southern experience, in which evil has an immediacy and reality that cannot be evaded or explained away. In that experience man is still confronted with the hard choice. He cannot simply call in the marriage counselor or the police or the psychiatrist. It is with this aspect of the Southern experience that "Dragon Country" deals.

We know, of course, that dragons simply do not exist. Yet what could have done the damage to Jack Simms' hogpen? And how account for some of the things that have happened since?

> So what, in God's name, could men think, when they couldn't
> bring to bay
> That belly-dragging earth-evil, but found that it took to air?

Thirty-thirty or buckshot might fail, but then at least you could say
You had faced it—assuming, of course, that you had survived the
    affair.

We were promised troops, the Guard, but the Governor's skin got
    thin
When up in New York the papers called him Saint George of
    Kentucky.
Yes, even the Louisville reporters who came to Todd County would
    grin.
Reporters, though rarely, still come. No one talks. They think it
    unlucky. . . .

Turned tongue-tied by the metropolitan press, not able to admit that the evil has reality, even the friends and relatives of the victims explain the facts away. When a man disappears, his family reports that he has gone to work in Akron, "or up to Ford, in Detroit." When Jebb Johnson's boot was found with a piece of his leg inside it, his mother refused to identify it as her son's.

Now land values are falling; lovers do not walk by moonlight. Certain fields are going back to brush and undergrowth. The coon "dips his little black paw" undisturbed each night in the stream.

Yes, other sections have problems somewhat different from ours.
Their crops may fail, bank rates rise, on rumor of war loans be
    called,
But we feel removed from maneuvers of Russia, or other great
    powers,
And from much ordinary hope are now disenthralled.

The Catholics have sent in a mission, Baptists report new attendance.
But that's not the point. We are human, and the human heart
Demands language for reality that has no slightest dependence
On desire, or need. Now in church they pray only that evil depart.
But if the Beast were withdrawn now, life might dwindle again
To the ennui, the pleasure, and night sweat, known in the time
    before
Necessity of truth had trodden the land, and heart, to pain,
And left, in darkness, the fearful glimmer of joy, like a spoor.

But this last difficult stanza is no Manichaean celebration of evil. The poem is not simply saying how much better off are the Kentuckians who inhabit the dragon's country, because they have to live so dangerously. The "fearful glimmer of joy" that the last line hints of comes not from evil as such but from the "necessity of truth." Admitting the element of horror in life, conceding the element of mystery, facing the terrifying truth—these are the only actions that can promise the glimmer of ultimate joy. . . .

Warren's characteristic theme—man's obligation to find the truth by which he lives—comes in for a fine restatement in a recent poem and a recent novel. Both put a young soldier's idealism to the test; both have a Civil War setting. The poem is entitled "Harvard '61: Battle Fatigue." The young Harvard man of the class of 1861 has died in the fight to free the slaves, but in death he is puzzled—even nettled—by the fact that others have died bravely for a bad cause—or perhaps, for no cause at all.

> I didn't mind dying—it wasn't that at all.
> It behooves a man to prove manhood by dying for Right.
> If you die for Right that fact is your dearest requital,
> But you find it disturbing when others die who simply haven't
>   the right.

The way in which certain "unprincipled wastrels of blood and profligates of breath" have flung themselves into death has confused the issues. There was, for example, the middle-aged Confederate soldier whom he shot and killed just before he received his own death wound. The man was, he exclaimed to himself, "old as my father" and the dying Confederate soldier, observing the boy's blanched face, had even given him a bit of fatherly advice, saying to him: "Buck up! If it hadn't been you,/ Some other young squirt would a-done it."

But even as the young Harvard idealist heard these words,

> The tumult of battle went soundless, like gesture in dream. And
>   I was dead, too.
>
> Dead, and had died for the Right, as I had a right to,
> And glad to be dead, and hold my residence
> Beyond life's awful illogic, and the world's stew,
> Where people who haven't the right just die, with ghastly
>   impertinence.

The young idealist has a case: he had indeed tried to slay "without rancor" and had striven to keep his heart pure "though hand took stain." In a sense, then, he has earned a certain right to his squeamishness. In any case, such squeamishness touches some answering chord in the hearts of all of us nowadays who regard war as the ultimate horror and justify, if at all, our participation in it only in terms of its necessity and our own purity of purpose. As for the poet's attitude toward the idealistic young fighter for the right, "Harvard '61" is only one half of a double poem, the other member of which has to do with the gnarled and bewhiskered Confederate whom the young man killed. The inclusive title for this double poem is, significantly, "Two Studies in Idealism: Short Survey of American, and Human, History." The poet is not condemning idealism but extending our conventional notions of it and in the process showing how deeply it is rooted in human nature. If the member of the class of '61 is being chided, it is not for his dedication or his bravery but for a too-simple view of reality and a certain pharisaical self-righteousness.

In his novel, *Wilderness,* Warren addresses himself once more to the problem of the idealist caught up in the Civil War. His criticism of idealism has not changed, but in this instance his treatment of the idealist is not glancing and ironic but direct, serious, and fully and obviously sympathetic.

The hero of the novel is a young Bavarian Jew, Adam Rosenzweig. He has a club foot, but in spite of this deformity and in spite of the bitter opposition of his uncle—his only close relative, for Adam's parents are dead—he makes his way to America in order to take part in the War to help free the slaves.

What Adam finds, of course, is the mixture of good and evil, the contradictions and cross purposes, that one always encounters in a great war. He finds, for example, that the inhabitants of New York City are not unanimous in regarding the conflict as a holy war for freedom. Some of them even resent the Negroes as being the indirect cause of their being conscripted to fight. Adam finds himself caught up in such a conscription riot on the very day that he lands. The mob is killing such Negroes as it can find.

The general situation in which Adam finds himself has an aspect more troubling still. As he makes his way toward the battlefields, his immediate companions turn out to be men who are vicious or cowardly or callous. Though he is sorry for the Negro Mose Talbutt and tries to teach him to read, he finds it hard to accept him fully or even to come to a genuine liking of him. Though he applauds Jed Hawksworth for having displayed the sense of justice and integrity that forced him to leave his native South, Adam cannot find in Hawksworth a brother idealist or even a warm human being. In sum, Adam's persistent difficulty is that of accepting man with all of his imperfections and believing that the ideal can have any place in a creature so faulty.

In the stinking mud of the army's winter quarters in northern Virginia, the sensitive young man is almost overwhelmed with the ugliness and cruelty and crassness of human life. A soldier celebrated for heroic exploits in battle turns out to be in the camp a drunken bully. An ignorant washerwoman who hangs around the camp is sentenced to the lash for prostitution and Adam hears her shrieks as the whip falls. The state of affairs seems to call in question everything that he has lived for up to this time and the whole meaning of his quest.

The last two chapters of this short novel bring to a head this crisis in Adam's affairs. He has slipped away from the wagon train and driven his sutler's vehicle into the Wilderness where the confused and bloody battle will be fought. He is at last alone. The battle will eventually reach into the glade where his team is tethered. There he will face an ultimate testing of his conception of human kind and of reality.

Few authors would have dared to compress so many successive states of mind into so short a time span, as Adam's mood shifts from dejected loneliness to tender affection, or from obsessive guilt to pride in his new-found masculine power, or from cynicism to human sympathy, before he finally attains to self-knowledge and through that knowledge to a way of accepting humankind. Certainly few authors could have brought it off. But Warren has earlier set forth very skillfully the circumstances which have made Adam what he is and the psychological pattern through which Adam will be forced to move. Moreover, the battlefield itself so eagerly sought by Adam, and won to with such difficulty, provides the necessary forcing bed for Adam's development. There he finds himself detached from and yet a part of the battle, in the "cold center of stillness in the storm which was the world." There is opportunity for thought, yet involvement is imminent. Finally, after the skirmishers strike into his hidden glade, fight over Adam's almost passive body, and then rush away, the burning forest, which has been set afire by the guns, forces Adam toward decision and action.

But unless the reader already possesses the supporting context, including Adam's earlier history, there is little point in trying here to lead him step by step through the drama of Adam's development. No summary, in any case, can preserve the drama. But it will do no harm to mention some of the elements at work in Adam's Wilderness experience.

The day begins with a pang of loneliness as Adam wakes from a dream of his mother, the mother who, he feels, had at the end come to hate him because he sided with his father in believing that it was right to sacrifice one's family in the fight for liberty. Though his mother had not forgiven him, he yearns for forgiveness. In the dream she has seemed to proffer tenderness and love.

There is Adam's sense of guilt. In particular, he feels remorse for the exasperation which allowed him to lash out at Mose Crawford, the freedman, the night before Mose murdered his tormentor, Jed Hawksworth. Adam believes that his bitter words may have actually triggered the deed. In the silence of the forest, Adam wonders about something else: why did not Mose kill *him*, the man who had actually uttered the harsh words, rather than Jed, and he reflects that the reason must be that Mose had once saved his life: "he thought, *you cannot strike down what you have lifted up.* So Jed, he decided, had had to die in his place." In a curious way, Jed's life has been sacrificed for his own, and he wonders whether "every man is, in the end, a sacrifice for every other man."

Adam's reveries are interrupted when the battle bursts in upon him. A handful of ragged Confederate soldiers overrun the glade, knock Adam down, and, while one of them, a mere boy, sits on Adam's almost passive body, these half-starved men stuff themselves from the supplies in Adam's sutler's wagon. But their hunger humanizes them for Adam: he "felt a sweet sadness fill his heart. He loved the boy because the boy had been very hungry and now had food." The psychology here is sound enough: it is always easier for the Adams of our world to accept the fact that they share a basic humanity with the enemy than to accept the evident bestiality within their allies or the latent bestiality within themselves. For Adam, that more difficult acceptance is late in coming.

First, a detachment of Federal troops surprises the Confederates; then in the ensuing fight Adam manages to reach a rifle and kills one of the Confederate soldiers. The Federal troops rush away in pursuit of the enemy, and Adam once more finds himself alone. He experiences a moment of pride in the proof that, though crippled, he is man enough to act and kill. But his momentary pride flickers out into dejection and bitterness. He is lost in the forest and barefoot—one of the retreating Confederates has taken Adam's boots, including the one carefully fashioned by a Bavarian cobbler especially for his deformed foot. Adam has lost his team: one horse has been killed; the other has run away. He finds himself again questioning his motives for having come to America. Perhaps he had come simply to justify himself. He weighs too the consequences of this coming: besides being responsible for the death of the Confederate soldier, is he not responsible also for the death of Jed Hawskworth?

In his bitterness he feels that the world has betrayed him—even his father, who bequeathed him the idealism that forced him toward the conflict for freedom but who also bequeathed the deformed foot that renders him unable to become freedom's soldier—even his father has betrayed him. For a moment he decides to accept the betrayal. Henceforth he will be tough-minded and hard-boiled. As he walks over to strip the boots from the dead soldier, he feels that he has at last discovered the nature of the world. All that he had previously believed was false. The bitter discovery actually gives him a sense of release and of power. Now at last he knows the truth about reality.

Hardened by this new and devastating knowledge, he tells himself, as he stares at the face of the soldier whom he has killed: "I killed him because his foot was not like mine." This remark is, of course, a fantastic over-simplification, but it does at least testify to Adam's having peered into the depths of himself and having glimpsed the dark side of his own motivation: specifically, the fact that his crippled foot has indeed had its part in his desire to engage in this war. But as he tries to put on the dead soldier's boots, his glance happens to fall upon the phylactery and the talith which he has brought from Bavaria and which, though he had given up his religion, he had never been quite able to bring himself to throw away. In the looting of the wagon, they have been tossed aside. Seeing them, he is suddenly smitten with a sense of desolation. He takes off the dead man's boots and sets them down tidily near the corpse. "In a numb, quiet way he thought how foolish this was." And yet he has to do it. He peers again into the dead man's face and tries to see whether it shows any mark of the young man's life. He wonders how his own dead face will look and asks himself the question: "Am I different from other men?"

The redness in the sky tells him that the forest is now on fire, set aflame by the guns, and he realizes that he ought to go and drag the wounded away from the flames. He strains his ears to hear the cries of the wounded, but he can hear only the imagined cries within his own head. Suddenly, he finds himself praying the prayers that he had learned as a boy: "Have mercy upon the remnant of the flock of Thy hand, and say unto the Destroying Angel, Stay thy hand."

As the book ends, Adam is ready to rise and try to make his rescue. In a sense it will be what he has to do, just as his coming across the sea and joining in the fight for freedom was what he has had to do. But he has broken "the compulsion of the dream" which has held him up to this time. It is not that his action in seeking to fight for freedom, because it was a compulsive action, has been wrong. He knows that he would do it again, but now he cries "in his inwardness: *But, oh, with a different heart!*" He prepares to pick up the dead man's boots (with a different heart he can now accept them), put them on, and hobble out of the forest glade.

What has happened, of course, is that Adam has discovered himself and, now understanding himself, can forgive, and ask forgiveness of, his parents; can accept the past; and can enter into communion with mankind. His experience parallels in general terms the experience of several of Warren's other characters— it is like that of Jack Burden at the end of *All the King's Men*, or that of the heroine of *Band of Angels*, who hates her father for what he has done to her and only at the end finds herself able to forgive him, to accept her past, and thus to find freedom.

This matter of man's relation to the ideal runs through the fiction and the poetry of Warren. A Christian may be tempted to transpose the problem into that of conversion or redemption. But if he yields to the temptation, he must take the responsibility for the transposition and not assume that it formed part of the author's intention. Still, there is no doubt that one can learn from Warren's fiction and poetry a great deal about the psychology of conversion and the cost of redemption even though Warren himself poses his problems in non-Christian terms—often in terms of the movement from ignorance to knowledge or from bafflement and confusion to order and insight.

Warren's poem "Walk by Moonlight in a Small Town" is a beautiful instance. The speaker returns to his boyhood home and finds the little town, in spite of all its tawdry "matter of fact," filled to the brim with mystery.

And pitiful was the moon-bare ground.
Dead grass, the gravel, earth ruined and raw—
It had not changed. And then I saw
That children were playing, with no sound.
They ceased their play, then quiet as moonlight,
    drew, slow, around.

Their eyes were fixed on me, and I
Now, tried, face by pale face, to find
The names that haunted in my mind.
Each small, upgazing face would lie
Sweet as a puddle, and silver-calm, to the night sky.

But something grew in their pale stare:
Nor reprobation or surprise,
Nor even forgiveness in their eyes,
But a humble question dawning there,
From face to face, like beseechment dawning on empty air.

Here the children remembered from his boyhood put the question to
him, not he to them. It is a question that he would answer, but obviously
no man can answer.

Might a man but know his Truth, and might
He live so that life, by moon or sun,
In dusk or dawn, would be all one,
Then never on a summer night
Need he stand and shake in that cold blaze of Platonic light.

But what the poet says here is humanly impossible. Man can never know
his truth so thoroughly that he will not need to shake in the cold blaze of the
light of the ideal. It is a beautiful poem and the Christian may perhaps be
forgiven for boldly appropriating it as a tender though completely unsenti-
mental statement of the way in which the whole human creation yearns
toward the truth that would give it significance and thus redeem it from its
all-too-evident mutability into eternity. But how honest the poem is! For
the desiderated truth is a judgment as well as a revelation.

Robert Penn Warren's *Night Rider:*
The Nihilism of the Isolated Temperament

by Alvan S. Ryan

In taking my sub-title from one of Mr. Morton Zabel's essays on the fiction of Joseph Conrad, I want to suggest that the similarity often noted between the themes of Conrad and Warren furnishes a valuable clue to the interpretation of Warren's first novel, *Night Rider.* The context of Zabel's phrase is his essay on *The Nigger of the "Narcissus,"* one of Conrad's earliest works. Zabel calls it "the work in which Conrad first defined the central motives of his art" and finds in it several of "the primary conceptions that were to be developed and given their full complexity of realization in his future novels." Similarly, *Night Rider* can be said to define the central motives of Warren's art, and I would add, too, that while the "full complexity of realization" found in Warren's later novels is not here, there is nevertheless an impressive unity of structure, a concentration and focus, that has its own artistic justification.

Zabel sees as central to *The Nigger of the "Narcissus":*

> ...that drama of man's destiny which Conrad repeatedly emphasized: the conflict between his isolation as an individual, the incommunicable secrecy of the self which begins and ends in loneliness, and his need to share his life with others, the force of that "solidarity" which Conrad insistently invoked as a human necessity, a mode of salvation from the nihilism of the isolated temperament. An "unavoidable solidarity," he called it, "the solidarity in mysterious origin, in toil, in joy, in hope, in uncertain fate, which binds men to each other and all mankind to the visible world."[1]

I would call attention especially to the word "nihilism" in this passage, because at least one critic (Norman Kelvin, in *College English,* April, 1957) has called Warren a "moral nihilist," whereas a careful reading of *Night*

[1]*Craft and Character in Modern Fiction* (New York, 1957), p. 182.

Rider shows that while the protagonist's nihilistic attitude is of central importance, this attitude is not at all to be equated with the novelist's vision. As I hope to show, the protagonist is torn by the conflict Zabel speaks of, and attempts to escape from loneliness and isolation. His failure is that he embraces a false solidarity, and, paradoxically, in so doing only increases his sense of isolation.

The theme of the novel is the search of the hero for self-definition and self-knowledge. This is Warren's first treatment of a theme that has frequently been pointed out as central to all of his fiction. The hero's discovery, under the pressure of moral choice and action, of what kind of man he is, of the terms within which he can act, and of what fulfills or destroys his search for meaning and significance, is the burden of the novel. From the outset Mr. Percy Munn is set apart from the other characters; he is always an isolated man. The theme is embodied in the action of the novel in a powerfully ironic way, for the action traces Munn's progressive discovery that in allying himself with a political and economic association calling itself a "Brotherhood" he discovers only his own emptiness in his relations with his mistress, Lucille Christian, and finally the very basis of his sense of selfhood, the relation between his present actions, his past, and a possible future, disintegrates completely.

What kind of man is Mr. Munn? The essential thing is that he is a divided man who does not know himself and the terms within which he can act. Yet he struggles toward this knowledge and broods over his acts after they are committed. It is, in fact, Munn's relentless self-scrutiny that makes him a character of essential dignity, and gives to the novel much of its impact. But his failure is due to a deep inner nihilism that is a kind of darkness. Images of darkness, of night, or of loneliness and isolation are associated with all of Munn's broodings, and perhaps nowhere more effectively than in the symbolic image of the grackles that opens Chapter 9:

> One clear afternoon, as he walked down a quiet street between the rows of dull-colored brick houses, the grackles came sweeping over the roofs, not flying very high, and settled in the trees of a little park just ahead. He stopped stock-still, one hand on the iron fence in front of a narrow dooryard. Then, slowly, he walked on down the street, toward the little park where the grackles were. In the overmastering loneliness of that moment, his whole life seemed to him nothing but vanity. His past seemed as valueless and as unstable as a puff of smoke, and his future meaningless, unless—and the thought was a flash, quickly dissipated—he might by some unnamable, single, heroic stroke discover the unifying fulfillment.[2]

His urge toward community with other men is counterpointed against this sense of isolation. What he does not learn until too late—yet, as I read the

[2]Robert Penn Warren, *Night Rider* (New York: Random House [; London: Martin Secker & Warburg Limited] , 1939), p. 208.

novel, he does at last learn it—is that the anarchic and immoral actions of the Association, however just the claim for a fair price for their tobacco crop, are only a travesty of the true search for community. The community or solidarity he wants is one that respects the individual human person and the imperatives of his sole self, not one that swallows up the individual in some absolute. Hence, as the action unfolds, Munn, far from being drawn closer to other men, is able only to give himself to the abstract idea of the Association of Growers of Dark Fired Tobacco, and his isolation is increased rather than diminished.

The opening incidents of the novel reveal an uncertainty in Mr. Munn that is immediately felt as having tragic possibilities. He is drawn into a leading role in the Association by a series of maneuvers which he momentarily resists, then gives in to. He is drawn in by the firm wills of other men, men like Mr. Christian and Senator Tolliver. He comes in to Bardsville for a meeting, but he does not want to be there; he resents the physical pressure, the pushing of the crowd to get out of the train, and we are soon aware that he gives way to a series of pressures, not of bodies but of wills, that are just as insistent. And the opening scene becomes an image of Munn's situation, of his essential isolation even when he is in the midst of men, and of his failure to define the way in which he would assert either his own identity, or his "solidarity," in Conrad's sense, with other men.

When Mr. Christian calls the first meeting of the Association, and asks Munn to come alone, Munn at first protests, but on Mr. Christian's assurance that "it's not official or anything" (p. 12) he assents. (Mr. Christian's daughter Lucille has already made the first advances toward Munn that foreshadow her own way of maneuvering him.) Christian breaks down Munn's resistance by flattery. "You're a smart man, Perse..." (p. 12). Later, Christian uses the same tactics to persuade Munn to join him, Senator Tolliver, and Captain Todd at dinner. We now see the root of Munn's conflict in his musing on what he wants from life. He is attracted to a life deeply rooted in Southern tradition, to a life of politics combined with the law and the management of his farm. Yet "if he desired anything of life, that thing was to be free, and himself" (p. 13). From the dinner he goes to the mass meeting, in which he has no intention of taking an active part. Yet he is ushered up to the platform, and in a state of bewilderment as to how he has been so deftly manipulated, he even makes a speech.

Later in his hotel room Munn thinks back on the speech and decides that "he had been drunk.... He felt cheated and betrayed" (p. 30). The two scenes suggest an undefined emptiness in Munn, even a readiness to be the prey of another's will. His passivity leads him away from the desire he had expressed "to be free and himself."

Munn takes a further step into the organization when he accepts membership on the board of directors of the tobacco growers' association. Yet here again he tries to refuse; and for months afterwards he speculates as to why he had not been firm in his refusal. "Mr. Munn's common sense, his logic, had conspired with his friends to force his acceptance. Such chances to get along didn't turn up every day to a young man of thirty. He had better grab it" (pp. 32-33). His response, however, is not this simple, but curiously ambivalent, for he also remembers months later—and the mood is precisely like the one that gripped him after his first speech—that in accepting "he felt unmanned and ashamed, as though an unsuspected weakness had betrayed him" (p. 33). When he tells his wife, May, that he has been named to the board, and she expresses pleasure at the news, he is disappointed at her response. Yet why should he expect her to detect the false impulse at the root of his acceptance if he could not define it himself? For Munn, there is defeat involved in his activities with the Association long before he has taken part in any violence. Even the rain on the roof over their heads at one of the meetings seems to beat on his mind, "dulling him, conquering him, and those other men, into a kind of immemorial passivity and acceptance" (p. 39).

It is a mark of Mr. Munn's inner division that another response, quite different, alternates with this one. He is frequently seized by a sense of exaltation and elation. As he watches farmers signing their names and joining the Association, he experiences "the grip of an absolute, throbless pleasure in which he seemed poised out of himself and, as it were, out of time" (p. 37). He lives in a state of excitement as though "poised on the brink of revelation"; his energy "seemed boundless" (p. 45). Why this elation comes to him he does not know, and when he tries to define it to his wife the words fail him. Here Warren touches on one of the deep moral issues involved in influence and persuasion, for Munn is not simply avid for power. On the contrary, it is usually his vision of some single person in his audience, his recognition of one man's significance as a man, that frees his tongue. It is this that he tries to tell his wife. But this sense of persons, which would have been Munn's salvation had he held onto it, is obscured by the clearer impulse toward power. Munn, in fact, is trying to define himself by his power over others. If he cannot see this himself, it is because of his infatuation. His elation comes from a sense of power over others, a sense that he is influencing their wills— even as his own is being swayed. And in this elation he forgets, or fills temporarily, the loneliness and emptiness within him. He is unaware of the irony of his inner division, of the fact that the elation he feels as others join the Association is the same sense of power felt by those like Senator Tolliver and Mr. Christian, who are using him; while, if he feels that another part of his being is betrayed, he is yet unaware that he must also in his success be betraying others. How much these pragmatic conquests mean to Munn is clear on the night when he is unable to persuade anyone to join. "It had gone black out for him, as suddenly and as irrelevantly as the man's face above the lamp the instant the flame was extinguished. ... At what moment could a man trust his feelings, his convictions?" (pp. 40-41).

The conflict of two selves in Munn is given dramatic form by his relationship to two men, Captain Todd and Senator Tolliver, who represent the two paths open to him from the outset of the action. The way which he rejects by a series of bad decisions is that of Todd, who has the "deep, inner certainty of self" (p. 43) which Munn aspires to but lacks. Todd is firm in his moral decisions. He is not an opportunist, and he will neither abrogate nor abdicate his freedom of decision and his sense of justice. Tolliver is the opportunist, the compromiser. His flattery probes and finds Munn's weakness, which is his inability to decide between his desire "to be free and himself" and his desire for public acclaim and for a political career like Tolliver's, even at the cost of compromise.

The scene early in the novel (Ch. 4), in which the members of the Association Board meet at Senator Tolliver's house, shows Munn poised between Todd and Tolliver, and fatally erring in his judgment of the latter. The bond linking Tolliver and Munn is Munn's ambition. Just as Tolliver, as a young lawyer, had been advised to enter politics, so Munn, himself a lawyer and thirty years old, has been tempted against his better judgment to accept a position on the board because it is too good a chance to miss. Now the Senator's flattery further infatuates Munn. When Tolliver introduces him as "my good friend Percy Munn" and adds, "We'll have him in Congress yet" (p. 93), Munn is pleased by the empty words and the hand on his shoulder. His moral vision obscured by flattery, Munn later sits at the meeting looking from the Senator to Captain Todd, and decides that "he was a good man, the Senator, but Captain Todd was a better. The best of the lot. But the Senator was a good man" (p. 95).

In this same scene Munn's uncertainty is again shown by his apologetic tone when he discusses with Captain Todd's son, Benton, his own decision to begin law practice, not away from home, as the young man decides to do, but in Bardsville. Perhaps, he says, it was a mistake. And when Benton compliments him on his speech at the mass meeting, Munn dismisses it as "an accident" and muses on "the accidents which were his history" (p. 103).

Looking back on this crucial Christmas meeting, Munn realizes that "he had been taken in" by Senator Tolliver. But it is important to notice that in spite of his frequent references to "accident" he does not call this accident. Only for a moment had he been struck by "the force of accident and change." "Later, he was to curse his blindness, his stupidity, and his vanity" (p. 113). He had not known himself, so how could he know the others? But this clear vision of his own weakness is after the event, and it does not govern his response to those of the same kind that follow. For when in early spring the association receives the rigged offers of several large buyers, Munn votes with Tolliver to accept them, though the vote is carried against acceptance. The Senator's subsequent resignation from the board and the discovery that he has been bought off are deeply disillusioning to Munn. Yet his response is ironically self-destructive, and a further evidence of Tolliver's role as his *alter ego.* Musing, on his return home, that Tolliver "was out to break what he had made" ("To destroy what you create—that was power, the fullest manifestation. ... The last vanity" [p. 126]), Munn purposely breaks the news to his wife in the most unsettling way possible. He realizes that he wants to make her suffer, yet he "enjoyed the moment, postponing consideration of the event, and of the judgment which, he knew, he would later bring to bear bitterly against himself" (p. 128).

Thenceforth Mr. Munn more and more gives himself to the "idea" of the Association, doing things he hates, yet doing them nonetheless. His awareness of his self-betrayal is shown by a whole pattern of incidents and images. He acts joylessly, reluctantly, often petulantly. He sullenly performs acts he does not believe in, and his inner division is made manifest in the physical revulsion of his own nerves and body. His nausea, his retching, and, after the lynching of Bunk Trevelyan, his vomiting show the price Munn is paying for his failure of moral will. Looking for a scapegoat, Munn comes to see in Tolliver the enemy on whom he would have revenge. His wife sees the change in him and though she senses its cause she no longer can reach him, while he knows that he is "destroying the promise of happiness" she had given him (p. 160).

With the formation of the Protective Brotherhood, farmers who refuse to join are forced at gunpoint to scrape their own plantbeds, and the violence of the night rider activities increases. Barn burnings and the dynamiting of warehouses are followed by the retaliatory burning of houses. Here again, the relation of Tolliver and Munn is developed through symbolic incident and through the very structure of the novel. Tolliver, now in the service of the buyers, makes a public address denouncing the night riders. Munn listens, and as he looks at the "somewhat stooped, sallow" man on the baggage platform he feels "the firmness of the hatred within himself" (p. 301), and relishes it as something he can depend on and cling to and cherish "as one fingers a token or a keepsake, which is nothing in itself, but which means the reality of one's past,...the fact of one's identity" (p. 302). Yet as Munn reflects on the change in Tolliver from the day of the first rally, he realizes how much he, too, has changed. "He hung poised on the brink of that thought, as on the brink of a blackness" (p. 302). (The sentence echoes with an ironic change the earlier one, describing his feelings as he watched men joining the Association, when Munn felt "poised as on the brink of revelation.")

That same night the Senator's house, Monclair, is burned to the ground, and Munn's place is next. This suggestion of the intertwining of the fates of the two men foreshadows the final confrontation between them. From the window of Mr. Munn's office Dr. Ball, in Munn's absence, fires from Munn's rifle the shot that kills Turpin, and the blame is placed on Munn. So Munn, who is certain it was his bullet that killed Bunk Trevelyan, and who feels remorse at the death of Benton Todd, is hunted now for a murder he did not commit. He flees and hides out at the Proudfit farm, where he is visited by Lucille Christian, who tells him of Senator Tolliver's advances toward her. Her twice repeated "He's nothing" defines the emptiness and the coldness of Munn himself, his betrayal of his own nature in favor of "events" and abstract ideas. And it plants in Munn the desire for final vengeance on Tolliver.

It takes Munn two days and two nights to reach the miserable house where the once lofty Senator now lies dying. Munn enters the bedroom and stares across the footboard at his enemy. Then he levels his revolver. But Tolliver's calm courage is unnerving. Munn's words, "If I didn't kill you, you'd lie here, in this house, and be nothing...you were always nothing," bring the one reply from Tolliver that echoes Munn's subconscious knowledge. "'Nothing,' the voice echoed questioningly. 'A man never knows what he is, Perse. You don't know what you are, Perse'" (p. 456).

Munn's resolve is gone. He sees now that to murder Tolliver would be a final act of self-destruction as well. The emptiness is in himself. The revolver slowly drops to his side, and Tolliver asks for a drink of water. Munn pours the water from a pitcher and hands the Senator the glass, but at this very moment the posse hunting for Munn approaches the house. Munn escapes out the rear door and heads for the woods, falling twice as he runs in the dark. He sees the form of a man "against the field and paler sky" and aims his revolver. But before shooting "he lifted his arm a little toward the paleness of the sky" (p. 460), and within this moment of hesitation and with this signal the shot is fired that kills him.

This final scene of the novel has been interpreted as suggesting that to the end Mr. Munn is without self-knowledge, that he remains a rider, as Eric Bentley has put it, "in the night of the spirit." Perhaps so. Yet if we return to the final paragraph of Chapter I, we see Warren using a device that Conrad uses in *Typhoon,* and that is the placing at the end of the initial chapter of a passage central to the entire theme. For the paradoxical relation between communion and isolation seems to me to be this theme. In the final scene of the opening chapter Munn stands at the window of his hotel room, looking down at the crowd milling around in the street near midnight. He remembers how he had spoken to them in the afternoon, and in retrospect the poise and exaltation he had felt now makes him feel cheated and betrayed. But then:

> He recalled that that afternoon he had said something about what one man owed to another. One man was very much like another. He was like those

men, one of them. Unbidden, warm and pulsing, that exaltation returned to him, more perfect than under the brilliant sun. . . . Involuntarily, he raised his arm as though to address a great multitude and tell them what he knew to be the truth. (p. 30)

One is tempted to say that this truth is the sense of communion, the sense of what one man owes another, but the very tone in which it is conveyed in this earlier passage of the novel shows that Munn does not really possess such a truth; rather, he knows it only in a confused and emotional way, and only momentarily. Throughout the novel this dimly recognized sense of true solidarity, while it troubles both Munn's proud isolation and his capitulations to a false solidarity, is always defeated. Yet in the final scene with Tolliver he recovers it, though the recovery comes too late. He realizes that to kill Tolliver would not make him "something," as he thought. He knows now that what he hates in Tolliver, his duplicity, his dependence on others for his existence, have their seeds in himself, and that in himself he must destroy them. Hence the importance of the single gesture of Munn's when he hands Tolliver the glass of water. It is significant, too, as indicating a momentary though unclear recognition of "solidarity," that the final gesture of the novel parallels the gesture in the passage just quoted from the first chapter. "But without thought—he did not know why—at the long instant before his finger drew the trigger to the guard and the blunt, frayed flame leaped from the muzzle, he had lifted his arm a little toward the paleness of the sky" (p. 460).

I interpret this gesture as symbolizing Munn's imperfect awareness of his predicament, not as an affirmative recognition. Returning to Zabel's comment on *The Nigger of the "Narcissus,"* it is clear that in *Night Rider* there is no movement from "the nihilism of the isolated temperament" toward such a sense of solidarity as is expressed in the narrator's final words to his shipmates on the "Narcissus"; "Haven't we, together and upon the immortal sea, wrung out a meaning from our sinful lives?" This is exactly what Munn has been unable to do. Nor does Munn, night rider that he is, ever win from his journey into the heart of darkness, or from his confrontation of his alter ego, the recognition and self-knowledge that Marlow returns with. It is rather the Jack Burden of *All the King's Men* who finally emerges from nihilism and isolation, to see the spider web image of Cass Mastern's diary as a symbol of what Conrad calls "the solidarity in mysterious origin, in toil, in joy, in hope, in uncertain fate, which binds men to each other and all mankind to the visible world." Yet *Night Rider* is a powerful dramatization of the efforts of a man deficient in self-knowledge to emerge from isolation into solidarity. His failure is that the solidarity he embraces is at its roots immoral and absolutist, a travesty of the true solidarity that begins with "the deep, inner certainty of self."

On the Politics of the Self-Created:

At Heaven's Gate

by James H. Justus

Robert Penn Warren's first two novels have often seemed better as the trying-out of *All the King's Men* than as novels in their own right. Certainly, as studies of the nature and uses of political power, *Night Rider* and *At Heaven's Gate* are anticipatory. Both touch on big bossism in its corporate and individual forms, and both dramatize the dangers to the morally insensitive individual posed by abstract embodiments of power: the Association of Growers of Dark Fired Tobacco in one, Bogan Murdock's financial empire in the other. And compared to the firm assurances of the third novel, both seem tentative: they lack a particularized, sensuously immediate politician whose motives and acts are examined in a context of rich circumstantiality, as well as an engaging figure who is articulate enough to justify his credibility as a man both morally aware and expediently knowledgeable. Willie Stark and Jack Burden, for all their foreshadowings, had to wait for *All the King's Men.*

Although we occasionally still hear opinions that *Night Rider* is Warren's best novel (opinions which become more assertive with successive appearances of Warren's later work), only one critic to my knowledge has suggested that *At Heaven's Gate* is even his *second* best. I do not believe that *Night Rider,* for all its precision and control, is Warren's finest novel, and at least two later titles can rival *At Heaven's Gate* for second place. But neither of his first two novels is apprentice fiction—we know that there were two earlier attempts which did not reach print—and both are works that deserve recognition without the inevitable use of *All the King's Men* as some kind of ultimate model.

There are flaws aplenty in *At Heaven's Gate,* not the least of which are the undisguised threads stitching the various segments together like a patchwork quilt. There are occasional spurts of fancy writing, and its more self-conscious effects are obviously derivative and uncertainly controlled.

"On the Politics of the Self-Created: *At Heaven's Gate*" by James H. Justus. From *Sewanee Review,* LXXXII (1974), 284-99. © 1974 by the University of the South. Reprinted by permission of *Sewanee Review.*

(The derivation is mostly from Faulkner: there are detectable echoes from *The Sound and the Fury, The Wild Palms,* and perhaps *Sanctuary.*) The whole of chapter 13, which contains the most pretentious writing of the novel, is also a technical shambles. In it are wasted closeups (for the first time) of Dorothy Murdock, who scarcely matters in the thrust of the plot, and the young Negro house man, Anse, who matters only in the final few pages because he is falsely accused of Sue Murdock's murder; it also contains scenes of Sue's final break with her family, which are jaggedly ineffective, even as melodrama.

Despite all these flaws *At Heaven's Gate* is finally more interesting than *Night Rider.* Its stylistic modulations, its scattergun point of view, and its deployment of multiple narratives can be seen as both untidy and typically Warrenesque. For the first time we see the rich profusion of favorite words and phrases—"the blind, unqualified retch and spasm of the flesh, the twist, the sudden push, the twitch, the pinch of ejection and refusal"—and the lengthy segments of second-person idiom, faintly ironic and precisely detailed, straight out of the tough-guy and private-eye tradition of the 1920s and 1930s. And, in its more discursive moments, *At Heaven's Gate* achieves a kind of lyric naturalism that becomes a hallmark of Warren's prose: periods of closely observed details strung out in an evocative rhetoric which invites nostalgia for a specific time and place or which invokes awe for a mythic history that seems to explain national and even human urges.

Someone once noted that *At Heaven's Gate* is Warren's only city novel. In a technical sense this is true. But it is also the closest Warren ever came to writing an agrarian novel. The values associated with southern Agrarianism —integration of personality, mutual responsibility, and a general harmony of man and nature—are conspicuously missing in the lives of the major characters, but their very absence is a measure of their importance.

The urban setting (a city like Nashville) and the time (the 1920s) suggest strongly that Warren's second novel establishes the New South as a home-grown wasteland. The novel is studded with physical and spiritual images of disease, perversion, filth; and its characters are dominated by movers and shakers who keep one eye on public relations and the other on schemes for maintaining wealth and power through abstract finance. *At Heaven's Gate* is Warren's only work in which the combined effects of technology, finance capitalism, and political power are examined so explicitly, even obviously. Bogan Murdock, the chief symbol of power, is a hollow man; and most of the other characters are fragmented people spiritually awash in a milieu stripped of the values that presumably once obtained in an agrarian mode of life.

The countryside is seen almost totally as remote, though not remote enough to escape victimization by urban greed. Surrounding land is foreclosed for commercial exploitation by functionaries within Murdock's empire. The solidity and specificity of the land are absorbed by abstract capitalism and retained only as ironic pastoral names of the major interlocked Murdock enterprises: Massey Mountain, Happy Valley, Pretty River. Mr. Calhoun is the only genuine countryman in the novel. Quiet and ineffectual, he is a reminder—hardly even a backdrop for important scenes—of simple and profound human values and an implicit model by which the lapses of others, including his son's, are contrasted. That standard is unobtrusive but pervasive.

The "Jesus-struck" hillman, Ashby Wyndham, is the only articulate spokesman for rural values, and that only secondary, since his chief concern is his moral failure in his role as wandering evangelist. His earlier sin is in striking his brother, who wants to retain the family farm despite Ashby's eagerness to sell, get his share of the money, and be off to the urban fleshpots. But one of Ashby's themes is the general decline in the quality of life after the coming of "newfangleness." The immediate source of his spiritual sloth he cites as "abominations under the ridgepole of the Lord's house," but he also looks back to earlier days before "the change of time," when the woods were "full of varmints yit, and squirrils fat in the trees, lak apples when the limb bends, and turkeys gabblin…[and] the skillit never groan[ing] empty." Jerry Calhoun's great-uncle Lew raves about land grabbing—a very real thing, since Murdock is engaged in seizing commercial advantage out of his apparent gift of a forest preserve.

The entire rural environment is threatened by "development." Massey Mountain is seen in terms of mines, timber, resources; and the promotional phrases for justifying its exploitation are "expansion and development," "haven't scratched the surface," "bold enough and farsighted," and "free flow of financing." Sweetwater, the union organizer, puts the matter bluntly: "They took the iron out and cut it over and blew the rock out and starved the folks to death and the ground's washed away." He is right in his charge, of course, though his function at Massey Mountain is just as manipulative as the capitalist owners. The total result is, predictably enough, radical dehumanization.

Given the lapse of necessary and sustaining values, what is left is manner—watching and learning "methods." The novel is a brilliant example of Warren's insight into the manipulative uses of technique. The roles his characters play are desperate, and the techniques of their playing serve to mask, distract, or deceive. The major psychological patterns of the novel involve rejection and repudiation, often in violent ways. In most cases what the characters react against is the continuing relationship of the individual with the home, the past, and tradition. In Warren's own Unreal City the uses of technique are necessarily efforts to remake the self after new images, to fill the gaps left by the repudiation, to heal what Jack Burden of *All the King's Men* calls the terrible division of the age. What usually results in these efforts to create the self anew is to widen the division and make it all the more terrible.

Warren returns again and again to the notion of how Bogan Murdock operates in abstraction without concern for human involvement. His manner with his subordinates is assured, cool, detached—and effective. Jerry becomes head of the securities department of a new Murdock bank *because* he knows as little about its operation as Private Porsum, the president, knows about banking generally. Jerry's decision to reject a career in geology (a science based on the tangible manifestations of nature) for the abstractions of speculative finance is symbolically confirmed at his graduation. There his geologist mentor meets and chats with Jerry's father; Murdock, glimpsed in the crowd, is mysteriously unavailable—and even unseen except by his future employee. And when Jerry becomes engaged to Sue Murdock, his cynical accountant friend, Duckfoot Blake, suggests that he ask for a cash settlement: "Cash, not paper. Not a scrap of Bogan's paper. Or some day you will be using it in the backhouse." (It is the prescient Blake who explains to Jerry: "Bogan is a solar myth, he is a pixy, he is a poltergeist. ... When Bogan Murdock looks in the mirror, he don't see a thing.")

Around this hollow man are gathered associates and even members of his own family who serve only as adjuncts to his power. Enormously polite, Murdock has a bland exterior which is of a piece with his speech patterns, a compound of clichés drawn from patriotic oratory and idioms drawn from indulgent parental lectures. This rhetoric and manner are tools, says his daughter, to make people do what he wants. And most people are gullible enough to be taken in by what Duckfoot Blake calls "the voice of the charmer" and "the smile of the Crucified Redeemer." Murdock is Warren's single most explicit exhibit of how substance has been reduced to salesmanship, and Jerry Calhoun is his fullest development of those figures who are unable to distinguish the difference.

Like Percy Munn of *Night Rider* Jerry Calhoun is unable to communicate to others what he is like or how he feels. To dramatize the state of the spiritual drifter, Warren shows how, almost unconsciously, Jerry falls into the styles of living which insure a blind security without the burden of human responsibility. Vaguely dissatisfied with himself and with only a blurred sense of identity, Jerry seizes upon certain kinds of patterns which land him a feeling of greater inner clarity and security. As a football player he cherishes certain plays because they permit him to be caught up into "a pure, rhythmic, fluctuating but patterned flow of being" which momentarily protects him from "the disorders and despairs of his life." Later his homework in the banking business—reading books and reports which Blake recommends—offers him something similar: "It was so clean and sure, that flow of unheard voice off the page—a guarantee that the world was secure, was a pattern which you could grasp and live by."

Jerry rejects the past because it is not a guarantee of security; his father's house, in fact, embodies the truth of man's financial precariousness and his physical imperfections. Only painfully does Mr. Calhoun make the family farm minimally productive. Within the household are two people, one embittered and lame, the other almost vegetablelike in her blindness and immobility. And the most painful sight for Jerry is his father, who performs simple chores clumsily, then goes about his tasks of caring for these people whose only actual relationship to him is through marriage. Such visible evidence of insecurity and imperfection is revulsive to Jerry, whose only alternative is withdrawal from all human relationships that demand responsibility. He therefore rejects his past because he equates it with inadequacy, imperfection, failure. To accept it would be to accept what he most fears. In denying that responsibility he also denies the mutual warmth and closeness which could purge his fears. There is, then, always a chilly impersonality in his friendships among the other Murdock boys, and Sue rightly detects that their affair is loveless and mechanical.

The past rejected (or, more precisely, avoided, since he is too passive to reject outright), Jerry has only the present, and, because he cannot endure meaningful relations with others, even that present is delicate and precarious. He moves smoothly on the surfaces, adopting the bland Murdock's speech patterns, gestures, attitudes, along with his New York tailor. Murdock is his model not merely because he is the top man but also because, psychologically, Murdock so successfully ignores the problems of emotional entanglements, a problem which the long-suffering Mr. Calhoun never acknowledges as a problem. His coolness is unruffled, his concern itself devoted only to making others help him to perpetuate his power. Jerry cherishes the present world, and he is discomfited by anything in it which recalls his past and the human imperfections associated with it: Blake's bumbling parents, for example, or Rosemary, Sue's painfully crippled friend. Particularly reproachful to him is the warmth of the Blake house: for hours after a visit he suffers from "elegiac melancholy" and "diffused despair."

Jerry Calhoun never knows with any precision who he is. In our first glimpse of him he is rehearsing available definitions ("Bull's-eye Calhoun," the boy who "brought back the bacon from New York") until his very name echoes in his head "like a set of nonsense syllables." And at the last scene he has become, literally, what Sue Murdock once accused him of being, an "emotional cripple" in the house of cripples, like Aunt Ursula and Uncle Lew, under his father's care. In between, to compensate for his avoidance of human involvement, he cultivates the manner of the progressive businessman on the way up.

Warren devotes most of chapter 5 to Jerry's training for his job. While he studiously learns the basic principles of economics and the technicalities of investments and securities, Jerry is most adept at learning the required amenities of getting along in his new milieu: what to wear, what to say to associates, where to live (Blake tells him that the smell of cabbage clings to his clothing if he lives in a boarding house too long). And, most important, he learns the trick of successful behavior with potential customers:

> It was all easier than he had imagined.... If they asked him questions or asked for his opinion, he would answer not too discursively, nodding slightly, his manner respectful but authoritative. He was not afraid to disagree with them. He knew football and fishing and hunting; and they knew that he knew those things. When the men talked to him about business or politics, he listened in the same way; and when they asked him a question he replied in the same way, rather briefly, respectfully, not afraid to disagree, not afraid to say that he did not know, nodding almost imperceptibly, with a slight corrugation of the strong, glowing flesh between his straight brows.

These are the resources of a not especially intelligent man who avoids the reality of his past (and sometimes fantasizes it into something more genteel) by steeling himself against involvement, a man whose fragmented identity is supplemented by a reliance on self-conscious tricks, manners, gestures.

His affair with Sue Murdock ironically undercuts Jerry's best efforts to achieve a harmonious, well-regulated, and "healthy" position within her father's organization. For Sue, like Jerry, is also repudiating home, past, tradition. Her restlessness, her refusal to accept an understood place in her family circle, is marked by several instances: her insistence on sexual intercourse at the most dangerous times and in the most dangerous places; her perverse taunting of Jerry, her brother, her father, her mother, and her grandfather. Moreover the second world which Sue enters impinges uncomfortably on Jerry's plans. It is precisely the phony world of the university and the little theater, the functions of which suggest the diverse and the tangential, which threatens the routine niche that Jerry is laboring to carve out for himself. Sue's strategies are more desperate than her lover's: having rejected an unsatisfactory definition of herself, she is still searching for a satisfactory one.

If chapter 5 shows Jerry learning the techniques necessary for a new self, chapter 7 and its extension in chapter 19 describe Sue's efforts. At play rehearsals Jerry wonders to what extent her reciting of fictional "sentiments and passions" is her own; even the "familiar fluent movement from the waist and shift of the shoulder" are convincing. But he is quick to detect the artifice of her special language which she uses with her new friends: "Oh, she was the queen, all right, Jerry thought. Bullying them and saying, 'Darling, darling, blessed one,' in that phony voice he hated, which wasn't her voice, which was a voice she never used except when she was with these phonies."

Under the tutelage of Slim Sarrett, Sue progresses from the early state of being unable "to put it into words" to that state which Jerry so despises: the carefully learned, calculated repartee which she develops by skimming through current issues and fads and applying to them fragments of wit and breathless pauses. The technique never wholly satisfies her, but since her goal of self-definition is so hazy, she must concentrate on the method to get as much as she can from the immediate moment. With cues from Sarrett she polishes her techniques:

> Something is *like* something else—oh, just like something—the "just" was important—and you shut your eyes and it popped into your head and you said it, and they would laugh. But you yourself did not laugh. You just sat there with your face straight, just as straight as you could make it. Unless nobody laughed at first. Then you looked off to one corner of the room, and smiled just a little bit to yourself, like you knew something, and then—it always worked that way—somebody laughed, like he knew something too.

It is ironic that Jerry, who perceives the artifice and the special language of Sue, takes Murdock's speeches and gestures at face value. The easy, seductive conversation, the confidential intimacy, the calculated show of emotion, the very stock speeches stitched with parental and political clichés: all are part of his actuating rhetoric, and all make Jerry "relaxed, patient, and strong." Sue's conversation and mannerisms simply make him nervous; but his failure to discriminate between the ploys of the political corrupter and those of the desperate searcher is radical.

One of the wiles of the political corrupter is the appeal to social egalitarianism. Murdock, who is pleased with his lack of snobbishness, reminds Jerry of a favorite story: "I think that the Emperor Tiberius was right in his reply to the courtiers who remarked on the poor birth of the favorite Rufus: Rufus is his own ancestor. I have always thought that a noble remark." *Man as his own ancestor:* both the concept and its verbal justification in anecdotal ancient history come easily to Murdock. The notion has always had special relevance for the American, of course, ranging from political and social independence to spiritual Self-Reliance, and to their economic vulgarization in the phrase *self-made man*. Murdock is the perfect manipulator of the doctrines of the New South apostles, his rhetoric a symbolic union of traditional sectional pieties and the promotional slogans of national big business. In Warren's context there is a further declension: the spiritual implications of the self-made man are both extensive and gloomy.

Their reliance on techniques betrays a fundamental lack of substance in Jerry and Sue. Warren's emphatic and iterated references to calculated effects, artifice, rhetorical patterns, deployment of manners and gestures, tricks of phrasing and bons mots, and cultivation of personal images for public consumption: all point up the plight of the fragmented self who is not at home even in the world it tries to make. In an urban milieu liberated from the demands of family, past, or tradition, values that celebrate man's responsibility for man are few and fragile. Techniques can only oil the machinery of an impersonal, dehumanized, and abstract society.

Except for Sue, who searches for a real human involvement outside the sterile managerial atmosphere of her father's house (and her options are less varied than they appear to be), all the great users of technique in *At Heaven's Gate* shirk any mutual responsibilities: Murdock, Slim Sarrett, Sweetie Sweetwater, Jerry, and Private Porsum, another of Murdock's less apt pupils. Sue's successive lovers—Jerry, Sarrett, Sweetwater—share a desire to revise their imperfect pasts, and for Sue all come to be in varied ways reflections of Murdock, who himself has revised the past (his father is a political murderer) into a chapter of heroism and local patriotism. Neither is a true alternative to her father; all three are merely fragmented replacements. All are moved by abstractions no less than Murdock: Jerry (like Porsum) is a poor boy turned hero, and the nature of his success is as mysterious as his identity; the dehumanization of her other two lovers is suggested by their obsessive devotion to abstract systems—Sarrett to aestheticism, Sweetwater to Marxism—and both share Murdock's talent for manipulating others.

During the same evening that Sarrett tells Sue, fresh from a dispute with Jerry, that she had created a version of Jerry to fit her needs, as well as a new version of herself to accommodate it, he tells her the version of himself and his past that he needs. It is a rich romantic story of the precocious child of a riverboat captain and a New Orleans prostitute. Once on his own, this young Sarrett knocks about the country, instinctively honing in on wealthy and influential patrons; "how easy it is," he tells Sue, "once you get the trick." Though the details of the narrative are fabricated, the governing motives are clear enough. Sarrett has so denied his home, past, and tradition that he must manufacture replacements; but his present world is not one in which he can immerse himself. He is too much the director, watching over the intricate interrelationships of his world. He is Warren's most dramatic case of alienation until the creation of Ikey Sumpter of *The Cave*. His actors—graduate students, professors, foundry workers, newspapermen—perform regularly, and he observes them with clinical dispassion. Though he mingles, he mingles to manipulate, pressing here, encouraging there.

One of the clearest examples of Sarrett's technique occurs when Sue tries to compare acting to her own personal development: Sarrett completes her simile ("Like first menstruation?"), and she agrees; Sarrett then congratulates her on that "subtle and precise" comparison, concluding: "You say very subtle and precise things, sometimes." But even Sue, for most of her association with Sarrett, is nothing more to him than the most important fixture in his studio world. Just as she is his biggest triumph, so she becomes his most significant failure after his past is exposed by the homosexual Mr. Billie Constantidopeles. As an impurity which has corrupted the pure world of his own creation, she must be either "remade" or removed utterly.

When this world collapses, she turns to Sweetwater; and for all his differences, he follows the same pattern as Jerry Calhoun and Slim Sarrett. In rejecting the world of his preacher father and his certainty of belief, Sweetwater eventually comes to duplicate it and can apply his father's proverb without irony: "A man cannot believe in himself unless he believes in something else." As a vehement unionist, Sweetwater plays his role with a fervor worthy of his father. Fleeing from rigidity, he embraces rigidity. He demands rights as a husband despite his principle that a mission as labor organizer precludes marriage.

Sue is attracted to both Sarrett and Sweetwater because they exercise discipline and self-control and because they have goals. The price is high for a woman with only an impulse toward independence. She has no external goals and little internal discipline; her lovers, no less than her father, supply her with the outline (and as much substance as they can) for the creation of a new self. They can mold new images for her, but they cannot offer her what she most desperately needs: the full unreserved commitment of love. Though it is Sarrett who murders her, in the context of mutual responsibility Sweetwater must also share the guilt. In the context of a rapacious world, however, both escape such judgment. As in most of his novels with strong political strains *At Heaven's Gate* is not about Warren's views of politics—even Agrarian politics—or politicians. It is a study of individuals who in the "blur of the world" strive to find a focus in their own shape and weight, apart from such piecemeal definitions as economic man or aesthetic man.

I have spoken of the gloomy implications of Murdock's example in this novel. One of them is that those who have successfully defined themselves are precisely those who fulfill a fragmented, specialized category; those who fail do not achieve even that. One of the maxims in the novel says that "no one who has succeeded in fulfilling his nature, whatever that nature is, needs sympathy. The man who has not fulfilled his nature is the man who needs sympathy." Though it comes from Sarrett, the crisply detached intellectual, the statement is ratified by the action of the novel. As monstrous examples of the self-created, Murdock, Sarrett, and Sweetwater need no sympathy; Jerry and Sue, whose natures are never fulfilled, are pathetic cases of individuals who ache for a human wholeness but who learn merely shallow skills for a kind of protective adaptation in the world of the self-created.

Ashby Wyndham, of course, is the one character who lacks even protective adaptation. In a world dominated by the self-created, his only tack is confrontation. And though he casts in relief the spiritual failures of the major characters, his career offers still another variation on their pattern of repudiation. Ashby's sin is in seeking his individuality outside the context of familial responsibilities; but, unlike the major characters, Ashby seeks help by holding his sin before him as a constant reminder of man's creatureliness. He succumbs to pride even in this, but he does achieve an identity less blurred than the others', and his sense of responsibility serves as a moral yardstick against which the other characters are measured.

Sarrett and Sweetwater (and to a lesser extent Sue and Jerry—lesser only because they are less intelligent) are merely dissatisfied with what they have been—and manufacture by their own wills, and in totally secular contexts, new personalities for themselves and new functions which are merely (and perilously) grafted onto the old. Self-convicted, Ashby knows precisely what is required for reclamation: a reconstituting of the self from the inside out. Of all the characters he is least equipped, socially and intellectually, to ease his way through the urban world of the self-created by judicious use of technique. His public role—a combination of the Ancient Mariner and the southern street preacher—and his general theme—"the pore human man"—are possible only because of private experience: the transformation of man's evil ("a hog hollerness and emptiness for the world's slop") into righteousness through traditional Christian regeneration. "He made the world and what walks on it," Ashby writes, "and it out of pure love." For him the world in all its variety is no place where the self can be defined in purely secular ways. His statement is his proof that the self is God-created.

As a confessional tract the statement is markedly free of rhetorical technique. "The Lord led me, and He laid the words on my tongue. I named them, and it was ample." Since the words are by inspiration, the style inevitably is unvarnished: "I will put it down, spare not, fear nor favor, and I will write it as fair as I can." But it is of course unvarnished only from an urbane point of view. In his hill-country way Ashby Wyndham is among the most articulate of all the characters: his script may be crabbed, but the rhetoric abounds with figures which accord perfectly with the man's earthiness, his deep involvement with other sin-prone men and women, and his abiding respect for the mysteries of God's love. At the furthest remove from Ashby's vivid specificity is Bogan Murdock's rhetoric of bland abstraction and generalization. In each case the rhetoric is an index to character, particularly the depth of concern of one human being for another. For Ashby

Wyndham death and violence around him stimulate a profound reordering of his own life; for Bogan Murdock they become occasions for further political opportunism.

At Heaven's Gate posits no easy solution to the problem of self-definition. Those who are most in need of solving it—Sue Murdock and Jerry Calhoun—are confounded by the complexity and try to accommodate their urgencies with the stopgap measures of surface technique. Slim Sarrett tells Sue that people talk about themselves not out of vanity but because "they are mysterious to themselves, and they talk just to find out something about the mystery." But even at the end, when Sue is murdered and when a broken and bewildered Jerry is returned to his father's house, neither has learned much about the mystery. On the other hand Ashby Wyndham accepts the mystery because man is not his own creature: "a man don't know, for he is ignorant," and he "don't know, nor was made to." God's will, he explains, "runs lak a fox with the dogs on him, and doubles, and knows places secret and hard for a man's foot. But a man wants to know, but it is his weakness."

Those who use technique most outrageously to manipulate others—Murdock, Sarrett, Sweetwater—continue their lives apparently without much readjustment of their personal goals and methods. In the world of rapacity, the ruthless rule, mouthing their rhetorical clichés so patly that the mask becomes the face. Swearing by the portrait of Andrew Jackson (or by theories of poetry or politics) comes to be the real as well as the fake, the goal as well as the technique.

Murdock, Sarrett, Sweetwater: their respective stewardships are all perverted because they avoid the high penalties for human responsibility. Jerry and Sue suffer the pathos of failure. Only Ashby Wyndham emerges with anything resembling tragic stature, and that because he pays dearly for a commitment which seems anomalous to the urbanized denizens of the Waste Land. His career anticipates that of Cass Mastern in *All the King's Men,* and his folk formula foreshadows that anguished patrician's spider-web theory of complicity: "When a man ever does a sin he ain't done it secret and him private. He has done taken his own sin on his shoulders, but another man's sin too to bear him down. You throw a rock in a pond and it don't make one splash but they is ripples runs out from it."

Robert Penn Warren:

All the King's Men

by Arthur Mizener

Robert Penn Warren has had at least four careers as a writer. He has written six volumes of poems, one of which, *Promises,* won him the Pulitzer Prize in 1957; his *Selected Poems* won the Bollingen award for 1966. He had already received the Pulitzer Prize for Fiction in 1946 with *All the King's Men,* the third of his [ten] novels. He has written a biography of John Brown and two books on segregation. He has been one of the important contributors to the critical renaissance of the Twentieth Century and found (with Cleanth Brooks) a way to make its insights available to students in the most influential textbook of our time, *Understanding Poetry.* There is something symbolic about this last achievement, for the most persistent of Mr. Warren's beliefs is that men must, at whatever cost, carry knowledge into the world, must live their daily lives by its lights and must subject it to the test of experience.

Mr. Warren is usually thought of as a member of the Fugitive Group that gathered in the 1920s at Vanderbilt, where the young Warren studied with John Crowe Ransom and roomed for a time with Allen Tate. It is difficult to imagine a better apprenticeship in the craft of writing than working with Ransom, and to have been exposed to the grace, the wit, and the violence of Allen Tate's mind must have been almost too stimulating. Yet the association of Warren with the Fugitives is misleading, too. There were other important influences in his life, at California and Yale and Oxford, where he did graduate work, and wherever it was that he acquired the attitude — very different from either Ransom's or Tate's — that he has always had.

The starting point for that attitude — as for the different one taken by Tate — is the problem of self-realization and self-possession. The speaker in Tate's "Ode to the Confederate Dead" can

"Robert Penn Warren: *All the King's Men*" by Arthur Mizener. From *The Southern Review,* III (1967), 874-94. © 1967 by *The Southern Review.* Reprinted by permission of the author and the publisher.

> praise the vision
> And praise the arrogant circumstance
> Of those who fall
> Rank upon rank, hurried beyond decision,

but they are not real to him; he cannot share their vision or even truly understand it, though for a moment of pious respect for the past he imagines them rising like demons out of the earth. What is real for him is their tombstones, as neatly aligned as their ranks had been, decaying slowly in a neutral air.

> Row after row with strict impunity
> The headstones yield their names to the element,
> The wind whirs without recollection

in a world where impunity is absolute and the idea of meaningful action ("yielding") a pathetic fallacy. The conception of nature that had given the lives of these Confederate dead coherence and value is gone. "Here by the sagging gate, stopped by the wall" of the cemetery, the speaker feels a despair at his situation that is intensified by his recognition of what the world buried there, and long since reduced by time to "verdurous anonymity," had been like. (Tate particularly likes barriers that emphasize the metaphysical impenetrability he is concerned with by their physical insignificance; the mirror of "Last Days of Alice" is even more striking than the sagging gate of the "Ode," in which a version of that mirror in fact also turns up in the passage about the jaguar that "leaps/ For his own image in a jungle pool, his victim.") For Tate the cost of losing an endurable vision of nature is the loss of the world; deprived of the vision of a community and its discipline, the individual sinks into the incoherent abyss of impulse where

> You shift your sea-space blindly
> Heaving, turning like the blind crab.

This is the nightmare in which George Posey, the hero of Tate's novel, *The Fathers*, exists. "But," says the narrator of *The Fathers*, "is not civilization the agreement, slowly arrived at, to let the abyss alone?" Tate's image of the civilized man is the narrator's father, Major Buchan, whose feelings have been perfectly disciplined to the expressive social ritual of antebellum life at Pleasant Hill. There is in *The Fathers* an understanding that a civilization is subject to time and change: George Posey destroys the life of Pleasant Hill even before the Civil War destroys the social system it is a part of. But for Tate that change is simply an occasion for despair, for the recognition that we can never be Major Buchan, only George Posey.

To Warren the world of our time seems a convulsion quite as terrible as it is for Tate. But for him the world exists beyond any conception of it we may have; and it always has. We cannot know the past—but only some destructive conception of it—until we recognize that Willie Stark of *All the King's Men* is right when he says of it, "I bet things [then] were just like they are now. A lot of folks wrassling around." That knowledge about the past does not make the past meaningless, any more than does the knowledge that for the same reason we will never create a Utopia makes the future meaningless. It only makes the past and future real.

In one of the several poems Mr. Warren has written about the maternal grandfather (he was a cavalry officer under Forrest) who is his Major Buchan, the grandson begins by thinking that

> life is only a story
> And death is only the glory
> Of the telling of the story,
> And the *done* and the *to-be-done*
> In that timelessness were one,
> Beyond the poor *being done.*

Then his grandfather describes how he and his men once hanged a group of bushwackers, and suddenly the boy understands that his grandfather's past life was not a story, not something that exists only as a timeless *done* but something that was once *being done* in the terrible now of time,

> Each face outraged, agape,
> Not yet believing it true—
> The hairy jaw askew,
> Tongue out, out-staring eye,
> And the spittle not yet dry
> That was uttered with the last cry.
>
> The horseman does not look back.
> Blank-eyed, he continues his track,
> Riding toward me there,
> Through the darkening air.
>
> The world is real. It is there.

But it is very tempting to deny that the life of the past took place in the real world of time, as life in the present does, and to reject the life of the present as inconceivable in the light of what one imagines the past to have been. That is what Adam Stanton in *All the King's Men* does all his life; it is what Jack Burden, the novel's narrator, does for a long time, so that when, for example, he meets the sheriff and Commissioner Dolph Pillsbury in the Mason City court house, he wants to believe such creatures do not exist. With repudiating irony he tells himself that Dolph Pillsbury is "just another fellow, made in God's image and wearing a white shirt with a ready-tied black bow tie and jean pants held up with web galluses." But he knows Dolph Pillsbury is real, even if he won't admit it to himself (it is the Jack Burden who tells the story, long afterwards, who does admit it): *"They ain't real,* I thought as I walked down the hall [of the courthouse], *narry one.* But I knew they were."

It is not that man does not need a vision of the ideal possibilities of life or that actual life does not often seem grotesquely horrible in comparison with that vision. It is not even that, for some men, it is not altogether too easy to accept the world as it is and forget its unrealized possibilities (as Willie Stark for a while does). The danger is that men who do not forget these possibilities may, like Jack Burden, refuse to understand that they are possibilities for the world and are real only in the world. The risk of trying to realize these possibilities in the world is destruction, but not to take that risk is never to live. "For if," as Shakespeare's duke says, "our virtues/ Did not go forth of us, 'twere all alike/ As if we had them not." (There are interesting similarities between *All the King's Men* and Shakespeare's "dark" comedies, *Measure for Measure* and *Troilus and Cressida*). But it is temptingly easy, too, to think that one must not enter the grotesque reality of the world if one has any virtues.

When, in *Flood,* a prison guard refuses to shoot a madman who is murdering another guard for fear of hitting an innocent man, the Warden says, "Jesus Christ, a innocent man! There ain't no innocent man! You are fired." Yet it remains true, as the novel's cultivated lawyer says, that "When I look out the window and see some pore misguided boogers doing the best they can—according to their dim lights...what you might call the pathos of the mundane sort of takes the edge off my grim satisfaction." No man can afford not to shoot a murderous madman on the theory that the bystanders who are sure to be hurt are innocent (no man is) or on the theory that, since no man is innocent, men are not worth his trouble. Both theories assume that one is innocent oneself and that this innocence can be preserved by avoiding the infection of a world that is not. But the world is made up of men just like us, guilty men in ready-tied bow ties and jean pants, certainly; and made in God's image, too.

For Mr. Warren the worst is not to go into the convulsion of the world, terrible as it is to do that. No one in fact exists anywhere else. But men can deprive themselves of the responsibility (and the freedom) of being there by refusing to submit their virtues to the test of action, as Jack Burden does, or by acting as if virtue does not exist, as do the host of small-time pursuers of happiness who people Mr. Warren's novels, such as Marvin Frey, "a sporting barber with knife-edge creases in his striped pants, ointment on his thinning hair, hands like inflated rubber gloves. ... You know how he kids the hotel chippies and tries to talk them out of something, you know how he gets in debt because of his bad hunches on the horses and bad luck with the dice, you know how he wakes up in the morning and sits on the edge of the bed with his bare feet on the cold floor and a taste like brass on the back of his tongue and experiences his nameless despair."

"Mentre che la speranza ha fior del verde," says the epigraph of *All the King's Men* (Per lor maladizione si non si perde/ che non possa tornar l'etterno amore,/ mentre che la speranza ha fior del verde. By their curse none is so lost that the eternal love cannot return while hope keeps any of it green. *Purgatorio*, III, 133-135). In this Canto, Dante sees his shadow and Virgil, confessing he is lost, knows he must consult the penitents. Sinclair observes that Dante's casting a shadow "illustrate[s] the dualism of flesh and spirit...which is not to be resolved in theory, only in experience"; and of Virgil consulting the penitents, he says, "In this need penitence is wiser than reason, and reason is then most reasonable when it looks beyond itself. The soul's life is experience, a given thing—a *quia*, in the language of scholasticism—to be known only in living, in the last resort as unsearchable as God." ("State contenti, umana gente, al *quia*," I. 37.)

One of Mr. Warren's major objects in *All the King's Men* is to make the world of time in which experience occurs exist for us in all its ordinary familiar, immediate reality. The novel's story of the typical political struggle in which the country boy, Willie Stark, rose to power and of his exercise of that power, of the career of Judge Irwin of Burden's Landing with its judicial integrity, its marriage for money, its deal with the power company —this story is representative of the public life of our time. It occurs in an American world that is shown in beautifully precise detail, a world of country farmhouses and county court houses and small-town hotels, of pool halls and slum apartments and the "foul, fox-smelling lairs" of cheap rooming houses, of places at Burden's Landing and the Governor's mansion and the state capital, of country fairgrounds and city football stadiums and endless highways. Moreover, this story is told us by Jack Burden who is (among other things) a trained historian and experienced newspaper man and can give us an authoritative account of the immediate meaning of the events, the tangled train of intentions and acts that cause them and flow from them. The world appears overwhelmingly real in *All the King's Men*. It is there. Because there is where experience, which is the life of the soul, occurs.

It is the wisdom of reason in looking beyond itself to experience that Jack Burden refuses—or is unable—to recognize until the very end, when he finally sees that, if knowledge is indeed the end of man as he has always believed, "all knowledge that is worth anything is maybe paid for by blood." Until then he cannot commit his soul to experience because he cannot face what experience will do to the perfection of the story his reason has made up about life. He struggles to keep his existence a timeless preserve of images of Anne Stanton afloat on the water with her eyes closed (but even then the sky was dark greenish-purple with a coming storm) and of ideas about the world that make it unreal. "I had got hold of [a] principle out of a book when I was in college, and I had hung onto it for grim death. I owed my success in life to that principle. It had put me where I was. What you don't know won't hurt you, for it ain't real. They called that Idealism in my book I had when I was in college, and after I got hold of that principle I became an Idealist. I was a brass-bound Idealist in those days. If you are an Idealist it does not matter what you do or what goes on around you because it isn't real anyway."

This Idealism was merely Jack Burden's excuse for living as if the world of time—where people try to do their best according to their dim lights and fail and grow old—were not real. He clung to this principle "for grim death" (of the soul, at least) and secretly fancied that his failure to do anything was a special kind of success. It was a way of hiding from the knowledge of experience that "was like the second when you come home late at night and see the yellow envelope of the telegram sticking out from under your door. . . . While you stand in the hall, with the envelope in your hand, you feel there's an eye on you...[that] sees you huddled up way inside, in the dark which is you, inside yourself, like a clammy, sad little foetus...that doesn't want to know what is in that envelope. It wants to lie in the dark and not know, and be warm in its not-knowing." (When Byram White's corruption is exposed he stands before Willie Stark "drawing himself into a hunch as though he wanted to assume the prenatal position and be little and warm and safe in the dark.") Jack Burden wanted to remain forever kissing Anne Stanton in the underwater world into which she took the highest dive of her life (but when they came to the surface she swam straight for the beach). He looked longingly at the May foliage of the trees and thought of himself "inside that hollow inner chamber, in the aqueous green light, inside the great globe of the tree...and no chance of seeing anything...and no sound except, way off, the faint mumble of traffic, like the ocean chewing its gums." (This lotus-eater's dream was interrupted by Sadie Burke, who told Jack Burden that Anne Stanton had become Willie Stark's mistress.)

Jack's Idealism allows him to reject as absurd caricatures of humanity the beings who fall below his standards, but it also costs him his capacity to feel, so that it is really he who does not exist humanly rather than the imperfect creatures he rejects. Anne Stanton understands this without being able to explain it.

> "Oh, you just think you are sorry. Or glad. You aren't really."
> "If you think you are sorry, who in hell can tell you that you aren't?" I demanded, for I was a brass-bound Idealist then, as I have stated, and was not about to call for a plebiscite on whether I was sorry or not. . . .
> "Oh, Jack," she said, "...can't you love them a little, or forgive them, or just not think about them, or something?"

Yet he can maintain this attitude only by an effort of self-persuasion. He has to keep telling himself that his mother is maddeningly stupid, because he is touched by the bravery of her defiance of age and wants to respond to her love when she smiles at him "with a sudden and innocent happiness, like a girl"; he dwells on the ludicrous horror of Tiny Duffy and the The Boys, only to find in the end that he cannot hate even Tiny. What is worse, he is often driven perilously close to recognizing that what makes him think others subhuman exists in himself. He will not touch Anne Stanton; if he does Anne will cease to be the sleeping beauty of heart-breaking innocence he has wanted her to remain ever since he saw her floating with her eyes closed that day. Instead he marries Lois who, he imagines, is merely a "beautiful, juicy, soft, vibrant, sweet-smelling, sweet-breathed machine for provoking and satisfying the appetite." But Lois "could talk, and when something talks you sooner or later begin to listen to the sound it makes and begin, even in the face of all the other evidence, to regard it as a person... and the human element infects your innocent Eden pleasure in the juicy, sweet-breathed machine." When Lois thus turns out to be—honestly and stubbornly—a kind of person intolerable to anyone of even moderate standards, Jack runs away, first into the Great Sleep and then to divorce. Whenever Jack Burden is faced with the dualism of flesh and spirit he runs away. His worst moment is caused by Anne Stanton's affair with Willie Stark, when he has to flee all the way to California and discover an entirely new principle, The Great Twitch, to hide behind.

Just as Jack will not go into the world of experience with Anne Stanton, so he will not give his ideals of personal conduct the reality of action. As long as he can convince himself that he is merely a technician, he can feel he is not responsible for what is done: he is just obeying orders. When he cannot—as when he is asked to put some real feeling into his column for the *Chronicle*—he quits. When he investigates Judge Irwin for Willie Stark, he is just exercising his technique. He had tried that once before, as a Ph.D. student, when he investigated Cass Mastern. But he laid that job aside unfinished because he wanted to keep his belief that "the world was simply an accumulation of items, odds and ends of things like broken and misused and dust-shrouded things gathered in a garret," whereas Cass Mastern had "learned that the world is all of one piece...that the world is like an enormous spider web and if you touch it, however lightly, at any point, the vibration ripples to the remotest perimeter." Perhaps, the narrator adds, the Jack Burden of those days "laid aside the journal of Cass Mastern not because he could not understand, but because he was afraid to understand for what might be understood there was a reproach to him."

With Judge Irwin he is again the researcher, with the research man's faith that the past is only a story, that "all times are one time, and all those dead in the past never lived before our definition gives them life, and out of the shadow their eyes implore us. That is what all us historical researchers believe. And we love truth." He does his job on Judge Irwin well: "It was a perfect research job, marred in its technical perfection by only one thing: it meant something." It had been easy to drop Cass Mastern when there arose a danger that the research job would be marred by meaning. Though

Cass Mastern had lived in time, it was not Jack Burden's time and it was easy to think of Cass as part of history, "the *done*." But Judge Irwin is still alive and Jack loves him, and in digging up his past Jack has brushed the spider web. He tries not to know that, but cannot escape when his mother says, "You killed him, you killed him. ... Your father, your father and oh! you killed him."

He has had his bad moments before, as when he caught himself defending what Willie Stark had done against the sincerely selfish business men at Judge Irwin's dinner party ("the bluff, burly type, with lots of money and a manly candor"). He hastened to absolve himself of responsibility ("I didn't say I felt any way," he insisted, "I just offered a proposition for the sake of argument"), but he had come very close to understanding the possibility that—as Cass Mastern puts it—"only a man like my brother Gilbert [or Willie Stark] can in the midst of evil retain enough innocence and enough strength to...do a little justice in terms of the great injustice." Jack Burden does not want to understand that; he wants to go on thinking that "politics is action and all action is but a flaw in the perfection of inaction, which is peace," wants to go on not knowing that his refusal to possess Anne Stanton "had almost as dire consequences as Cass Mastern's sin" with Annabelle Trice, his friend's wife, and far more dire consequences than the sin of his father, Judge Irwin, with the wife of Judge Irwin's friend Ellis Burden.

The real reason Jack Burden works for Willie Stark, just as it is the real reason Adam Stanton does, is the fascination for him of *doing* good, not just imagining it. But he does not want to recognize that to do good he must involve himself in the world where power is acquired, not without dust and heat, and what you do has all sorts of unexpected consequences for which you must take responsibility. So Jack Burden has to persuade himself that he is just Willie Stark's research man. It is not until Willie is dead and Jack discovers the part Tiny Duffy played in killing him that Jack considers acting on his own. Then he comes very close to telling Sugar Boy about Tiny. He knows that will make Sugar Boy shoot Tiny, exactly as Tiny had known that telling Adam Stanton about Anne and Willie had made Adam shoot Willie.

But Jack does not tell Sugar Boy. Before he gets a chance to, he has gone to see Tiny and given himself the unearned pleasure of setting Tiny straight. Then Sadie Burke writes him that it would be foolish to expose Duffy "just because you got some high-falutin idea you are an Eagle Scout and [Anne Stanton] is Joan of Arc." That is the truth, and it makes him think of his own responsibility for Willie's death, and suddenly he feels himself caught in a "monstrous conspiracy whose meaning I could not fathom. ... It was as though in the midst of the scene [with Tiny Duffy he] had slowly and like a brother winked at me with his oyster eye and I had known he knew the nightmare truth, which was that we were twins bound together more intimately and disastrously than the poor freaks of the midway who are bound by the common stitch of flesh and gristle and the seepage of the blood. We were bound together forever and I could never hate him without hating myself or love myself without loving him."

That is the moment at which Jack Burden faces the truth. But until it arrives, he is a brass-bound Idealist filled with something like despair by the insignificance of the existence he has been so careful to persuade himself is the only reasonable one, so that when Anne Stanton says to him, "You are such a smart aleck.... Aren't you ever going to grow up?" he says, "I reckon I am a smart aleck, but it is just a way to pass the time." But it does not even do that, for he wakes each morning to look out the window and see "that it [is] going to be another day" in the endless series of insignificant tomorrows. Or he watches from a train window a woman empty a pan of water and go back into her house—"To what was in the house. The floor of the house is thin against the bare ground and the walls and roof are thin against all of everything which is outside, but you cannot see through the walls to the secret to which the woman has gone in.... And all at once you feel like crying." For "the soul's life is experience, a given thing ...to be known only in living...." That is what makes Willie Stark so fascinating.

Willie Stark has a gift for acting in the world. As a country boy he had studied law and history with the passionate intensity of one who instinctively feels that knowledge is, not so much a means of understanding as an instrument of power. "Gee," he says later with amiable contempt, "back in those days I figured those fellows knew all there was to know and I figured I was going to get me a chunk of it." What he knows by then is that you can use certain kinds of knowledge to make men do what you wish, but that is quite another thing. "No," he says to Hugh Miller, "I'm not a lawyer. I know some law. In fact, I know a lot of law. And I made me some money out of law. But I'm not a lawyer."

He began his political career with a farm boy's naïveté by trying to get the Mason City school honestly built. When the courthouse crowd kicked him out, he ran against them on his own. But nobody listened to his story about the school and he was badly beaten. His wife Lucy, who lives to remind him of the values power exists to serve—as Anne Stanton lives to remind Jack Burden of the power values exist to direct—reminds Willie that he did not want to be elected to a government of crooks anyway. But all Willie can remember is that the courthouse crowd had "run it over me. Like I was dirt," because they had the power. Then, with the collapse of the school's fire escape, Willie becomes a hero and it almost seems as if not mixing with crooks is the way to achieve power as well as virtue, for in no time there is the city politician, Tiny Duffy, on his doorstep asking him to run for governor. He never suspects Tiny is merely looking for a way to split the opponent's vote. "For the voice of Tiny Duffy summoning him was nothing but the echo of a certainty and a blind compulsion in him."

Willie sets out to campaign for governor with his earnest, boring, true speech, and Jack Burden and Sadie Burke watch him, full of the easy cynicism of the irresponsible wise. Yet they are reluctantly impressed by Willie. "You know," Sadie says one evening, "...even if he found out he was a sucker, I believe he might keep right on." "Yeah," Jack says, "making those speeches." "God," she said, "aren't they awful?" "Yeah." "But I believe he might keep right on," she said. "Yeah." "The sap," she said. When Sadie turns out to be right, they both yield to the fascination of Willie's gift for action. Sadie gives herself wholly to Willie, enduring his trivial infidelities but reacting fiercely to the real betrayal of his affair with Anne Stanton, only to discover in the end that she has helped to kill the man who, whatever he had done, she could not live without.

Willie does keep on; but not making those awful speeches. The discovery that he is once more being run over like dirt strengthens his feeling that power is all that matters, and slowly, even unconsciously, he drifts away from Lucy's understanding of the values power exists for. We watch him— as he talks to Hugh Miller, to Judge Irwin, to Adam Stanton—developing his theory that the law and the good are things men of power make up as they go along until he is—in fact if not wholly in intention—merely a virtuoso of power, half believing that, by its mere exercise, men can give power a purpose, as Jack Burden, his counterpart, is merely a virtuoso of speculation, half believing that by contemplating an ideal men can change the world. When Willie reaches this point, Lucy refuses to live with him any more. But when their son, Tom, is paralyzed for life and Willie, like some pitiful Faustus, cries out that he will name his magnificent new hospital after Tom, she is there as always to remind him that "these things don't matter. Having somebody's name cut on a piece of stone. Getting it in the papers. All those things. Oh, Willie, he was my baby boy, he was our baby boy, and those things don't matter, they don't ever matter, don't you see?"

There is something in Willie that always recognizes that, too, even when he is exercising his political skill with the least regard for it. When his cunning but unscrupulous maneuver to save Byram White leads Hugh Miller to resign, he says to Miller in semi-comic woe, "You're leaving me all alone with the sons-of-bitches. Mine and the other fellow's"; and when he blackmails the legislature into voting down his impeachment, he says to Jack Burden that Lincoln seems to have been wrong when he said a house divided against itself cannot stand, since the government he presides over "is sure half slave and half son-of-a-bitch, and it is standing." When he begins to plan his great free hospital, he refuses to allow it to be built in the usual crooked way. He is not just remembering the collapse of the Mason City school's fire escape; he can prevent Gummy Larsen from building shoddily even if Gummy does take a cut of the school contract. What he is remembering is what made him want that school built honestly. This insistence that the hospital be built without graft is, as Jack Burden says, "scarcely consistent" with Willie's constant assertions that you always have to make good out of bad, but it maddens him that Jack Burden—who has not yet learned to look beyond reason—cannot understand why, just after Willie has saved Byram White from his deserved punishment, he wants to build that hospital with clean hands.

Thus, in the confrontation of its two central characters, *All the King's Men* poses what is for Mr. Warren the central problem of existence, the irrepressible conflict between the conception of life that gives action meaning and value and the act of living in the world in which meaning and value have to be realized. This conflict appears unendurable. Yet both Jack Burden, who tries to exist in the conception without accepting the responsibility of action, and Willie Stark, who drifts into acting effectively for its own sake, find it impossible not to know that it must be endured.

"This," as Jack says near the end of the novel, "has been the story of Willie Stark, but it is my story, too." As Willie, living the practical life of power, is haunted by a desire to use his power in a virtuous way he denies is possible, so Jack Burden, prevented from acting by his concern for the virtue he can imagine, is haunted by a desire to realize himself in the world he denies is real. This is the story the novel tells about Jack Burden. But the novel is Jack Burden's story in another sense: he tells it. It was a risk to use as narrator a central character whose changing conception of the nature of experience is the main issue in the novel. It is like making Emma Woodhouse, Lambert Strether, and Lord Jim the narrators of their novels. If it could be brought off, the meaning of the action could be revealed dramatically, from within and behind the view of a character who is limited by his own nature and does not understand that meaning for a long time; and when this meaning finally emerges on the surface of the novel, it will be the product of an experience that has been fully represented in the novel and will not be arbitrarily given, as is, for example, Marlow's view of life in Conrad's *Lord Jim.* But it is very difficult to keep separate the limited view of the events a character has as he is living through them and the view he finally takes, when the events are all over and he sits down to write the story. Mr. Warren brings off this difficult maneuver, and it is well worth what it costs. But that cost is nonetheless the considerable one of making the novel very easy to misunderstand.

The voice of Jack Burden conveys three distinct feelings about the events he describes. It is, most obviously, the voice of Jack Burden the Idealist who sardonically points out the plentiful evidence that life is grotesquely absurd. He does that very effectively and what he shows us is hard to deny. At the same time the tone of his voice is almost hysterically extravagant.

That extravagance gives a hectic rhetorical brilliance to his descriptions of the world's absurdities, but why should he care that much if the world is beneath contempt? His extravagance is really the expression of the second of Jack Burden's feelings, his longing to reach beyond reason to the secret of experience that he is debarred from by the refusal of Jack Burden the Idealist to believe experience is real.

The Idealist's rhetoric always belittles the world by contrasting the indignity of its shoddy physical nature with some dignified image of the soul.

> I'd be lying there in the hole in the middle of my bed where the springs had given down with the weight of wayfaring humanity, lying there on my back with my clothes on and looking up at the ceiling and watching the cigarette smoke flow up slowly and splash against the ceiling…like the pale uncertain spirit rising up out of your mouth on the last exhalation, the way the Egyptians figured it, to leave the horizontal tenement of clay in its ill-fitting pants and vest.

How silly to describe men in grand terms when they are all what Jack says Lois's friends are: "There was nothing particularly wrong with them. They were just the ordinary garden variety of human garbage"—whose "wayfaring" produces nothing but broken springs in cheap-hotel bedrooms, whose "pale, uncertain spirit" is only cigarette smoke, whose "tenement of clay" is dressed in ill-fitting pants and vest.

The Idealist Jack Burden is, then, always saying, "Go to, I'll no more on't." But just the same "it hath made [him] mad," or nearly so, and like Hamlet, once he is launched on a description of it, he cannot stop torturing himself ("Nay but to live/ In the rank sweat of an enseamed bed,/ Stewed in corruption…"); until slowly, as we listen, we begin to feel, not that men's lives are less horrible than he says they are, but that there is some imperfectly fulfilled intention in them not unlike Jack Burden's own—some dim light—that makes them pitiful rather than disgusting. Consider, for example, Mortimer Lonzo Littlepaugh who was fired by the American Electric Power Company in order that Judge Irwin might be paid off with his job "at a salary they never paid me." Mortimer is almost as absurd as his name, and his indignation is a fantastic mixture of "confusion, weakness, piety, self-pity, small-time sharpness, vindictiveness." "I gave them my heart's blood," he writes his sister just before he commits suicide, "all these years. And they call him vice-president, too. They lied to me and they cheated me and they make him vice-president for taking a bribe. … I am going to join our sainted Mother and Father who were kind and good…and will greet me on the Other Shore, and dry every tear. … P. S. If they [the insurance company] know I have done what I am going to do they will not pay you." "So," as Jack Burden observes, "the poor bastard had gone to the Other

Shore, where Mother and Father would dry away every tear, immediately after having instructed his sister how to defraud the insurance company" —to no purpose, he might have added, since Mortimer had borrowed practically the full value of his insurance. Mortimer Lonzo Littlepaugh was certainly grotesque, but with a passionate sincerity that is, however absurd, also pitiful.

The same double response is evoked by the tone of the narrator's voice as he describes the characteristic life of his time. "A funeral parlor at midnight is ear-splitting," he will say about a cheap joint, "compared to the effect you get in the middle of the morning in the back room of a place like Slade's.... You sit there and think how cozy it was last night, with the effluvium of brotherly bodies and the haw-haw of camaraderie, and you look at the floor... and the general impression is that you are alone with the Alone and it is His move." Or, driving past the comically tasteless and pitifully decaying Victorian houses of Mason City, he will notice "the sad valentine lace of gingerbread work around the veranda"; or he will observe the absurd and touching awe of the girl in Doc's drugstore who, seeing Willie Stark standing there at the counter, "got a look on her face as though her garter belt had busted in church." People are certainly ridiculous— vain, pretentious, foolish—as Jack Burden, who is being a smart aleck to pass the time, can see very clearly; they are also pitiful—sincere, eager, committed—as another Jack Burden cannot help feeling.

The third and most important feeling Jack Burden's voice expresses is the feeling that ultimately resolves the conflict between these two, the feeling of the Jack Burden who is telling us this story. This Jack Burden seldom speaks to us directly, and when he does it is mainly to remind us that what Jack Burden felt when he was living through these events was different from what he feels now, as he tells about them. "If I learned anything from studying history," he will say, "that was what I learned. Or, to be more exact, that was what I thought I had learned." Or he will say, "at least that is how I argued the case then"; but he does not say how he argues it now.

Only at the end of the novel do we learn that, discover that Jack Burden, without ceasing to believe in the reality of man's reason, has come to believe also in the reality of experience. Life, he now knows, is not "only a story" in the timelessness of which "the *done*" and "the *to-be-done*" are one. But if he now knows that "the *being done*" exists beyond any story man's reason invents about it, he also knows that story represents man's idea of it and determines the way he will act in it. The very existence of *All the King's Men* demonstrates that, for the controlling element in the narrator's voice is not Jack Burden the Idealist or Jack Burden the historian but the Jack Burden who has come to understand that "the soul's life is experience," and thus believes, "in my way," what Ellis Burden says as he is dying, that "the creation of evil is...the index of God's glory and His power. That had to be so that the creation of good might be the index of man's glory and his power. But by God's help. By His help and in His wisdom."

We sometimes hear the man who knows that in the way the narrator puzzles over an ostensibly virtuous act, as when he says of Jack Burden's conduct that night in his bedroom at Burden's Landing that Anne Stanton "trusted me, but perhaps for that moment of hesitation I did not trust myself, and looked back upon the past as something precious about to be snatched away from us and was afraid of the future. ... Then there came the day when that image was taken from me. I learned that Anne Stanton had become the mistress of Willie Stark, that somehow by an obscure and necessary logic I had handed her over to him." Sometimes we hear it in an ostensibly accidental observation, as when he notes that "later on love vines will climb up, out of the weeds," around the sign of the skull and crossbones put up where people have died on the highway. Jack Burden does not notice that because it is irrelevant to his sardonic description of life in the age of the internal combustion engine; it is the image of some larger meaning of experience.

This larger meaning is in fact present behind everything he tells us, as it is behind the whole description of that drive up route 58 with which the novel begins. There is Sugar Boy taking every risk he can in order to exercise his uncanny skill as a driver and satisfy his naïve need to act effectively in the world by slipping between truck and hay wagon with split-second timing ("The b-b-b-b-bas-tud—he seen me c-c-c-c-com-ing"). There is Willie Stark enjoying every minute of this dangerous game. There is Jack Burden thinking it was a pleasure to watch if you could forget it was real, but not willing to know, as Willie Stark does, that only if it is real does it have what Cass Mastern calls "the kind of glory, however stained or obscured, [that is] in whatever man's hand does well."

That drive was a wholly natural event, the politician being driven at politician's speed to his home town to get himself photographed at his pappy's farm for the newspapers. But it sets Jack Burden brooding about the age of the internal combustion engine and the cars whirling along the new slab Willie had built for them, the boys imagining themselves Barney Oldfields and the girls wearing no panties "on account of the climate" and their knees apart "for the cool." It is an absurd way for human beings to behave; and yet Jack Burden knows too that "the smell of gasoline and burning brake bands and red-eye is sweeter than myrrh" and that the girls "have smooth little faces to break your heart." It is all very like the life of man, which moves through time at a breakneck clip that some enjoy too much and some are too frightened by but which is the unavoidable condition. It is far more dangerous than the gay ones suspect, for the sheer speed of it can easily hypnotize you and "you'll come to just at the moment when the right front wheel hooks over into the black dirt off the slab, and you'll try to jerk her back on. ... But you won't make it of course." Probably not; but, as the frightened ones refuse to admit, you have to risk it if you are ever to smell the frankincense and myrrh.

In this way the whole story of *All the King's Men* becomes a kind of metaphor. The events of the novel are the incidents of a journey every man takes up that highway toward the River of Death (if not so surely to any Celestial City beyond it). For each wayfarer the other characters represent different ideas of how to get there as incomplete and partial as his own is for them. Each of Willie Stark's women, for example, represents a mode of travel he adopts for a time. Lucy, the school teacher, has the country people's simple notion of virtue and lives by it with unfailing integrity, leaving Willie when he discovers he cannot hold onto it and gain power; but Lucy has to go right on believing that Willie, whom she had loved and married and borne a son to, is, with all his faults, a great man. When Willie discovers how to gain power, he takes up with Sadie Burke who, having fought her way up from the bitter poverty of her childhood, plays the game of power with fierce determination; and when Willie takes Anne Stanton as his mistress and Jack Burden, seeing Sadie's suffering, says characteristically, "If it's all that grief, let him go," she says, "Let him go! let him go! I'll kill him first, I swear"— and does. Willie makes Anne Stanton his mistress when he discovers in himself a need not just for power but to do good with clean hands. Anne Stanton has shared something of her brother Adam's dream of an ideal past in which those who governed were heroic figures; she has always known it is not enough, but it makes her able to give those who, like Willie, govern now a sense of greatness. Anne comes to love Willie when she learns that he, whom she had supposed a wholly wicked man because he was not perfectly good, has done much good—"Does he mean that, Jack? Really?"—and that her father, whom she had supposed perfectly good, had done evil. Each of these women is for Willie Stark the embodiment of the idea he lives by while he loves her, as Willie is for each of them. So each character is for all the others he knows.

Through most of the novel, Jack Burden is suspended between Adam Stanton, the friend of his youth, and Willie Stark, the friend of his maturity, and between Ellis Burden, the father who had loved to make the child Jack Burden happy and lived only to care for the helpless children of the world after he learned that his wife had become the mistress of his best friend, and, Judge Irwin, the father who did not scare but loved Jack's mother and took her, was an upright judge all his life except once, when he was desperate, and taught Jack to shoot ("You got to lead a duck, son").

For Jack, Adam Stanton is the romantic who "has a picture of the world in his head, and when the world doesn't conform in any respect to that picture, he wants to throw the world away. Even if it means throwing out the baby with the bath. Which...it always does mean." Jack ought to know; it is what he did when he refused to touch Anne Stanton. Adam Stanton refuses to believe people need anything but justice. But Willie Stark who, like Judge Irwin, has the courage to act what he feels, is one of the people and knows that "Your need is my justice." Jack Burden is, to start with, too like Adam Stanton to believe that the grotesque world he lives in can be put together again, even by all the king's men, and for a long time he refuses to touch it. But in the end he is too much like Willie Stark not to understand Willie's dying words—"It might have been all different, Jack. You got to believe that"—and to know he must try. As the novel ends, he has married Anne Stanton and is living with her in Judge Irwin's house, that relatively permanent—and lifeless—expression of the values handed down to him from the past, writing the history of Willie Stark's life. But he and Anne are about to leave that house and the writing of history and to enter the process of history, the life of their times. "And soon now," as Jack says in the novel's last sentence, "we shall go out of the house and go into the convulsion of the world, out of history into history and the awful responsibility of Time."

The Required Past:
World Enough and Time

by Robert Berner

That which hath been is now; and that which is to be hath already been; and God requireth that which is past.

—Ecclesiastes

In Robert Penn Warren's novels the relationship of characters with their fathers is related to their achievement of identity and self-knowledge. Amantha Starr is plunged into the dilemma expressed in the opening sentence of *Band of Angels* ("Oh, who am I?") when her father dies. In *Night Rider* Percy Munn tells Senator Tolliver, his father-surrogate, that he wants to kill him in order to achieve identity. ("It came to me, Do it, do it, and you'll not be nothing" [*Night Rider,* p. 457].[1]) In *At Heaven's Gate* Jerry Calhoun is a rare figure because he achieves some sense of identity when he returns to his father and his home and its traditional values. The rest of the characters in that novel reject their fathers and fail to achieve any such identity: Sue Murdock remains in opposition to her father to the last; Bogan Murdock conceals his father, who had once murdered a man, from the world as though to deny his father's crime; and Slim Sarrett tells Sue a cock-and-bull story about how his fathers were all the men who had visited his mother in her New Orleans crib, when actually his parents are middle-class Georgians. In *All the King's Men* Jack Burden rejects the Scholarly Attorney, whom he supposes to be his father, and finds a father-surrogate in Willie Stark. But he achieves self-knowledge when he discovers that his real father is Judge Irwin. Norton Girault has

"The Required Past: *World Enough and Time*" by Robert Berner. From *Modern Fiction Studies,* 6, no. 1 (Spring 1960), 55-64. *Modern Fiction Studies,* Copyright © 1960 by Purdue Research Foundation, West Lafayette, Indiana, U.S.A. Reprinted by permission of Purdue Research Foundation.

[1]Page references are to the first editions of Warren's works: *Night Rider* (New York, 1939), *Selected Poems, 1923-1943* (New York, 1944), *All the King's Men* (New York, 1946), and *World Enough and Time* (New York, 1950). [All of these works have been published in Great Britain by Martin Secker & Warburg Limited.—Ed.]

shown that the symbolism of birth and rebirth is developed throughout this novel,[2] and at the moment his father kills himself Jack is born into self-knowledge, into an awareness of his responsibility for his own sins, into what might be called moral maturity. The relationship of Jeremiah Beaumont to Colonel Fort in *World Enough and Time* is again that of the "son" to the father-surrogate, and the implications (psychological, philosophical, and finally moral) are similar to those in Warren's other fiction, though the symbolic structure of his fourth novel is more complex than that of any of his other works. Most critics have agreed that the essential conflict in the novel is between the "world" and Jeremiah's "idea." Robert Heilman, for example, has appropriately stated the theme: "the failure of a private, subjective, 'ideal' realm to come to terms with, to be integrated with, to be married to a realm of public life and activity, the realm of politics and society and group action, of law and justice."[3] I intend to demonstrate how Warren works out this theme in terms of what is essentially a realistic view of human nature and a philosophical view of history (both with theological overtones) and to show how he accomplishes this by dramatizing the relationship of Jeremiah to his "father," Colonel Fort.

The father is a metaphor in Warren's work for time, for the past, for an awareness of man's place in relation to the past and the future. As Jack Burden says, "I tried to tell her [Anne Stanton] how if you could not accept the past and its burden there was no future, for without one there cannot be the other, and how if you could accept the past you might hope for the future, for only out of the past can you make the future" (*All the King's Men*, p. 461). Just before one of his crises Jack is a student of history writing a dissertation on the life of Cass Mastern. He drops the subject "because he was afraid to understand for what might be understood there was a reproach to him" (201). He digs into the pasts of Cass Mastern and Judge Irwin and finds the same thing: crime. History is a record of man's crime, and to understand that fact, Jacks tell Anne, is to be realistic enough to live in the present and plan for the future. As Hugh Miller, the Attorney-General who resembles Judge Irwin in attitude, says to Jack, "History is blind, but man is not" (462). This means, I take it, that against the moral neutrality of history, against the fatality of the past, man must oppose his will. This blind history is like "the innocent savagery of Time," as Warren calls it in "The Ballad of Billie Potts." Time is innocent because it is morally neutral, because it is determined by a necessity outside the control of man's will—it is not to blame for anything—but Time is savage because it *is* innocent, in the sense that nature is innocent; thus when man submits his human nature to savage nature, when he ceases to constantly

[2]Norton Girault, "The Narrator's Mind as Symbol: An Analysis of 'All the King's Men,'" *Accent*, VII (Summer 1947), 220-234.

[3]Robert B. Heilman, "Tangled Web," *Sewanee Review*, LIX (Winter 1951), 107.

oppose his moral will to the moral neutrality and blindness of fate, then he ceases to be human and becomes morally blind. (This function of nature in the novel will be taken up later.) The father is symbolic of the past because he is a person's link with the past just as the son is the link with the future. The person who becomes aware of that fact also becomes aware of his share in the common guilt of man. It is for this reason that Percy Munn, in *Night Rider,* kills Bunk Trevelyan, of whom he dreams as of a son and to whom he literally gave life when he saved him from the gallows by pinning his murder-charge on a Negro sharecropper. When Munn realizes that the Negro's seemingly preposterous claim of innocence was true and that he has condemned an innocent man and given life to a Bunk Trevelyan who is completely lacking in moral sense, he kills him as though to kill an evil future which he helped to create.

Thus in *World Enough and Time* Warren frequently brings the past up to date by showing how the past has affected the present. The "sluttish wench from the inn" whom Jeremiah's grandfather Marcher marries gives him descendants who include a governor of Kentucky, a Confederate hero, a railroad president, and a Montmartre Bohemian suspected of pederasty. Gran Boz, the river pirate, fathered a mixed and incestuous breed who survived him, and Warren suggests that these descendants became part of the westward movement and prospered, entering all ranks of society.

> So Ole Big Hump was forgotten, but more than a century later, lying under the earth on his island, he might grin to think that the joke, in the end, was not on him but on the world, for those most respectable descendants, who did not know him and would have denied him with shame, still carried under their pink scrubbed hides...the mire-thick blood of his veins and the old coiling darkness of his heart. (433)

Big Hump's respectable descendants would not accept their evil ancestor; and yet the father, in Warren's view, must be recognized by the son before the son can achieve identity and moral maturity. When Jeremiah is thrown into the Frankfort dungeon, he remembers a similar experience when he was a child; the passage invites comparison with Jack Burden's symbolic rebirth when he finds his father:

> ...he had crawled back a long way, through winding, cranky gullets that constricted breath...he had felt along the wall, inch by inch, to another aperture...he had crawled again, deeper, deeper, and narrower, and had come at last to a place where he could crawl no more, it was so close, "So I lay there, and breathed the limey, cool inward smell of the earth's bowels.... It is a smell cleanly and rich, not dead and foul but pregnant with a secret life.... And while I lay there I thought how I might not be able to return, and would lie there forever, and I saw how my father might at that moment be standing in a field full of sun to call my name." (312)

This cave is clearly symbolic of the womb and to be in it is to be outside of human responsibility and outside of time (he "would lie there forever"). And it is the father who calls him to life and into a juxtaposition with the past and future.

But though man must recognize and accept the evil of the past (and the crimes of his father), he must not surrender to this evil. Nature, in Warren's work, is like the past: it is part of man, but man must resist it with his will. Thus Jeremiah is unable to achieve salvation when he hears Corinthian McClardy preach. McClardy's converts manifest their religious experience in both physical and spiritual ways, and the body for McClardy seems to be the way to the soul. (This is related to Dr. Burnham's interest in the relation of the mind and body.) But though Jeremiah's soul is shaken by the preaching, his body leads him into the woods and into a hideous coupling with a hag. This natural experience in a natural setting amid "festoons of grapes" is related to the flight in the last chapter into "innocence" and nature on Big Hump's island, a kind of upside-down Eden which is a frightening parody of the related notions of the noble savage, human perfectibility, and the Golden Age. The "innocence" which Jeremiah achieves is not of men but of animals and vegetables. It recalls the moment just before he kills Fort, when he seems to sense qualities of the vegetable world in himself. Standing outside Fort's window, "he had the fancy that he was growing into the ground, was setting root like the plants of the thicket, was one of them groping deeper and deeper into the cold, damp earth..." (235), a thought related to the passage about the cave quoted earlier. He finds companionship with a dry lilac stalk which touches his cheek, and he remembers his pantheistic feeling when he was a boy moved by McClardy's preaching: "he had touched the ice-ridden beech and had felt his being flow out into the shining tree...and into the sunlight from every lifted twig, and down the trunk into the secret earth so that he was part of everything" (235). But he does not remember the lesson which Brother Trotter ("learned in doctrine") had tried to teach him: "the saved man... should not enter into nature, for the kingdom is not of this world" (29).

It is also important to notice the place of the past in this complex of symbolism; to kill Fort is, for Jeremiah, to kill the past. "Then, he thought that after the event to come he would never again have to cringe and fawn at some reference, however innocent, to the past. ... The past would be dead" (213). The decision to destroy Fort, then, is a move toward nature, toward "innocence," toward timelessness, toward the animal state of total unconsciousness of birth or death or anything but the moment, and *away from* the father, the human community, guilt and the responsibility toward past and future which makes man human. All of this is contained in a few lines in "The Ballad of Billie Potts" where Warren says,

> Think of yourself riding away from the dawn,
> Think of yourself and the unnamed ones who had gone
> Before, riding, who rode away from *goodbye, goodbye,*
> And toward *hello,* toward Time's unwinking eye;
> And like the cicada had left, at cross-roads or square,
> The old shell of self, thin, ghostly, translucent, light as air,
> At dawn riding into the curtain of unwhispering green,
> Away from the vigils and voices into the green
> World, land of the innocent, land of the leaf.
>
>   (*Selected Poems,* p. 7)

The journey west ("away from the dawn") is a journey into nature ("land of the leaf") and innocence and away from consciousness and identity ("The old shell of self") and the human community of "cross-roads or square." It is the same journey which Jack Burden takes west to Long Beach, where he sleeps to escape from the fact that Anne Stanton has become Willie Stark's mistress. And it is the journey which Jeremiah takes down the river to Big Hump's island. There he discovers "a kind of peace...a peace with no past and no future" (435). But what does this timeless and unconscious peace amount to? Jeremiah reaches what is probably his deepest degradation when he lies with a syphilitic slut behind a shed where a man who had been knifed in a quarrel is bleeding to death. At this point, as he admits later, he has managed to "embrace the world as all...to seek communion in the blank cup of nature, and innocence there" (459). He is able to escape from the island and from his false view of reality only when he learns from One-eye Jenkins the full extent of Wilkie Barron's treachery. This brings him to a knowledge of Fort's nature and of his own relationship to him. He tells One-eye, "I have killed one man. ... With my hands. ... He was a man. A great man. He was my friend and benefactor. He loved me like a father, and I killed him" (457). (Of Judge Irwin, Jack Burden says on several occasions, "He was a man.")

Colonel Cassius Fort must be understood in terms of what Charles R. Anderson calls the "men of principle" who appear frequently in Warren's novels: Captain Todd (in *Night Rider*), Judge Irwin, Hugh Miller are others.[4] Anderson quotes the "stand" of the Twelve Southerners, who wrote in 1930 that "man must accept his middle place in 'nature' between the animals and the angels, neither sinking into naturalism nor aspiring to perfection, but creating the best possible order out of his recognized limitations and preserving it." Warren's "men of principle" believe in what Anderson calls "the general or accepted laws governing conduct that have

---

[4]Charles R. Anderson, "Violence and Order in the Novels of Robert Penn Warren," *Southern Renascence: The Literature of the Modern South,* ed. by Louis D. Rubin and Robert D. Jacobs (Baltimore, 1953), pp. 207-224.

come down through history." Warren clearly demonstrates that the alternative to this is to be either a Wilkie Barron or a Percival Skrogg. Barron is a man of the "world" without the "idea," a cold manipulator of souls who seeks a political end with absolutely no regard for the means he must employ. Skrogg, on the other hand, is of a race that "has multiplied and become the glory and the horror of our time" (79). He is the pure idealist, a man of pure "idea" without "world," but he is a perfect complement of Barron and seeks the same end.

But Fort is a "man of principle." He understands political realities without becoming an amoral monster like Wilkie Barron. Like Judge Irwin (who tells Jack Burden that "politics is always a matter of choices, and a man doesn't set up the choices himself. And there is always a price to make a choice" (*All the King's Men*, p. 364), Fort has the conscience to change his political course when he thinks he is wrong. When he decides that the New Court party is wrong he espouses the Old Court though his own Relief faction has declared for the New Court, and he runs for office because "thought without action I deem disease of will, and no virtue" (190). The political spirit of compromise (repugnant to an idealist like Jeremiah) enables him to conceive of a plan to end the New Court-Old Court squabble to everyone's satisfaction, a plan which, appropriately enough, Jeremiah foils by murdering him the night before he was to present it to the Legislature. In fact, this particular political conflict is related to the whole question of traditional values. The New Court party wants to destroy the court and the Constitution too, if necessary, to make it possible for debtors to postpone payment of their debts. Wilkie Barron, the political amoralist, says, "For what is our constitution for? It is to protect the people of the state. And when it does not protect, it is not valid" (151). Jeremiah has the sense to see that Wilkie is saying that "the voice of Justice [is] in the belly," a "wicked parody" of his own belief that "the voice of Justice [is] in the heart" (152).

Furthermore, Fort is aware of his own guilt in regard to Rachel Jordan. When he rejects Jeremiah's challenge to a duel, he says, "I cannot fight you. I cannot fight any man on this point. If a man should come at me with a penknife and the name of Rachel Jordan on his lips, and I held a sword, I could not lift it" (128). Jeremiah is at his worst in this scene, threatening to horsewhip Fort in the streets, and, when Fort asks him to let him keep his "good name," accusing him of cowardice; and it is to Jeremiah's credit that he vomits in the blackberry bushes when it is over. Fort's attitude toward his sin with Rachel and toward the world is summarized in his letter to her:

> I confess me wrong, and bitterly. ... I betrayed you and betrayed others who trusted me, compounding betrayal by betrayal, and for those months lived in a dream outside the hard world and its duties. Then I came back into the

world, and hope to do my duty still, whatever it may be and bear with fortitude the ills and losses. ... You sent me back into the world to play what part
in it I could with my poor rags of honor left. ...
... Take happiness with Beaumont, and do not stain your heart or his hand
with blood—however guilty that blood may be. And it is guilty blood. But
it came to guilt, not by coldness and in the calculation of man's vanity, but in
hotness and folly, forgetful of the nature of things, and the debt it owed the
world.   (135)

Considering the line "You sent me back into the world," Jeremiah's charge
that Fort abandoned Rachel sounds more romantic than accurate. It is
further to Fort's credit that the novel clearly demonstrates that only
Jeremiah hates Fort. He tortures Rachel to cry out for Fort's blood, and just
before her death she tells Jeremiah that he killed Fort, not for her, but for
himself. "You made me hate Fort, and you used me. Oh, I didn't hate him,
I loved him..." (452).

At the end of the novel Jeremiah has realized his sin against Fort, against
Rachel, against Dr. Burnham, against Hawgood and Madison, a sin which
he says is "the unpardonable...crime of self" (458). But he does not know
how "the word becomes flesh" and "the flesh becomes word." He has not
learned what the novel makes clear: the dualistic view that a man must be
both guilty and innocent of self simultaneously. "For all men believe in
justice," says the narrator. "Otherwise they would not be men" (463). Men
must believe in justice even though they cannot always agree as to a just
way to get it. Men must live in the world without becoming monsters like
Wilkie Barron; they must have ideals without becoming monsters like
Percival Skrogg. Even Barron and Skrogg finally come to realize this:
Barron, after great worldly success, kills himself; and Skrogg, with apparent contempt for the world and even life itself, loses his great reputation as a fearless duelist when it is learned after his death that he wears a
chain-mail vest. Even they attempt to heal the split between "world" and
"idea."

As I see it, *World Enough and Time* poses the question: In a world run
by Wilkie Barrons and Percival Skroggs, what does a man do? Of the various world-views presented by the novel, only two receive the implicit
benediction of the novelist. One of them is the view of Tom Barron or of
Munn Short (or of Willie Proudfit in *Night Rider*), a view similar to the
line from *Ecclesiastes* which serves as an epigraph for this essay, a view
expressed in the same poem by the admonition, "Fear God, and keep his
commandments." Old Tom Barron explains to Jeremiah why he plants:
"It come on me long back that all for a man like me was to set his strength
to whatever come to his hand. ... I have seen days I cried out against God
for the grief laid on me. But what I learned I learned. ... And son, I aim
to take me one more crop. It may be the best I ever made. Under God's

hand" (140-141). This view of the world is what John Crowe Ransom, in *God Without Thunder* (a work which must sooner or later be mentioned in a discussion of Warren) calls "the tragic spirit."

> Tragedy exhibits always the failure of secular enterprise. In tragedy the mind makes the critical confession that human goodness, and intelligent work, a combination popularly supposed to be the sufficient cause of prosperity, do not actually produce their triumphant effect upon the material world. Or: *The moral order is a wished-for order, which does not coincide with the actual order or world order.* And having made this confession, what can the mind do about it? I would suggest the simple answer: the mind must accept the world order.[5]

And yet Tom Barron's view of man's condition, though it is a more intelligent one than Jeremiah's, has its limitations. If the "world order" is the world as it is willed by God (or fate or whatever we may wish to call it), that is one thing; but if this "world order" is the world as it is ordered by Wilkie Barron, then living in that world may be intolerable. The moral order *is* a wished-for order, and yet man *must* wish for it. As Warren says, "All men believe in justice. Otherwise they would not be men." The alternative is to give oneself over to the world either like Wilkie Barron, or like Jeremiah in his false Eden on Big Hump's island, that is, either to pragmatically accept the evils of the world because they do exist, or to retreat into the womb of false innocence.

Therefore the only other acceptable view of man's condition presented by the novel is that of Colonel Fort, who falls in spite of (and because of) his principles and devotion to duty. His sin against Rachel Jordan, like the sin of Hester Prynne in *The Scarlet Letter* committed "in hotness and folly, forgetful of the nature of things," can be forgiven (like all sins of the flesh); yet it destroys Fort, while Wilkie Barron's long, continuous sin of pride (recalling Fort's words about "coldness and the calculation of man's vanity") gives him at least temporary success in the world. Unfortunately this is frequently, perhaps usually, the way it goes. *World Enough and Time* presents a realistic, and that is to say painful, view of political action in particular and man's fate in general. Warren's capitalization of words referring to Satan in the Corinthian McClardy section and the general violence of the novel show that in *World Enough and Time* Satan is a powerful reality. In fact, the final scenes on Big Hump's island and the fine Shakespearian thoroughness with which Warren kills off his characters may make it appear that perhaps God is out of His league in this contest with Satan. But to say this is to forget Warren's view of the function of Satan. In *All the King's Men* the Scholarly Attorney (another Tom Barron) dictates to Jack Burden a paragraph on God's creation of sinful man, in

---

[5]John Crowe Ransom, *God Without Thunder,* 2nd edition (London, 1931), p. 49.

which he says, "The only way for God to create, truly create, man was to make him separate from God Himself, and to be separate from God is to be sinful. The creation of evil is therefore the index of God's glory and His power. That had to be so that the creation of good might be the index of man's glory and power" (462-463). This is the tragic view: man must fail, but it is his "glory and power" to aspire to "the creation of good."

It is an aspect of what Jeremiah calls "the doubleness of life" (140), and the last page of his manuscript shows that he still has doubts whether this "doubleness" can be integrated.

> I had longed to do justice in the world, and what was worthy of praise. Even if my longing was born in vanity and nursed in pride, is that longing to be wholly damned? For we do not damn the poor infant dropped by a drab in a ditch, but despite the mother's fault and tarnishment we know its innocence and human worth. And in my crime and vainglory of self is there no worth lost? Oh, was I worth nothing, and my agony? Was all for naught? (465)

Warren leaves the final judgment of Jeremiah to the reader; but the novel has clearly shown that though Jeremiah has failed to make the word flesh and vice versa, though he can only seek expiation and is beyond redemption for his crimes, though he fears his dream of justice may have been a completely false one, still he, like all men, must dream of justice. Not that this is easy, but that it is necessary. It is much easier to sink into nature, which, Warren seems to say, is the democratic temptation. Thus when the Court of Inquiry tries to determine whether Bump's measurement of the footprint found outside Fort's window matches Jeremiah's boot, Hawgood proves it does not while four other witnesses who have already hanged Jeremiah in their hearts claim that it does. "But some in the crowd cried it was four against one and one man's word was as good as another's or it was no democracy" (280). This is perhaps the ultimate perversion of the ideal of justice—irrationality and hatred in the name of the democratic ideal—and unfortunately, judging from the novel, it is the greater temptation to be like the four false witnesses than like Hawgood.

And yet Hawgood, though a political friend of Fort, can defend Fort's murderer in court "for truth," joined by Madison, a personal friend of Fort; Fort himself does good in the world though painfully aware that the good must be tainted by the sin in his past; and though Jeremiah sinks into the mire of animality on the island and calls it "peace," he can still rise out of that mire into an awareness of Cassius Fort's humanness and a faith in the "innocence and human worth" of "the poor infant dropped by a drab in a ditch." The reader is certainly aware of the agony in *World Enough and Time:* this is the worth of that agony.

Carrying Manty Home:
Robert Penn Warren's
Band of Angels

by Allen Shepherd

> I don't think I do write historical novels. I try to find stories that
> catch my eye, stories that seem to have issues in purer form than
> they come to one ordinarily. ...I hate costume novels, but maybe
> I've written some and don't know it. I have a romantic kind of
> interest in the objects of American history: saddles, shoes, fig-
> ures of speech, rifles, et cetera. They're worth a lot. Help you
> focus.[1]

> ...out of Margaret Mitchell by Mark Twain![2]

The progress of *Band of Angels* (1955), Robert Penn Warren's fifth
novel, suggests that of an aerialist pedaling along a wire over Niagara
Falls. He is an accomplished professional, but you fear for him nonetheless. He wavers, seems almost to stop, disappears into the mist, and finally
reaches the end. He then gets off his bicycle and trips over a rock. Time
and again Warren saves the novel as it threatens to fall into steamy sen-
sationalism or trite melodrama. In the end, however, he seems to lose his
nerve, and the novel dives into a false and one must say sentimental
resolution.

Band of Angels is in a number of ways both an ambitious and an impressive performance. The story, like most of Warren's stories, is fast-
paced and exciting, the plotting is intricate yet coherent. Warren's sense

Carrying Manty Home: Robert Penn Warren's *Band of Angels"* by Allen Shepherd. From
Four Quarters, XXI (1972), no. iv, 101-9. © 1972 by *Four Quarters*. Reprinted by permission
of the editor and La Salle College.

[1]Malcolm Cowley, ed., *Writers at Work: The Paris Review Interviews* (New York: Viking
Press, 1959), p. 188.

[2]Leslie A. Fiedler, *Love and Death in the American Novel* (Cleveland and New York: The
World Publishing Co., 1962), p. 393.

of place is as keen as ever, his linguistic powers are sometimes startling, his fund of antiquarian lore is formidable, and his tragic sense often succeeds in infusing new meaning into the clichés of the historical novel. Warren's interrelated themes are for the most part familiar ones: the meaning and achievement of freedom and identity, the dangers of untutored idealism, and the necessity of integrating past and present. The principal defect in the novel, however, is a radical one: its protagonist and narrator, Amantha Starr, is notably unattractive, often insensitive, full of self-pity given to constant evasions, practicing one betrayal after another. She is also not a credible woman, and might indeed be made to fill out an illustrative page or two in *Sexual Politics.*

Band of Angels, as a popular philosophical novel, asks to be read, in an eighteenth-century phrase, as "pleasant instruction": to be successful, it must be both. Thus the question of the novel's focus. Warren attempts to control and deepen his story by internalizing the struggle, yet fast-paced action, bizarre characters, and vividly realized setting all tend to over-shadow Manty's problems, largely passive as she is. There is at times such a claustrophobic density of detail, such an insistence on background authenticity, that one loses sight of Manty. One has in *Band of Angels* an extensive and crowded panorama, from Starrwood, a small, backwoods Kentucky plantation, to pietistic, Abolitionist Oberlin, to New Orleans, to bloody African slave-gathering expeditions, to Halesburg, Kansas, in the 1880's. If some of the detail seems to come from *Godey's Lady's Book,* if some descriptions (of Manty's flight through the swamp, for instance) are rather labored, one is struck time and again by the felicity of Warren's selection of surface detail. Walter Sullivan puts the case well when he says that "in at least one way he [Warren] is as well qualified as any living American novelists to write about the past."[3]

A question raised by *Band of Angels,* however, is whether such richly rendered authenticity aids in or militates against the creation of a novel of ideas, which is what this novel purports to be. Allied to the physical data of Manty's story, but seeming almost to possess an independent life of its own, is Warren's unflagging concern with problems of freedom and identity, the nature of reality, the goodness of evil intentions and the evil of good ones. There is evident throughout the novel a kind of stratification in which the line of demarcation between event and the meaning of event is often distinct.

Manty forthrightly addresses herself to the novel's two principal themes on the first page: "Oh, who am I? ... If I could only be free..."[4] The achieve-

[3]"The Historical Novelist and the Existentialist Peril: Robert Penn Warren's *Band of Angels," The Southern Literary Journal* II (Spring 1970), 109.

[4]*Band of Angels* (New York: Random House, 1955), p. 3. Subsequent quotations from this edition will be identified in the text.

ment of identity and freedom, as becomes evident, troubles not only Manty, but nearly all the novel's characters, indeed the generality of men. It is on this or a related issue that Sullivan pursues his examination of the novel, concluding that the existential terms in which Manty's dilemma is cast are essentially anachronistic and that Warren is unfaithful to the spirit of her time. Had it been published ten years later, *Band of Angels* would also surely have had—along with Styron's *Nat Turner*—its ten black critics to respond.

Manty's progress to identity and freedom is tortuous and crab-like, a step forward usually followed by a half-step backward. This until the great leap forward of the novel's conclusion. Central, of course, is her half-caste status; the Civil War goes on within and without her, and the primary question is "Oh, whose side am I on?" (276) In the end, however, she is a white woman, with a white father, white husband, and white child. Never, as Leslie Fiedler observes, can she bring herself to say, "I am a Negro."[5] Yet as Manty finally realizes, freedom does not inhere in the possession of manumission papers. "Nobody," she concludes, "can set you free,… except yourself." (363-364)

Prerequisite to self-hood, or the achievement of freedom, is the rejection of a number of self-enslaving alternatives. Manty, like many of Warren's characters, is not immune to the attraction of mechanistic philosophy; so long as she believes that "…you are, therefore, only what History does to you," so long as she thinks that "…everything in the world is just something that happens…to you," she can reject all responsibility, for her own actions, and for those of others. (112 and 309) She seeks to withdraw from the public world, the world of war and the Freedman's Bureau and the Constitutional Convention, but "the world was there creeping in like cold air under a door. …" (257) Although her future husband, Tobias, after his first call, leaves her feeling "weak and pure…and ready for life," (223) Manty in a subsequent evasion, learns "the trick of sinking into the day's occupation," which she calls "the human commitment," but which is in fact a sanctified retreat from involvement. (250-251)

Frequently she reflects on the complexities of cause and effect, on Flag-Officer Farragut's fine gold braid bringing her Tobias, John Brown being responsible for her rape, the infinitely complicated causal chain of the New Orleans riots of 1866. Always the thread which she follows leads away from her. For a long time her father is a dumping ground for all responsibility, and as "poor little Manty" she proclaims her hatred for each of the men in her life. Fastening the blame for her condition on one person (her father) or on a series of people (Seth Parton, Hamish Bond, Tobias Sears) is easier than admitting that cause and effect are not precisely definable, or that one

[5] *Love and Death in the American Novel,* p. 304.

is inescapably involved in and responsible for what happens to oneself and to others as well.

Although Manty is plagued by guilt feelings, she is also troubled by the presence of another self, "that cold-eyed *not-you*," (161) which rejoices in the avoidance of responsibility which derives from "poor little Manty's" power over others. These others—her father, Hamish Bond, Tobias Sears —are all made to feel that they have wronged her, that they are guilty. Thus after her father has apologized,

> there came to me some hard sense of an advantage just gained, not to be exploited yet but held in reserve, some possibility of self-justification and of revenge. (32)

Recuperating from Hamish Bond's first attack, she seeks to "confirm my sweet advantage of having been little and precious and wronged." (162) During Tobias Sears' first call upon her, her heart leaps as she realizes that she "had touched some secret spring that gave me power over him." (224)

With each accession of power, Manty seeks a new focus of responsibility. Repeatedly she seeks freedom in flight from the past: to be "free from everything in the world, all the past, all my old self, free to create my new self." (234) In the past lies the physical cause of her bondage, her father's bankruptcy and untimely death, but also the fact which denies the rationale of her life, that her father had loved her, had not been able to consider her as less than his daughter, had not been able to bring himself to draw up manumission papers, and thereby risk alienating and losing her. In their final conversation, Miss Idell begins to tell Manty this, but she cannot accept it, since it involves not only acceptance of responsibility for her own situation but forgiveness of her father.

This forgiveness is what Manty finally achieves, and *Band of Angels* is the only one of Warren's novels which deals specifically with this problem. Manty's resolution, whatever its defects, is significant because it contrasts so markedly with much of Warren's earlier work, poems and novels, in which he found the condition of horror almost unendurable, yet not admitting of resolution. Forgiveness of her father entails Manty's acceptance of responsibility, acknowledgment of the purposiveness of her acts, the achievement of that limited freedom which is man's condition, and the recognition of her own identity.

Since virtually all of the major characters in *Band of Angels* seek freedom and identity, it would be well to consider the nature of their struggles and achievements. Their struggles are designed to complement and illuminate Manty's own, but as will be seen, they tend rather to contradict or undercut them. Miss Idell and old Mr. Sears possess a sure sense of their identities; Manty naturally hates the one and fears the other. For many men, Manty fancies, the war offers a promise of fulfillment: "Perhaps this was the deepest and dearest promise, the most secret—the brute, communal roar, the dancing, the flames leaping in darkness." (174) The war offers fulfillment to emptiness, commitment to a cause, however ill-defined, self-realization in action, much like that which Percy Munn sought in *Night Rider.* Hamish Bond seeks freedom in expiation, through benevolence to individual victims of the institution from which he has profited. Kindness in him is like a disease. Bond's *k'la,* or bound brother, Rau-Ru, seeks freedom through political action, a new definition in a new name, Lt. Oliver Cromwell Jones. Two idealists, Seth Parton and Tobias Sears, seek freedom through imposing pure idea on the world; "the idea," in Jeremiah Beaumont's phrase, "must redeem the world."[6]

None of them succeeds in finding either freedom or the desired identity. At his death, Bond finds himself, as he had bitterly promised his mother he one day would, "ass-deep in niggers." (324) All his life he has been haunted by his denial of his parents, even as he blames them and others for his career as a slave-trader, thinking "I didn't make myself and I can't help what I am doing." (189) It is those to whom Bond most consistently extended his kindness and protection, Rau-Ru and Manty, who preside at his hanging, each blaming the other for his death. Rau-Ru had long occupied a peculiar situation in Bond's household. As a boy, he had been saved from certain death by the intervention of Bond, then engaged in an African slave-gathering expedition. In defense of his newly acquired chattel, Bond had been wounded and lamed for life. Thus was Rau-Ru's bond established.

His owner strengthened the tie by educating him, by appointing him an overseer, by offering his friendship and protection. And it is "Old Bond being good" (271) that makes Rau-Ru hate him most. This and the beating which he receives for defending Manty, Bond's other favorite, from the advances of Charles de Marigay Prieur-Denis. This is the event—not Mr. Lincoln's Proclamation—which Rau-Ru tells Manty had set him free. Free for what, to do what? Free eventually to return, a hunted outlaw, to Bond, this time himself the master, to hang Bond, or to feel that he could if he wanted to. Yet it was Manty's presence, Rau-Ru asserts, which drove Bond to jump from the wagon with the rope around his neck. Rau-Ru cannot forgive the kind father-master, and his final gift to Manty, saying that she is, as she desperately claims, white, is more a gesture of contempt than forgiveness. Who is the victor, who is the victim?

Seth Parton, the sanctified Oberlin farm boy, sought absolute purity, but ended in absolute impurity, giving up theology for the stock market. Seth, who prayed with Manty in an Ohio glade to be shown "the performance of sanctification," in New Orleans attempts a ritualistic coupling with

[6]Robert Penn Warren, *World Enough and Time* (New York: Random House [;London: Martin Secker & Warburg Limited], 1950), p. 505.

her, after discovering that "only in vileness may man begin to seek," and finally marries the sensual Miss Idell. (52 and 284)

Tobias Sears, the most fully developed and longest enduring of the novel's supporting cast, suffers a more equivocal fate. Warren's later essay, *The Legacy of the Civil War,* provides an illuminating gloss on this student of Mr. Emerson. Influenced initially by his father, who in his detachment reflects the "are they my poor?" side of Emerson's thought, Sears is one of the "higher-law" men, to whom the attraction of a total solution is strong. This predilection, together with the objection of the corrupt Colonel Morton, explains Sears' embracing of total Negro suffrage and his joining the Freedman's Bureau. Sears is one of those who, as Warren observes in his "Meditations on the Centennial," "had lost what they took to be their natural and deserved role."[7] which is to say a traditional sense of identity. He is one of "an elite without function, a displaced class."[8] Bereft of his class identity, and frustrated in the attempt to achieve personal freedom, Sears commits himself to the political implementation of the Fourteenth Amendment, only to conclude in despair that "...we undertook to do good in the world, but we had not purged our own soul." (294)

A prototype of Sears would seem to be the Abolitionist Theodore Weld, who as Warren records in *The Legacy of the Civil War,* found that "he himself needed reforming," and that "he had been laboring to destroy evil in the same spirit as his antagonists."[9] Sears' post-war literary activities reveal the essence of his character: in *The Great Betrayal* he denounces the Gilded Age for the corruption of the ideals for which he had fought, and in his poetry, published occasionally in the *Atlantic,* he is himself the ever recurring protagonist, "dying always into the beauty of Idea, into the nobility of Truth, dying into the undefiled whiteness of some self-image." (346) This is Warren's higher-law man, who "had withdrawn, and all that was left was 'the infinitude of the individual'—with no 'connections,' with no relation to 'dirty institutions.'"[10] The West to which Sears withdraws is not—and this is typical of Warren—the great good place, not Frederick Jackson Turner's land of golden opportunity, but a place in which Manty and Tobias fail and grow old. Yet Warren is not content to leave Sears in a state of moral narcissism, but rather leads him into conversion to the Thingism which he had indicted in *The Great Betrayal.*

The fervor of the convert is relieved by his sardonic realization of the depths to which he has fallen, and it is this protective self-satire which largely defines him until the end of the novel, when he is retained by Josh

---

[7]*The Legacy of the Civil War: Meditations on the Centennial* (New York: Random House, 1961), p. 26.

[8]Ibid.

[9]Ibid., p. 23.

[10]Ibid., p. 30.

Lounberry, a Chicago Negro who has grown rich by selling a device to put kinks in white folks' hair (this is the sort of pointless irony which Warren unfortunately sometimes cannot resist). Lounberry's father, it develops, is Uncle Slop, the local garbage man, whom Sears and Lounberry contrive to outfit with a suit of new clothes, after washing him down and dousing him with cologne.

Sears is also involved (I use the word advisedly) in Lounberry's accommodation problem at the local hotel, during the settlement of which he uncharacteristically becomes involved in a fight. I provide this summary because it is necessary to the understanding and evaluation of the novel's conclusion, since little Manty (a name which she at last symbolically rejects) is much impressed by her husband's new manner, and concludes that she, too, can learn something from Mr. Lounberry, "not merely because he could honor his father, but because he could honor the father who had rejected him." (373) It would appear that in Tobias' hosing down the old man and engaging in a fistfight the reader is to perceive a dramatization of his conversion, an image of idealism consorting with mundane reality. To support the novel's resolution, some such reading is in fact obligatory. It should be observed, however, that Sears is not radically changed, that his uncustomary violence derives from his being treated as a disprized equal by Lounberry ("Then I saw the colored man looking at me. It was a look that said, plain as day: *you, too.*") (370) On the matter of the novel's conclusion, which he nicely anatomizes, Walter Sullivan asserts that "it is hard to see how she [Amantha] is much freer on the last page than she was on the first."[11] It is indeed, though contrary to Warren's manifest intent.

What Warren has attempted to do is to carry off a black tragedy with a white joke. The ending is forced, hurried and derives from no logical or psychological precedent. *Band of Angels* aspires to be (and often is) more than the conventional historical novel which Warren has understandably said he dislikes. Certainly he undertook to write an anti-historical novel, his subject the plight of the white Negro, that is, Manty's radical division, this plight symbolic, in Warren's formulation, of the human condition. Hanging over the novel is the aura of miscegenation, the gothic horrors of Faulkner's *Light in August* or Twain's *Pudd'nhead Wilson*, but Warren rejects the unavoidable implications of Manty's situation, so that the novel more closely resembles the barely sketched fate of Cassy, in *Uncle Tom's Cabin*.

Warren has evidently been annoyed by those critics who have asserted that *Band of Angels* is a partisan Southern statement. "One reviewer," he recalled in a *Paris Review* interview, "a professional critic—said that *Band of Angels* is an apology for the plantation system. Well, the story of *Band*

---

[11]"The Historical Novelist and the Existential Peril: Robert Penn Warren's *Band of Angels*," p. 115.

wasn't an apology *or* an attack. It was simply trying to say something about something."[12] There have been and doubtless will continue to be comparable remarks, even from sympathetic critics; one thinks of Stanley Edgar Hyman's characterization of what we read as "the peculiar tendentiousness"[13] of *Wilderness* (1961), in which, he said, Warren overemphasized Northern sins.

The point is not Warren's partiality or impartiality but would seem rather to be that Manty does not know what to believe, who she is, and that her radical division cannot be healed. Her enlightened and pious education in the North has equipped her with a set of Abolitionist suppositions which are as useless and pernicious in understanding the realities of slavery and of being a Negro as the contrary clichés dispensed by Southern slaveholders. Time and again Manty's consciousness of her Negro blood drives her to repudiate the white men who try, however mixed their motives, to help her, but when she tries to join with the Negroes (teaching Negro refugees, responding to Dollie's final pleas, fleeing to Rau-Ru) consciousness of her white blood moves her, despite herself, to disgust and terror. Her situation is not amenable to Warren's solution.

The biggest chance Warren takes in the novel is in the selection and development of his narrator. Manty is not the compulsive righter of wrongs with which we are familiar; she is not roused to fury by the presence of evil in herself and in the world. She is instead a pallid and passive and egotistical sufferer. She is no match for Sue Murdock or Rachel Jordan or Cassie Spottwood, nor has she even the staying power of Maggie Tolliver. Perhaps she most closely resembles May, the wraith-like wife of Percy Munn.[14] She has little substance of her own and derives her being from her successive masters. For all her pondering, she remains strangely anonymous; we do not even know what she looks like.

When she is sold at Starrwood, she is a young girl, about sixteen; when the novel ends in Kansas she is in her mid-forties. Yet one has no impression of her growing older, and little evidence of maturity. Manty is articulate, or at least voluble, and indeed as first-person narrator she has to be. Warren entrusts his thematic statements as forthrightly to her as to his other first-person narrator, Jack Burden, but oh! (as Manty would say) the difference. She goes obediently through her paces, addresses herself to the problems Warren sets her, but seldom is she even a credible woman.

Although *Wilderness* is the account of an idealist's education, it rather closely resembles *Band of Angels* in several respects: a Civil War setting, a search for freedom and identity, and the special burdens of the protagonists

---

[12] *Writers at Work: The Paris Review Interviews*, p. 194.

[13] "Coming Out of the Wilderness?", *New Leader*, XLIV (November 13, 1961), p. 25.

[14] Characters in respectively, *At Heaven's Gate*, *World Enough and Time*, *Meet Me in the Green Glen* (1971), *Flood* (1964) and *Night Rider*.

(Adam Rosenzweig's deformed foot and his Jewishness, Manty's pliant femaleness and her mixed blood). More significant, however, is the novel's most evident similarity: the tone of their conclusions, which is uncharacteristically affirmative. The chances of man's prevailing in Warren's fiction were rather slim before *Brother to Dragons* (1953), which concludes with R. P. W. announcing his reconciliation with the world, now "prepared/ to go into the world of action and liability."[15]

Perhaps brief reflection on the conclusions of Warren's novels antedating 1953 will suggest the extent to which they differ from those of *Band of Angels* and *Wilderness*. Percy Munn, protagonist of *Night Rider* (1939) is finally shot down like an animal, which in fact he has virtually become. At the end of *At Heaven's Gate* (1943), Bogan Murdock's empire is tottering, but he has brought about, directly or indirectly, the death of his daughter, the alcoholism of his wife, the destruction of several of his collaborators, and the subjection of his employee, Jerry Calhoun. Calhoun and Ashby Wyndham may go on, but Calhoun is weak and Wyndham finds that he cannot pray, without which he is powerless.

In *All the King's Men* (1946), the recovery of Jack Burden, in his marriage to Anne Stanton and his prospective return to politics, remains distinctly problematical. Jeremiah Beaumont, of *World Enough and Time* (1950), is murdered on his way back to the world of responsibility, and one could readily imagine, had he lived, his return to monomaniacal idealism. This is all to say that *Brother to Dragons* witnessed a shift in Warren's moral vision. Previously it might have been summed up something like this: those who have denied their place in a sinful community (mankind), out of disillusionment, pride, or irresponsibility, must learn that they cannot remain apart; they must enter into life, take up their burdens, and suffer, in the possible hope of eventual redemption. Warren, before *Brother to Dragons*, had tried on a number of meanings, held them up, examined them, criticized them, but had not committed himself.

In *Brother to Dragons, Band of Angels* and *Wilderness*, one has the sense that Warren intends an answer, that these works represent an advanced stage of public self-study, but that he has not found an adequate vehicle, that his paradoxes are at war with one another, that he cannot integrate the affirmative conclusions he desires. The result is a series of conclusions which tasks our credulity: always the conversion of the protagonist is suspect. So Manty's reclamation is not simply artificial, though it is that, but destructive of the tragic premises of the novel. No band of angels, alone and unaided, could ever carry Manty home.

---

[15](New York: Random House [; London: Martin Secker & Warburg Limited,] 1953), p. 215.

The Uses of Gesture in Warren's *The Cave*

by James H. Justus

In his essay on *Nostromo,* Robert Penn Warren observes that Conrad was more interested in the kind of experienced humanism typified by Emilia than he was in the more flamboyant "radical skepticism" of Decoud or Monygham. Such a humanism, he concludes, emerges only out of character-in-action, when the human will meets the hard, sometimes intractable facts of other human wills in particular situations. From the clash, the recoil and clash again, comes that reward of the active consciousness: an understanding of "the cost of awareness and the difficulty of virtue."[1] The observation is useful for our reading of *Nostromo,* of course, but the double fascination is perhaps more Warren's than it is Conrad's.

In most of his novels, Warren sends his protagonist out of an intensely private world, where commitment has been either ill-defined or too easily pledged, into a public world where, if he is strong, his experience will enrich and validate that personal vision of self. The search for self-knowledge is a response to two contradictory desires: the searcher's need for a definition of his private being that will isolate him from the mass and celebrate his uniqueness, and his need for immersion in the group, the cause, the spirit of community. If in the search for self-knowledge he arrives at the clearing, the needs of identity and community will have been harmonized. The protagonist may succeed or, more often, fail, but in each case he will come away from his experience with an appreciation of the high cost of awareness. From *Night Rider* (1939) to *Flood* (1964), the protagonist resembles a Decoud or a Monygham more than he does an Emilia, a circumstance that sheds a particular light on how, in Warren, the strenuousness of human effort often outstrips its rewards. Perse Munn, Jerry Calhoun, Jack Burden, Jeremiah Beaumont, Amantha Starr, Adam Rosenzweig, Bradwell Tolliver—all achieve self-knowledge, but only after the most painful, prolonged, and costly exertion, which is to say that Warren, like

"The Uses of Gesture in Warren's *The Cave*" by James H. Justus. From *Modern Language Quarterly,* XXVI (1965), 448-61. © 1965 by *Modern Language Quarterly.* Reprinted by permission of the publisher.

[1] "'The Great Mirage': Conrad and *Nostromo,*" *Selected Essays* (New York, 1958), pp. 48-49.

Conrad, goes "naked into the pit, again and again, to make the same old struggle for his truth" ("'The Great Mirage,'" p. 58).

None of Warren's novels demonstrates the strenuousness of human effort, the defining of self through community, quite so insistently as does *The Cave*.[2] Here, failure after great struggle is still seen as a dismal fact of man's lot, but a viable, even impressive success is dominant for the first time in a Warren novel.[3] Because it is the only one of Warren's novels which lacks a true protagonist, the structure of *The Cave* suggests that all characters, however different they may be, are equally illustrative of the theme. By exploring them from multiple angles, Warren emphasizes both the strenousness and the reward of human effort. Reward commensurate with that effort comes to no fewer than seven characters (Jo-Lea, Monty, Jack and Celia Harrick, Brother Sumpter, Nick, Bingham). Two minor characters (Nick's wife and Dorothy Cutlick) achieve less, but their efforts are also less intense. One minor character (Mrs. Bingham) and one major (Isaac) make "wrong" peaces, but they are exactly the right peaces inasmuch as these characters inevitably fulfill their separate natures.

The entire plot of *The Cave* is an exploitation of the problem of reality (announced clearly in Warren's epigraph from Book VII of *The Republic*). It posits man's difficulty in separating shadow and substance and ominously suggests that even the removes from reality are reality too. Warren's techniques for this exploitation are therefore appropriate: the choice of characters who often seem drawn from a ragbag of caricatures and stereotypes; the language which, in juxtaposing cadences of ceremony and the hokey folk idioms of realistic action, ends up as stylized artifice unifying a vision of man that is itself stylized; the mood created by a mannered prose richly studded with the metaphors of reality-shadow *(image, shadow, dream, ritual, fantasy, impromptu drama, the fusion...of the dream and the actuality)*. There are caves and typal caves—all those cool, remote, pastoral glades and green back rooms of houses and banks where Keats is either read or acted out and where competing identities, personae and

---

[2]*The Cave* (New York, 1959); page references are to this edition.

[3]*The Cave* marks a crucial shift in Warren's technique. In *Wilderness* (1961) and *Flood* (1964), the same pattern emerges: the gray fact of existence resists man's control or even his understanding, but the dedicated human effort, in the midst of failure, can provide tentative success in the overwhelming concern for wholeness. Philosophically, Warren sees this success as being as difficult to attain as that in *All the King's Men* and *World Enough and Time;* however, in its dramatic working out, in its novelistic force, the success is much easier: the hurdles come down against the reiterated onslaught of rhetoric. This thickening of philosophic statement and the corresponding dramatic thinning out have been cited most often as the reasons for the relative failure of Warren's recent fiction. I believe that an investigation of Warren's strategies in genre and his tactics in technique will show that these later novels are more substantial than has been generally believed, but the subject is not appropriate to this essay. For the best presentation of Warren's weakness as a "philosophic novelist," see Madison Jones, "The Novels of Robert Penn Warren," *South Atlantic Quarterly,* LXII (1963), 488-98.

selves, are met and clarified. These identities emerge by gesture, the expression of the personal and the particular in meaningful patterns, the
personal and particular responses to given situations. Gesture, though it is
Warren's most successful method of delineating character, is also, in *The
Cave*, the manifestation of the indirect, the oblique: gesture *shadows forth*
the reality of the gesturer.

Obvious difficulties arise for the reader. Warren here lavishes his considerable energies on a created world that itself is almost an image of his
customary world of politicians, cranks, agrarian exploiters and reformers,
and commercial wizards and failures. However perfectly harmonious the
novel becomes on its own terms, the reader is forced to accept an artistic
artifact that is finally richer in statement than in drama. He may refuse to
accept it, of course, particularly if he is impatient with an author who tends
to transform a perfectly useful genre—the novel—into something resembling the parable or morality play. To remember the work of others who
have appropriated the novel form for their own purposes may not lessen
his distaste. But the fact should be made clear anyway: Warren's adapta-
tions in *The Cave* suggest more the occasional practice of, say, Kafka, Sartre,
Faulkner, Camus, Porter, and Golding than they do his own earlier practice
—or, more accurately, that tradition of gamy Southern naturalism into
which many critics have been content to place Warren. Stylization has always
been a Warren hallmark; in *The Cave* it guides characters and shapes their
actions and knits together both theme and structure into what is finally a
cohesive, comprehensive work of art.

One of the more remarkable aspects of stylization in *The Cave* is the
structural, metaphorical, thematic figure of Jasper Harrick, a non-character
almost in the same sense that James's Mrs. Newsome of *The Ambassadors* is
a non-character. His compulsion as a separate identity we know only at
secondhand; yet we see the pervasive power of that compulsion informing
the acts of every one who *is* a character. His experience is the paradigm of
self-definition. He is metaphorical, archetypal, mythical, bigger-than-life,
even stereotypical; and it is against him that "real" people test the validity
of their own more fragmented searches for self-definition. Jasper Harrick,
it should be noted, never appears except in the flashbacks of other characters; he says very few things, even by report, and only one statement is note-
worthy: his mother remembers his explanation for being a compulsive
caver—" 'in the ground at least a fellow has a chance of knowing who he is' "
(p. 241).

This motive of self-definition becomes the impulse of all the other prin-
cipals; in Jasper's fatal act, his own entombment, the motive suddenly is
manifested in a physical, tangible way, which in turn supplies the others
with both motive and act. Around the cave mouth Warren assembles his
congeries of searchers. Those who enter the cave in search of Jasper do so

frankly in hope of redefining their own identities; but even those whose quest takes them no farther than the cave mouth are searchers as well: they use Jasper's definitive gesture as a device for orienting their own attempts at self-definition.

The assembly at the cave mouth is the central fact of the action, the clearing where the paths of many searchers converge and where all participate in a ceremony of identification and confirmation. It is the place of grand gestures, where the two impulses toward identity and community are either harmonized or permanently shattered.

These searches, moreover, are underpinned by earlier and less grand gestures, which not only reveal motive of the acts and speeches of the individual searcher, but also supply a texture of motif that anticipates, corroborates, and intensifies the structural climax at the cave. The who-am-I theme is imaged in characters who realize, however dimly, that their present identity must be validated both verbally and physically.

In Warren's fictional world, speech accomplishes what it has always done for man in the real world: it makes subjective emotions external and objective facts internal. In answering the double needs of a Warren protagonist—his impulses toward identity and community—the verbal gesture possesses the double function of marking individual boundaries and erasing them. It not only defines the gesturer, but also suggests something of his dilemma in establishing intercourse between his private world and the public world in which he seeks to justify himself.

Those Warren characters who are blessed (or cursed) with the gift of vision, imagination, intelligence, or simply the mysterious compulsion to do right by a standard equally mysterious, are those who place the most value on *saying,* as if the words themselves may somehow act as agents for completing an experience still in the future. This largely unconscious use of verbal magic is an attempt not only to communicate wishes and desires, but also to establish the word as a coextension of the reality it names, to underscore the belief that by saying certain things in certain agreed-on ways, the *sayer* can shape his future and force events to turn out the way he wants them to. "Words," says Warren in a recent essay on Dreiser, "are not only a threshold, a set of signs, but a fundamental aspect of meaning, absorbed into everything else."[4]

In *The Cave,* Jasper's entombment provides not only the orienting scene, but also the chief orienting symbol by which an individual's sense of his own identity is tested. The entombment, for example, is the occasion for the restaurant owner to assert his identity, to deny that *Nick Pappy,* even though it is "what Johntown had decided was a good enough name for

---

[4]*"An American Tragedy," Yale Review,* LII (1962), 9.

Nicholas Papadoupalous" (p. 41), is either proper or adequate. He asks Mrs. Harrick to pronounce his name, since no one in Johntown had ever done that. His argument is as poignant as it is simple: "'they got things they call you. Like Nick Pappy. But if it is not your right name, it looks like sometime you don't know who you are, maybe'" (p. 304). It is Celia who remembers the shrug and the strange look of her son as he had explained his need for proper identity. It is Celia who sympathizes with, even though she cannot understand, the central problem so massively symbolized by her son's gesture. So even though she is "not handy with Greek," she tries three times to pronounce *Papadoupalous*, and Nick is satisfied.

For Monty Harrick, the problem of identity is even greater than it is for Jasper. He must not only live in the shadows of a legendary father and a well-known brother; he must also resist two versions of the public consensus: to the town generally that he is not even a chip like Jasper, and to the Binghams, old blocks and chips notwithstanding, that he is still a hillbilly. Monty's maneuver is to seize upon the epithet *hillbilly* and force Jo-Lea to repeat it, as if an aggressive, willed iteration will somehow substantiate his reality and transform an epithet of alienation into one of acceptance and union.

Monty's search for an identity that will satisfy both his private and public needs is paralleled by Jo-Lea's insistence that she and her father are separate identities. She can use the phrase "I'm me" with repeated firmness and act upon it, whereas Monty in the beginning qualifies the phrase for himself with "I don't know who I am." He remembers Jasper's assurance (rather, he literally interprets it)—"that trick of being himself so completely"—and then falls into the self-pitying depression of a younger brother because he "couldn't even be himself, whatever that was" (p. 19).

Jo-Lea's success and Monty's momentary failure in "naming" an identity are similar to Goldie Goldstein's success and Isaac's failure. Goldie can say firmly to Isaac, "'I want you because you are you'" (p. 113), but Isaac, who carries the burden of ill-defined identity, can respond only with indecision. Like Monty to Jo-Lea, he confesses to Goldie that he does not even have a sure identity to give her. And of all the characters in *The Cave*, Isaac is the one who is most concerned about his name. Even before his embarrassment at being taken for a Jew in college (Goldie is the first to call him "Ikey"), his concern is more deep-seated. Because he has an obsessive fear that he was named Isaac to be sacrificed, he taunts his father: "'Personally, I don't think you'd be up to it. ... Assuming that you really heard the voice of God putting the bee on you, would you really cut my throat?'" (pp. 96-97). All his moments of regret, however, when he wishes he were someone else, are offset by his dreams of glory, of seeing his by-line over a sensational story which he partly creates. He becomes, finally, shoddily, what he fears—the stereotyped Jew. His exploratory gestures before the mirror are a psychological rehearsal for building up the shabby commercialism which attends the search for Jasper:

> Isaac Sumpter drew himself up to his height, which was five feet, nine inches, straightened his good shoulders, curled his lip with the sardonic incisiveness, and with a tone that seemed to say that now he had, indeed, discovered all, said: "Isaac Sumpter."
>
> Then added, in a conniving whisper, with the pitying smile into the glass: "Ikey—Little Ikey."
>
> He shrugged, dropped his hands, palms outward, in a parody of the classic gesture of the Jew's resignation and irony, and repeated, in the accent of the stage Jew: "Ikey—Little Ikey." (pp. 99-100)

The opportunity at the cave gone, Isaac flees to New York, fulfilling himself at last not in other individuals (an obviously inadequate formula in itself) and not even in a stereotype, but in his particular image of a stereotype. He breathes life into a copy of a copy of his identity. The vision of himself in the mirror is transferred to his mind as the defining name and epithet by which he will complete his search for identity. In a shockingly appropriate way, Isaac's search is successful.

Monty's success in establishing a clear identity is of a different order. The words of Jasper should provide the principal impulse toward self-identity for the other characters, but since his few speeches are reported from at least two removes—and deliberately faked as well—their importance is diluted by charges, countercharges, and recriminations. Warren's scheme, using an almost non-character—long on symbolic ramifications and short on realistic life—is a bold and imaginative one in the contextual drama of *The Cave;* but it is also troublesome. The figure of Jasper, with his very absence, his thinned-out abstractness, becomes in his life and death less convincing for the reader, perhaps, than for the other characters, whose full-bodied response may strike us as slightly disproportionate to Jasper as stimulus. Credibility—and thus dramatic force—is strained. What is not strained, however, is the symbolic spinning-out of Jasper's role; and in this Warren makes him a figure of impressive dimensions, a mythic, though perhaps tawdry, hero capable of legend.

The task of verbally creating the symbol of transformation finally falls to Monty, who in his improvised ballad sings both for and about Jasper. Chapter VI is essentially Monty's; here, for the first time, the guitar becomes the explicit vehicle for the gift of song, the talisman of creativity. Standing in new boots that are catalogue duplicates of Jasper's, Monty takes the initiative by stationing himself at the cave mouth; soon encouragement comes flowing from the bystanders, some of whom had previously been friendly, some hostile or indifferent, some merely curious. As he dignifies his brother in song, he simultaneously forges his identity, an independent one that harmonizes both his separateness from and his continuity with Jasper's. The conclusion of this chapter is a kind of premature Orphean triumph in which the entire assembly rises to sing the stanzas which Monty has just created.

Names and epithets, then, enriching or diluting one's sense of self, become significant indexes for several of these searchers. For many of them, identity resides only tentatively, even uncomfortably, in the name. The restaurant owner must be satisfied to be identified more by his yellow Cadillac than by his name; his wife must answer to many ersatz identities required by both herself and Nick (*plain* Sarah Pumfret, *artiste* Giselle Fontaine, *fantasy* Jean Harlow, *tubercular* Mrs. Pappy); Dorothy Cutlick can assign no more meaning to her own name than she can to the Latin declensions which she repeats silently during her dutiful sexual sessions with Nick ("a person's name is not a good enough name for the ache a person is" [p. 40]); Jasper Harrick, vital as he is, struggles to retrieve an identity from the community's fiat that declares him the shadow of his father ("a chip off the old block"); and even the old blacksmith himself remembers the uncertain reality of the tribute paid to him in Johntown's legends for the identity he prizes ("old heller of high coves and hoot-owl hollows" [p. 135]), since to Celia he is not Jack Harrick but John T., and since he himself doubts "who Jack Harrick was, or if Jack Harrick had ever existed" (p. 148).

Words, whether used to cloak or to reveal, place their users in the position of declaring themselves; and when motives are made manifest, they stand as a defining trait of the characters who manifest them. The insistence on exploring names or epithets (most dramatically in the cases of Monty and Isaac) is the verbal gesture that particularizes the individual search for identity: the public correlative of a private need. But more: in Warren's dramas of confrontation, when the self seeks to focus more sharply its own blurred identity, words are not the only vehicle for this special communication. There is also the language of hands, the physical acknowledgment of the human need to know and to be known. The touch of a hand—or even the perfunctory handshake—possesses a certain residual value as a timeless symbol for human communion. In Warren's novels, such a touch functions literally—as physical gestures must in any novel. But Warren extends the literal gesture to its traditional symbolic function and then rings his own changes on that: the human touch may herald the visible need for that communion, the fear of it, or the doubt that communion is even possible. Its function is simultaneously literal and symbolic.

If entrapment in *The Cave* is the central metaphor for the difficulties of establishing personal identity, the human touch becomes the central metaphor for exploring the struggle to release, enrich, or redefine that identity. It can particularize a universal feeling of what might be called secular sacramentalism, the notion (more instinctive than rational) that not only one's health but also one's salvation depends on a right relationship with his fellows. It can also be used to pervert that notion and serve selfish purposes; even then, however, it reminds its user of what he should know at all times: that communion is possible but difficult. Touch symbolizes the greatest corporate virtue—human communion—but the rich, diverse, and complicated motives for touch dramatize the difficulty of that virtue.

Of all the characters who place importance on touch, Celia Harrick is consistently defined by that gesture. She sees the touch of the hand as necessary for herself, to complete herself within the entire spectrum of humanity. She must declare herself a part of the weakness of being human, and she offers her own weakness as a test for others who would share their strengths. She knows that touch is contaminating, but she senses that it is also regenerative.

The love and devotion she feels for her husband are accompanied and undercut by a sympathy for his weakness, a spiritual weakness which is magnified by his disease. Since Jack Harrick's image of himself—as Hillbilly rouster—has never included the intimation of weakness, he is the type (so Celia reasons) who "does not know that he has a cracking point" (p. 152). She prays that she may be the one to hold his hand when he does uncover that human flaw in himself. But her reiterated whisper, "'I want to hold his hand,'" is something more than spiritual prayer. Verging also on the memory of sexual desire, it reminds her of her own weakness, her own "breaking point" in succumbing to the sensuality of Jack Harrick; and the memory at one time causes her to bite the flesh on her arm and at another to press closer in the arms of Nick Papadoupalous.

In moments of accusation, she blames Jack Harrick not only for the blatant vulgarity of his heller role, but also for establishing the standards for Jasper, who, fulfilling expectations, became successively a favorite with the Johntown women, a hero in Korea, and an obsessive caver. She condemns the social pressure from the town which forced Jasper to respond appropriately to the nudgings and chuckles over "old Jack's boy." And she remembers the touching: "'They would put their hands on him—that awful old drunk Mr. Duckett, he put his hands on him...'" (p. 297). For Celia, this leering, winking, joking relationship was the reason for Jasper's caving —"'To get away from the hands on him'" (p. 298). At the same time she feels that she has failed Jasper precisely because she did not reach out her hand and touch him: "If only she had touched him. If only she had been able to reach out and touch him, then everything might have been different" (p. 241).

The difference here is not merely the difference between the reactions of the wife and the mother. There is a kind of maternal protectiveness about Celia, to be sure, but her desire to touch Jasper is essentially the same as her desire to hold old Jack's hand; it comes from a simultaneous perception of weakness—justifiable or not—and as impulse to ally her own weakness with what Nick observes as "the humanness" of these situations. In an early chapter, when the blacksmith suddenly drops to his knees with a near-incoherent proposal, the "heller of high coves" succumbs to the stereotyped humble lover in need of encouragement from his lady. When the war hero and carbon-copy heller suddenly turns serious, when his pinched and quiet face looks as if he might cry out in anguish, he communicates the need for touch even without words. In the first case, Celia responds with a hand in the lover's hair. In the second, she fails to put out her hand to touch her son. This at least is Celia's point of view. The failure of that gesture toward her son accounts in part for the intensity with which she repeats that gesture toward her helpless husband in his wheelchair. As they sit waiting in front of the cave, she crouches beside Jack Harrick's wheelchair, "one hand on the old man's right knee, supporting herself, comforting him, in that contact defining their oneness in the moment of sad expectancy and tremulous hope..." (p. 208). Touch, then, goes out not only in response to human weakness, but also as the manifestation of human weakness itself. The need is to be comforted as well as to comfort another:

> *This is my life,* the woman was thinking. *I can live it if he puts his hand on my head.*
> He laid his hand on her head. She had been staring toward the cave mouth and that touch on her head was a complete surprise. The tears were suddenly swimming in her eyes....(p. 208)

The aura about Celia extends to others. And as she becomes the focus for a kind of sacramental impulse, the touchstone which reveals human need in all its manifestations, so Warren tactically transforms the gesture of touch into a radial metaphor. The narrative is laced with hands that touch or fail to touch. As a technique, this gesture functions both literally and symbolically; and, diffused as it is among many characters and episodes, it is most successful in establishing coherence of theme. Warren begins with a commonplace, the most obvious physical act in the social world, and ends with an aesthetic device which, through parallels, repetitions, and variations, makes a profound statement on man in a chaotic world of competing realities.

At the entrance to the cave, for example, Celia cries out that somebody must go after Jasper, and it is Isaac who agrees: "'Yes, yes...'" and puts his arm around Mrs. Harrick's shoulder. "Then he jerked away from her, as though, very suddenly, he couldn't bear to have his arm there" (p. 227). For all his own deliberate toying with human privation, even Isaac feels the simultaneous need to comfort and to be comforted, but he also feels guilty in his willfulness. Further, the display of weakness threatens to tarnish the public image he has carefully created. Isaac's sense of deprivation, however illogical, suggests Celia's concern with having failed to reach out her hand to touch Jasper. In both instances the gesture of touching, if followed through, would have recognized the human need and, in recognizing it, gone far toward satisfying it. Isaac, however, is too committed to an image of himself to allow public airing of private fancies. Not even the momentary guilt of being a manipulator of Jasper's accident can deter him from that manipulation.

It is finally only Jack Harrick who can achieve a satisfactory reciprocity with Celia, and this can come only with his regeneration. Significantly enough, the closing scenes are sustained by a series of gestures of touching, where ambiguity is resolved in mutual recognition of human inadequacies. Old Jack Harrick reminds Jo-Lea that Monty, in the cave, "'will hold his Big Brother's hand, and tell him good-bye.'" He asks her to spend the night at his house with Celia "'and hold her hand'" (p. 392). Since Jo-Lea is pregnant with Monty's child, this invitation marks the strengthening of a family relationship that has been endangered and fragmented for many years. Finally, once alone, Jack sings as he strums the guitar:

> "He is lying under the land,
> But I know he'll understand.
> He is lying under the stone,
> But he will not lie alone—
> I'm coming, son, I'm coming, take your Pappy's hand."   (p. 402)

And when Celia comes to him, he lays "his hand on her head, not the weight of it, just lightly." The respect for mutual weakness engenders its own strength: the strength of acceptance without despair.

The artistic strategy in *The Cave* is clear. In sacrificing a dominating protagonist, Warren chooses to divide the dramatic interest among seven major characters and a host of minor ones, all of whom share in varying degrees the common search for self-identity. The tactics used to implement this strategy are also clear. Warren attempts to solve a built-in narrative problem—an inevitable dispersion of dramatic force—by using a kind of conceptual shorthand which will thicken the thematic statement. Thus, he uses verbal and physical gesture to externalize individual dilemmas in accommodating private and public needs. It is a familiar Warren technique, observable in such an early work as *Night Rider* and used perhaps most effectively in *World Enough and Time*. His success with gesture as an artistic tool has always depended on a dual function: giving circumstantial fullness to an individual character, who, however much he shares in the strengths and weaknesses of the human community, emerges as an independent creature worthy of having a story told about him. He can be realistic-naturalistic in the machinery of his story and still posit characteristic stances of his species; he can be a reasonable imitation of a man and still come to be a viable symbol of Man. In this sense, *The Cave* is an important departure from Warren's previous novels, and the choice of multiple protagonists is more crucial than it first appears to be. One result of this technique is that the dramatic power is diminished, and "rich meaning" is forced to take up the slack. An important indication of this shift may be seen in the reiteration of gesture and its distribution, sometimes without effective discrimination, among all the characters. At their best, they become more typal than human; at their worst, more stereotyped.

One of the more successful of these manipulations of character types through physical gesture revolves about the Sumpter-Isaac plot. From Brother Sumpter's point of view, the entire struggle to save Jasper is merely an elaborate drama, divinely ordained and staged, to save his son Isaac. It is not clear whether Sumpter believes he is acting out of a figural Abraham role or not, but Isaac accuses him of it even before the incident occurs, and Sumpter says to himself: *"He is my son, and he is beautiful, and God will give him back to me"* (p. 190). And, in an almost stupor-like voice, he says to Celia and Jack Harrick: "'It is my son who will be saved'" (p. 206). But to whatever degree he is conscious of his role, the drama does offer a testing of both father and son. Isaac has accused his father of not having the courage to kill him as a sacrifice in response to God's command and has speculated, half-seriously, that "Little Ikey is the one better pray hard" for a substitute sacrifice. He taunts his father with the possibility that there "'might be a snafu in the celestial bureaucracy and somebody might not deliver that miraculous ram in time to save bloody little miraculous Isaac's little neck'" (p. 97). Isaac gets his chance for salvation when Jasper in the cave becomes the substitute sacrificial ram. But if this is a miracle, Isaac never recognizes it. In manipulating the occasion for his own material advantage, in transforming himself into a stereotyped Jewish opportunist, he further alienates himself from the human communion.

Isaac's failure compels his father to go into the cave, to act not out of, but against, his own faith and morality to save Isaac: he lies and rearranges the evidence in the cave to substantiate Isaac's lie. After his father emerges from the cave with the report that Jasper is dead, Isaac reaches out his hand to touch his father's arm:

> The old man looked down at the demanding hand. Then, effortlessly, he reached his own free hand around, lifted his son's touch from him, meeting no resistance, and without a word...rose into the open air beyond. (p. 334)

There is more than a reversal of roles here. The old man does not sacrifice himself for his son. Out of an overwhelming love for Isaac, he sins against the merciful God in whose name he preaches; he chooses human loyalty over divine loyalty, and in that act tastes the bitterness of human weakness more strongly than ever before. In the horror of his own act, however, he cannot yet show his solidarity with human weakness, and he shrinks from the touch of it, even when it comes from his own flesh. Even the love of his son is no excuse for the guilt he feels. Isaac's sin is less than his own, and all others' as well. Old Sumpter feels that all other people, even with their imperfections, are superior to himself. When Nick tries to support him at the cave mouth, he jerks away, yelling, "'Don't touch me! ... I am not worthy...of your touch!'" (p. 349). And in the moment when he confronts old Jack, he asks him not to shake his hand but to spit on him.

That confession to Jack Harrick in turn stimulates old Jack's confession that he actually wanted to love his son. Such a confrontation, with its admission of error, paves the way for the regeneration of both men. Paradoxically, through his perception of weakness, when he recognizes his involvement in the human condition, Sumpter is better able to purge himself of spiritual pride and to attain a strength previously unknown to him. His sympathy for weakness can now gain for him a strength which will lead to his salvation. That sympathy, on the other hand, has only confirmed Isaac's scorn for weakness, including his own, and fostered an attitude that will lead him to codify the means for manipulating human weakness and to remove himself further from any hopes of salvation.

In *The Cave* more than in any of his other novels, Warren uses gesture— both verbal and physical—to objectify the personal response to moral challenges brought about by man's constant nature working itself out within necessary human contexts. On this matter Warren lavishes most of his energies, and though his particular interests do not give this novel the usual solid circumstantiality of Warren's world, they do go far in making *The Cave* a durable novel with its own impressive scaffolding. The *donnée* requires and receives from the reader not natural identification with the things and peoples of a "natural" place, but an astonished and even compassionate confirmation that psychic truths still coil and recoil in a natural world that has been imaginatively shattered and reassembled. The familiar Warren search for the "true" self continues, but here there is even more insistence (dramatically possible because of the large group of characters) that the "true" self lies in a mysterious but real concern for the non-self. Fathers must come to terms with sons, and sons with fathers; women with their men's adulteries, and men with their women's compromises; and brothers with their brothers' achievements and failures. In the shared commonality of weakness and imperfection lie strength and, perhaps, even regeneration.

Trial by Wilderness: Warren's Exemplum

by Leonard Casper

Wilderness is a novel written by a poet-dramatist, whose selective
method attempts "to write the particular story," free from all distractions.[1]
As if to avoid the sort of excessive introspection which sometimes clouded
such earlier historical fiction as *World Enough and Time* and *Band of
Angels*, Robert Penn Warren has chosen a narrator who is only self-
conscious and thoughtful, without being capable of either total recall or
gratuitously perfected self-knowledge. He has refrained from romantic
melodrama of the order which the Civil War readily makes available to
the American folk imagination. He has foregone erotic passages such as
those in *The Cave* which alienated monocular critics. Although *Wilderness* has somewhat more scope than *The Red Badge of Courage*—primarily because, as Don W. Kleine points out,[2] its anti-hero is a kind of
picaro-pilgrim with a doleful countenance—nevertheless its modest panorama is held deliberately remote from front-line thunder. The poet in
Warren does not even resort to lyric streams-of-consciousness, in order to
provide continuity and to compensate by emotional intensity for episodic
brevity. Instead, the art of Warren's poetry is perceptible in image-
becoming-motif; and his sense of dramatic investiture, in scenes hieratically
conceived. His hope has to be that this philosophical poem becomes a
"blooded abstraction" and not transparent allegory or costumed morality
play.

The extent of the author's gamble is perhaps most evident in his choice
of narrators. Adam Rosenzweig is presented from the first in a typical
stance, alone outside the house where his father lies dead. His role throughout the novel is that of the outsider, in search of the light of a livable self,
resurrection from the limbo of his inheritance. Despite his deadening
Bavarian ghetto, some dreaming part of himself was liberated and sustained by his father's sacrifices to Freedom and Justice, on the barricades of

"Trial by Wilderness: Warren's Exemplum" by Leonard Casper. From *Wisconsin Studies in
Contemporary Literature,* vol. III (1962), 45-53. © 1962 by the Board of Regents of the University of Wisconsin System. Reprinted by permission of the publisher.

[1]Correspondence with the author, March 17, 1962.
[2]*Epoch*, XI (Winter 1962), 264.

Berlin in 1848 and, for thirteen years, in prison. But the shared ideal becomes exclusively his own; Adam is born into nakedness, when his sickly father lets his brother force him to admit that his life has been blasphemous. He has trusted man more than he has trusted God; he has not lived resigned to the Law. And man has betrayed him: the German uprising has brought some degree of freedom to all but the Semitic peoples. From that moment, six months before his funeral, Adam's father was dead: "To be dead, [Adam] thought, that was to know that nothing would ever be different." Adam looks at his boot, cunningly designed to disguise his foot's deformity. He looks up to the splendor of mountain peaks, above the conspiring aloofness of the ruling houses. Assuming the obligation repudiated by his father, he too steps outside the Law (although accompanied by phylacteries, shawl and prayer book in a borrowed satchel): he enlists as a mercenary, to assist the Union cause.

Adam, whose untraditional name suggests his alienation even from his people, suffers additional exclusion by removal to foreign shores. When his foot's defect is discovered, he is not permitted to remain in the hired ranks. Nevertheless, still an idealist—in the absence of any experience (he is nearly thirty and yet has never known wealth or a woman, in part because a German-Jew needs a family-founding permit before marriage is allowed), he moves like a hermit figure through the American wasteland. Always he is someone else's shadow—rescued by a Negro from drowning in a cellar shortly after himself having helped "Shag them niggers!" in the slums of New York; adopted by Blaustein, the store prince, to replace a son killed in battle; reduced to assistant on a sutler's wagon, feeding the mouths of suffering soldiers, and not their souls. Only by an act of completed violence, when Adam actually kills a berserk scarecrow trooper and with one shot betrays what was so long chambered in his heart, does he finally achieve some degree of manhood and person.

How is it possible to sustain a novel of *in*experience, told from a nondescript point of view? Can any author make credible the sudden emergence of identity in a *naif* whose first thirty years were so unremarkable that they seem to constitute a case of arrested development? Apparently Adam lived so much in his father that there is nothing recorded of those long years except Adam's daily labor with timepieces and his lonely nights in the dark, awaiting the broken old man's return. (One would like to believe that Adam's assigned age is not mere convention, designed to abstract him further into a crypto-Christ; but that the space between the related civil wars in Germany and America requires that Adam be older than he seems. In any case, the thirty years are a statistic only; and Adam, before he sees the mutilated Negro hanging like an effigy in the mob-emptied streets, is static, a non-person.) Is Warren's central character so much an Everyman that he is no-man; so universalized in name and heritage and ritual action that he is never realized in full-blooded particular?

In *Moby Dick* the narrator, Ishmael, is rapidly exchanged for an omniscient point of view and is not recovered until late in the novel. The fact that readers seldom notice this conversion is surely due to the larger-than-personal nature of Ishmael, most evident in the sperm-squeezing scene. Outcast Ishmael is even Ahab written small and humanely. He is so easily absorbed into the communal figure of the crew and, by extension then, of mass mankind that the change in narration is apparent only. In *Wilderness* Adam's role is somewhat analogous. He is so much the unit-itiate, the inexperienced idealist, that events impress themselves graphically on him. Because his nature is unformed, Adam does not even exist as some personification; and the subjective readily yields to objective narration. In Chapter IX there is an unequivocal shift in point of view from Adam to Jed the sutler who, behind barred doors in winter quarters, paces the cage of his cabin, trying to fathom his own childhood. Adam could never have had access to such privacies. Yet the shift, since it occurs gratuitously, would seem a matter of indifference even to the author.

Although Adam at first appears disembodied, defined as he is by deformity, by lack, by otherness, by the dream unfulfilled and disregarding, his final emergence is not unprepared for because his sap and substance, his body, is composite of each of those graphic persons he has known. They are stages on the journey across what only seems a wasteland but what is actually a trial by wilderness, to the burning bush of achieved knowledge and to parturition (only a thin "diaphragm of lyric green" separates him from the powerful noon, at first; then his whole world burns) in the last chapters. The novel moves quickly from scene to scene, sometimes with no more transition than continued intensity: like a poem committed to images rather than to grammar or scansion; like a play, willing to foreshorten everything but dramatic truth. It is precisely the absence of distraction—the starkness of Adam's undefended response—which thrusts so many of *Wilderness'* moments forward into memorability.

The mutilated Negro hanged from a lamppost by a Northern mob weary of war; the dark rising flood, man-made, in the cellar trap; the aftermath of Gettysburg, the body-robbers; Mose at his alphabet; Simms Purdew, battle hero, ramming the heads of tied Negroes into washtubs of flour and buried greenbacks; Adam's bugle-sharp outcry at the heavens, from the animal-pen remains of the broken winter camp; the endless cavalcades "winding into the anonymity of distance"; the homely, maniacal attack of the scarecrows.... All these are the fire-seared and sharpened conditions of Adam's birth. On a variety of occasions Adam ponders the *ifs* of his strange passage. If the mountain had not gleamed so white; if the *Elmyra* had not rolled and betrayed him to a fellow-cripple.... Each of these and other moments is not a fatal accident enforced on inert man. Warren's canon has never been committed to determinism; but to causality, yes. And at the hour of illumination when Adam, having killed and having thus fulfilled the hate and fear of otherness that masked itself as ideal devotion, admits too the role he played in the murder of Jedeen Hawksworth and the subsequent flight of tortured Mose Talbutt, he takes on himself his share in the moral linkage of events. "He knew that, in the end, he would have to think every *if*—every *if* which was life." Every flaring detail, however detached it seems from Adam, becomes his secret motive, his *if*. Finally he accepts his flaw as his fortune, and moves on—towards the grandeur that the epigraph from Pascal implies: towards an awareness of human misery, without selfpity but with gratitude. Here is Warren's recurring version of *felix culpa*—Abel improved for having been Cain.

The theme of the oneness of man is glossed by this gradual transplanting of flesh onto Adam's archetypal spirit. At intervals the other characters have already shown their solidarity, even in seasons of most grievous mutual revulsion. From the instant that he first conceives of joining the conflict between the States, Adam wants to believe that his purpose is pure—the deliverance of Freedom and Justice—because he cannot bring himself to confess his innermost motive: the desire to kill a world that is different from himself, and from his dream. Only at the end can he say, *"I killed him... because his foot was not like mine"*: and so the end becomes his beginning. He has become the true proxy son of Blaustein who knew so well that "The hardest thing to remember is that other men are men." There is Herr Zellert who keeps pigs on the streets under the Schloss, so that he will not be mistaken for a Jew; bald Duncan with the stiff knee, wounded when he fled Manassas and bitterly reminded by Adam's supposed mockery aboard ship; Blaustein who unjustly calls the Plattdeutsch rapists and runners, because his son died at Chancellorsville when Stonewall Jackson broke their hired ranks; Jedeen Hawksworth (described as a "centaur," at one point, for his mismatched clothes) who resents his dependence on "Mr. Blow-steim," the rich Jew, and is even more confused about his own motives for having once defended a slave who struck the son of his owner; Mose proves to have once been an army deserter, but defends his action by insisting that Negroes had not been allowed to do anything else except dig privies; Monmorancy Pugh is trapped into killing conscriptors lest they send him to kill in daily combat. All these and others are flawed, like Adam himself (whose name in Hebrew means *man*): but what man who confesses and is contrite cannot be forgiven?

Adam the innocent eats finally from the tree of the knowledge of both good and evil; and is redeemed. He becomes Slew, for Old Slewfoot, and for his climactic performance as slayer-Cain as well. Yet in that supreme act of hate, at last he understands love, the power of forgiveness, and its superiority to self-righteous, untempered crusades in the name of Freedom and Justice. Having come his long pilgrim's way and having slain in defense of another's life, Adam knows he would do it all again: "But, oh, with a dif-

ferent heart!"—with all the difference that distinguishes conscious from unconscious act.

It is the heart that rescues, the Original Goodness—perhaps more immemorial and ingrained than Original Sin itself. Man's inarticulateness,
his failure to find fullness of expression (much less satisfaction) for his
deepest needs to know and to be known, finds repeated metaphor here.
America, first seen, appears as a green shore on which a dog barks unheard;
Maran Meyerhof's imploring O of widowship-to-be remains unvoiced;
Mose works his bits of alphabets as if in search of a name that will identify
him beyond the brand (W for Worthless) that he bears; Adam awaits a voice
crying in the Wilderness that will set him free:

> To shut the eyes—that was a mistake. For immediately the darkness of his
> head rang with a thousand cries. The cries had the strange, clear, bountiful,
> vaulted and vaulting hollowness of a cry uttered in the deep woods.... The
> red reflection of the flame glowed on faces from which the eyes distended
> maniacally, and in which the mouth made the perfectly round O of the
> scream, the scream he could not, in fact, hear.

There are the cave images too, dark inward places where man confronts
some portion of truth's terror—in that nearly fatal New York cellar; in the
cavernous dwelling of Monmorancy Pugh, driven underground by the
ironies of militant pacifism; in the scrub and blight pine of the Wilderness
itself: "...going in them woods after Ginnal Lee—it is like crawling in a
cave at night to wrassle a bear and it the bear's cave." And there are recurring references to the groping combat of civil war as an elephant, unknow-
able to the blind walking-wounded, trampled by its passage...So dark is
human understanding that men scarcely know their own worth. Goodness
has to be engrained, to advance against such ignorance.

If violence abounds, and rationalized hate, so too does kindness, welling
as unexpectedly as grace and revelation from secret springs. A seaman instructs Adam in ways to escape being returned to Europe when his deformity is discovered. In the aftermath of Gettysburg, preacher Mordacai
Sulgrave is acknowledged as one who hid from battle beneath a bed; yet
once he sucked pus through a tube from a man's swollen throat. On the same
occasion, Jed Hawksworth who has long dreamed vengeance on the North
Carolinians who ostracized him protects the corpses of the brave Carolinian
dead. Beneath the vile face of Simms Purdew, Adam sees the simple trust-
ful boy Simms must have been. Adam is able to move Millie the Mutton, to
expose the upward gaze in the camp-follower's roving eye. Pugh's wife finds
it in her heart to forgive her husband's failure to weep when their son dies
during their doomed running feud with the conscriptors. Pugh himself,
recalling the recoverable good days of his marriage, lets Adam escape him
alive.

Charity such as this vindicates human yearning for faith and hope. It is the other half of Blaustein's warning: the hardest thing to remember is that other men are men (the problem, in its fullness, of man as Negro). It is in Original Goodness, which conjugates God and man, that Adam finally discovers an end to the division which had torn his spirit at the beginning of his pilgrimage. Against his uncle's injunction that wisdom is total resignation to the Law, he had weighed the advice of Jacob the cobbler that life robbed of ambition—the right to dream, to choose—is trivial. The uncle's satchel, the cobbler's boots Adam has carried all the way, into the brightening knowledge of his mystery. Because there is love, the Law itself requires something far more difficult than resignation: will, action; and responsibility for consequences. Not will unbounded, but will limited by and attracted to that example of love. To wear the boot as disguise is to risk messianic vanity. Adam, pure idealist, longs to be heroic sacrifice, to suffer in public splendor; but finally knows that of him a more heroic decision is demanded—to be unheroic; to be like all others, in a way unforeseen, deformed and nameless; in humility, to be worthy "of what they as men and in their error, had endured." They are all parts of an alphabet constantly reshaping itself into a single run-on expression of human mingling and meaning. If Mose and Jed and kindred figures are the body of Adam, he is their conscience—a ritual of expiation in search of a guilty act to atone; he is their intelligence, capable of seeing their sameness.

Adam is capable, therefore, of realizing what so many of these other blind men measuring the elephant could not realize, the extent and meaning of their goodness which justifies forgiveness. And he is capable of altering his heart in accord with this knowledge. As in Warren's earliest novels, in *Wilderness* we do not see the last stage of revelation tested. Nevertheless, that stage has been attained creditably, without the fullness of its philosophical burden's having to be borne by one young and average man. Every occasion confirms every other, and informs on Adam. If he still seems undersized at novel's end, the cause may be that the book is not Adam's, but he is the book's.

Wilderness is, in one sense, the fictional counterpart of Warren's other 1961 volume, *The Legacy of the Civil War; Meditations on the Centennial.* Modestly avoiding any delusions of definitiveness while massive commemorative histories and commentaries are being published, *Legacy* is as finite in scale as *Wilderness* is and as subject therefore to the charge of slightness and abstraction. It is content to summarize without preference the moral positions of North and South in the 1860's and to establish similarities in the apparent extremes of the "irreconcilables." The Abolitionists, appealing to an absolutist "higher law" (Garrison was prepared to burn the Constitution), reserved the role of the Pharisaic avenger to themselves, although by the same token they became defenders of dissent and the right to conscience. The South, to the extent that it defended slavery, denied the concept of an open society which, otherwise, states' rights required. Both positions were self-contradictory and unrealistic. In their often uncompromising excesses, they crystallized life into brittle frailty. In the aftermath of Civil War, both sides permitted themselves hypocritical stances. Defeat became for the South its "Great Alibi," excusing all things and rendering its citizens playactors in the role of the pure victim. The North, meanwhile, has remained the "Treasury of Virtue" whose material prosperity has confirmed the sublime innocence which the self-righteous always find in themselves.

What has saved America from complete self-deception and the catastrophes attendant on living lies, Warren argues, is the development in certain men of a moral awareness responsive enough to inner contortions, to be able to find charity in the wilderness of war—the capacity to understand and to forgive. Lincoln had a laborious ethic—an appreciation of expediency but a delicacy also for the turn of consequences. The breakdown that he suffered before Gettysburg is to Lincoln's credit. Grant likewise, a former alcoholic, fought with dignity and magnanimity. The constitution of the Confederate States of America opposed further slave trade. There was such honor among enemies in battle, that we can view the Civil War now nostalgically. It has become a prototype for the ambivalence of love and hate in man: innocent men stumbled into the "crime of monstrous inhumanity," as surely as Adam did. But, however sobering, the war also presented lasting proof that we are not just victims of nature and history, but salient participants in its movements. It is this faith, in the possibility of being instructed by suffering, that validates any meditation on the very real deaths of human beings. From this "image of the powerful, painful, grinding process by which an ideal emerges out of history," man can find dignity in his existence and even some grandeur. Perhaps, Warren says in *Legacy,* that is "what we yearn for after all." Ambition is man's hope, although, in excess, his flaw.

Wilderness' epigraph from Pascal is a continuation of the same thought: "Tout ces misères-là mêmes preuvent sa grandeur. Ce sont miséres de grand seigneur, misères d'un rio dépossédé." Here is the basic expression of the novel's faith; just as the other epigraph from *Henry V*—so often human ends find imperfect means—states the condition preliminary to any faith. Accept the deformity, and many things are possible. *Wilderness* can be read as a dramatization of the ironies of the American Civil War, in which idealists had to hire foreign mercenaries or stoop to forceful conscription, and in which the freed slave remained a non-person even to those allegedly dying in his cause. Yet such ironies are only symptoms of the whole agony of human existence, the essential tentativeness of knowledge and the recalcitrance of experience. Negro—or Jew—epitomizes reduction of the individual through abstraction, for example, through imposed specification. These are tactics of evasion natural to men who, deficient in comprehension or over-proud, must invent simple explanations for the agony of life, including scapegoats for all error and annoyance. They must kill what is other. Evil becomes the exclusive property of some harassed and damnable few.

The method of the novel is, by poetic selectivity and specification, to translate *Legacy's* discourse into narrative action and then to compress the moments of action further into decisive, living metaphors—vicarious gestures. In his longer novels Warren used to insert an *exemplum,* to inform anticipatorily on the distraught narrator's dilemma. *Wilderness* resembles just such an *exemplum,* expanded and extracted from its other shell.[3] It is a play within a play removed; it is a metaphysical poem, deliberately freed from the high circumstance of history without sacrificing history's availability as myth. It is what any critic's reading of a worthy novel ought to be—one man's cautious record of the feel of an elephant in the dark.

[3]At a reading of his poems at Boston College, April 12, 1962, Warren revealed that he suspended the writing of short stories when he realized that the abridged, graphic impulse which animates many of his stories was better suited to lyric poetry. Perhaps *Wilderness* marks an attempt to reverse this process: to restore partially the conditions of space and duration to otherwise essentially static poetic images.

The Uncorrupted Consciousness

by Arthur Mizener

The initial reception of Mr. Warren's novel [*Flood*] was lackluster and uncomprehending. Perhaps the reviewers would not have liked it even if they had seen what it is; the philosophical romance may not really be popular today (if it ever was), despite our academic enthusiasm for safely dead examples of it like *The Scarlet Letter* and *Moby Dick* and *Light in August*. But at least readers would have known what Mr. Warren has been up to, even from unfavorable reviews, if reviewers had made it clear that *Flood* is, as its subtitle plainly says, "A Romance of Our Time," not a Marquand novel that has somehow got buried under a load of philosophical commentary.

It is pointless to get worked up about this misfortune: most reviewers do not write out of personal malice or wilful misunderstanding; but there is no use pretending (as some of us often do) that we do not concur with the all too common reader more than we can rejoice to believe. It is worth reminding ourselves what the cost of such misfortunes may be. Mr. Warren is a gifted writer; he will not cease to be so because one of his major novels has been misunderstood and under-valued. But he may be affected by this experience in ways that are not good. Leon Edel has pointed out the extent to which Henry James was affected, in ways that are at least complicating, by the "very big tempest in a very small teapot" stirred by his *Hawthorne*. It brought James, as Mr. Edel says, "to a strange turning point in his inner development which was reflected immediately in his work"; from then on James used up a great deal of creative energy, both in his life and in his work, hiding from people in elaborately mannered ways. Such turning points in authors' lives, for all our tendency to make the best of them afterwards in histories and biographies, are by no means all gain.

There is no use looking in *Flood* for the virtue of the Marquand novel— the vivid, detailed, representative image of the everyday world; *Flood* has its own kind of vividness and relevance, but it is not the realistic novel's.

"The Uncorrupted Consciousness" by Arthur Mizener. From *Sewanee Review,* LXXII (1964), 690-98. © 1964 by the University of the South. Reprinted by permission of the publisher.

The title alone, without the subtitle, ought to warn us what kind that is: can anyone think "flood" without thinking of The Flood? Immediately, of course, the title *Flood* refers to the literal events of the book, which is about a Tennessee town called Fiddlersburg that is going to be flooded by the building of a dam—a means of "getting shoes on the swamp rats...teaching 'em to read and write and punch a time clock, and pull a switch," as an earnest young engineer puts it. Socially speaking it is all very well meant and, as far as it goes, good. One of the major points about the world Mr. Warren is making is, that, however intimate a man becomes with the "black beast with the cold fur like hairy ice that drowse[s] in the deepest inner dark, or [wakes] to snuffle about" in his own nature, he must accept—indeed love—the outer world where time always moves and very ordinary people go about their well-intentioned business of destroying what has become precious to make way for dams and highways and motels; he must "know the *nowness* of God's will."

But if *Flood* has its consistent commentary on society and history, what it is most deeply concerned with is consciousness. Consciousness exists in time; with all its realized accumulations from the past and its active hopes for the future it must live in the actual present. But it is the consciousness, not the world, that counts. It must somehow survive with hope the flood of time, recognizing, as the dying country preacher of Fiddlersburg says, that the life one has lived, whatever it has been, is blessed. The essential story of *Flood* is the story of how Brad Tolliver, trying desperately to avoid this knowledge, struggling to conceal himself in a series of delusions, and in his struggles blundering about destructively among the lives of those he loves as much as he can love anyone, learns gradually to accept "the secret and irrational life of man." "Being you," as the blind Leontine Purtle says, "[is] like being blind," and Brad with all his human pride of intellect cannot endure the thought of it. The country that is being whelmed by Mr. Warren's flood, that is forever being lost under the irresistible flow of time, is the consciousness. But it is not until the last page of the novel that Brad admits to himself "there is no country but the heart."

From the beginning he has sensed that there is not, but since he had as a college boy written his book of short stories about Fiddlersburg, *I'm Telling You Now*, he has been trying to escape knowing it. One way he has done so is by becoming an expert at his trade, and the history of the movie script he tries to write about the flooding of Fiddlersburg shows us the result. First he offers himself a sardonic parody: "[Writer] comes back to Fiddlersburg, sees sister, becomes aware that he admires her legs, discovers she is really his mother in disguise, which explains everything. End: view of healing waters rising over Fiddlersburg in the dawn." Then he admits to his producer that he is stuck, unable to write merely expertly about Fiddlersburg and unable to face going back to the vision of *I'm Telling You*

ly being defeated, but he does his best to use even his awareness of the
he shouts), he does produce an expert script—not "a bolt out of place or a
nut loose." Yasha Jones, his producer, turns it down, and when Brad defends it on the ground that the plot is "exactly the way things have a way of
happening." Yasha says, "It doesn't matter.... What matters is the feeling.
Where in this is the feeling we want? Where is Fiddlersburg?" "You have,"
as he says elsewhere, "to document things. But if you depend on the documentation, then the real thing—all right. I'll say it—the vision, it may be—"
To be overwhelmed with the multiplicity of the world, as he reminds Brad,
"is the last sin for people in our business—no in any business—the sin of
the corruption of consciousness."

Brad's struggle with this script is one image of *Flood's* meaning. As with
all his other experiences, Brad knows, even as he tries to hide behind his
expertise, the truth Yasha Jones is insisting on. Only at moments can he
take comfort in remembering the reviews of his most recent Hollywood
success, *The Dream of Jacob;* "Dear God, it was an awful movie," his sister
Maggie says to Yasha. Brad knows that too. "An expert," he says, "is a man
who can do something on an artificial leg almost as well as you can do it on
a real one...practice a lot and learn to do the rhumba with it, and give
exhibitions in hospitals to hearten the inmates in their infirmities and he
will get his picture in the papers. He will be an expert." This remark is a
typical example of the way Brad, the ingenious intellectual, uses his awareness of the real nature of man's consciousness and his world to avoid
facing it.

From the novel's cunningly timed beginning square in the middle of
Brad's struggle, when he drives from Fiddlersburg to the Nashville airport
to meet Yasha's plane, we watch him seeing everything with this double
vision. We do not yet know why he does, but we see how he is using irony at
once to recognize and to deny the realities of the world and himself. "If
everything is fake then nothing matters," he tells himself comfortingly as
he passes a horrible new motel called The Seven Dwarfs, where no expense
has been spared. But a stream beside the motel bothers him: it is unavoid-
ably real. In this way his attempt to believe that nothing matters is constantly being defeated, but he does his best to use even his awareness of the
reality of the world to sustain his hope that it is fake. So, as he watches the
stewardess opening the door of Yasha's plane, he thinks, "would she fly off
and bring back an olive branch in her beak?" What a marvelously absurd
ark a DC-7 is; as long as Brad can hold on to that sense of the world's absurdity, he can avoid admitting the truth. This is a powerful help to him,
since the world is ridiculous—tasteless, pretentious, stupid, corrupt in
nature. When a guard at Fiddlersburg's penitentiary refuses to shoot a madman who is murdering a guard for fear of hitting an innocent man, Mr.
Budd, the Deputy Warden, says, "Jesus Christ, a innocent man! There ain't

no innocent man! You are fired." Mr. Budd knows this because in his way he also knows what Fiddlersburg's cultivated lawyer puts more elegantly when he says, "I look out the window and see some pore misguided boogers doing the best they can—according to their dim lights…[and] what you might call the pathos of the mundane sort of takes the edge off my grim satisfaction. …." It takes the edge off Brad's too (Mr. Budd is too "simple" a man ever to have felt any).

But Brad's most powerful help in maintaining his grim dissatisfaction with himself and the world is the way he has reduced his originally uncorrupted consciousness, the consciousness that went into *I'm Telling You Now*, to romantic idealism. For twenty years he has been turning Fiddlersburg into a sentimental myth that in its more sophisticated way bears the same relation to truth as the pathetic dream of happiness expressed by the Seven Dwarfs Motel. So long as he can define goodness as this unrealizable myth, he is safe from having to believe the actual world is good, can see it as material for romantic irony. He expends a great deal of creative energy on doing so, and the effect is formidable, for Mr. Warren is an impressive wit. Yet there is always a disturbing hum of suggestion behind Brad's ironies, a hint that in the end the joke is on him, that his irony is not a way of dissociating himself from the homely, vulgar, shocking world but a way of acknowledging its blessedness, though he does not consciously take that hint until the end of the book.

So powerful is this romantic irony that it is almost as easy for the reader as for Brad to be lulled by it. When, for example, he observes that "the whores of Nashville, it was officially stated by Federal authorities, did more than the matchless cavalry of Nathan Bedford Forrest to stem the tide of human freedom and hard money" and adds that the United Daughters of the Confederacy ought to put up a monument "to those gallant girls of the VD brigade who gave their all to all," it is hard not to be convinced of the adequacy of this view of history. It is funny and, as far as it goes, right. The same thing is true of his remark that modern Nashville "aspires to be the Kansas City of the upper Buttermilk Belt"; yet he refuses to go on to subject Nashville's absurd replica of the Parthenon to the same irony: something stops him. It is hard not to accept the bitter truth of his assertion about Fiddlersburg's Confederate statue that "he's been standing there a long time now, holding off gunboats and Yankee investors and new ideas" and easy to ignore it when he adds that the statue stands for "the lie that is the truth of the self." Romantic irony is Brad's defense against recognizing that truth; but we ought to recognize it.

The design of *Flood* surrounds Brad with characters who in their various ways have faced that truth—like the intellectuals Yasha Jones (in realistic terms the least plausible of Mr. Warren's characters) and Blanding Cottshill (who has to suffer not only the loss of the Negro mistress he loves but the knowledge that he is to blame for that loss), like Brother Pinckney, the cultivated Negro preacher, and Brother Potts, the uneducated white one who is dying of cancer. In Brother Pott's life Mr. Warren gives us his plainest image of the desperate difficulty of accepting the truth. Brother Potts has seen it as his duty to go to the penitentiary to pray with a condemned murderer, a Negro who "with a claw hammer of the value of six dollars... did with malice aforethought and against the peace and good order of the State of Tennessee, beat the pore bleeding be-Jesus out of the head of pore old Mrs. Milt Spiffort. All he could say in court was that she made him do it." As Brother Potts is on his knees in the cell praying, Pretty-Boy leans forward and carefully spits in his face. "But I didn't get off my knees," Brother Potts says. "Something held me down and I name it Glory. ... I did not make a motion to wipe that spit. I let it run. And I was praying again, out loud. ... I was praying for God to make me know that what happened was right because it was His Holy Will." Brother Potts "is merely a good man, full of suffering and befuddlement, doing his best to walk in the steps of the Master. He has no irony...[no] awareness of that doubleness of life that lies far below flowers of rhetoric or pirouettes of mind." He is incapable of the pirouettes by which Brad avoids this knowledge. But even Brad cannot avoid it when his Lady of Shalott from Fiddlersburg, the blind Leontine Purtle, turns out to be real.

The most important human experience for Mr. Warren appears to be sexual experience; it is perhaps a romantic attitude. For all his major characters, especially for Brad and his wife Lettice, it is the testing occasion. Brad and Lettice, the beautiful New York girl, were strongly attracted to each other, and for a while that was enough. But it had gradually gone bad because Brad used it more and more as a momentary release from the knowledge he could not get out of it. At the end of the novel, years after they have parted, Lettice realizes that "we could have had a life together... and been happy, even if I got old and slow, for we might have loved one another" (as Yasha Jones does Maggie, despite "the infinitesimally sagging, scheduled failure of her body"). When they are driving to Nashville for the last time, Lettice asks Brad to make love to her one last time; "in a sardonic trance" he takes her into a "grassy glade by a stream under a cedar bluff." That sardonic trance is a major rejection. "Wouldn't you like to remember us really ourselves?" Lettice says; but Brad says, "God damn it, I don't want to remember a God-damned thing!"

That was twenty years before the present time of the novel (1960), but Brad has never been able to endure the thought of that grassy glade since. He cannot stand it any better now that it is occupied by the Seven Dwarfs Motel, where a bright Fisk student leans against the high-test pump in an Elizabethan fool's costume and pretends to be a "Yassah, boss" Negro—and as Brad drives away from the pump in his white Hollywood Jaguar the

Negro says, "Thanks, Mac." This is part of Mortimer Sparlin's revenge, *his* romantic irony (and it is part of Brad's awareness of his self-deception that when Yasha Jones pays him a compliment he grins boyishly and says, "Thanks, Mac"). The other part of Mortimer Sparlin's revenge is to sleep with aging white patrons of the Seven Dwarfs and then have to go "out into the pre-dawn dark, hating the world and himself."

When Brad returns to Fiddlersburg, he focuses his romantic myth on Leontine Purtle; when he was fifteen "there had been a promise in the moonlight that spread all over the world westward without end. Where had that promise gone?" Now he persuades himself he has found it in a pure and innocent blind girl. He has had plenty of warning; Leontine has bothered him badly by showing him she understands what he was saying about Fiddlersburg in *I'm Telling You Now*. She is, like Brother Potts, wholly her limited self and therefore without despair or shame. But she is no Lady of Shalott. So desperately does Brad cling to his illusion about her that he does not even notice the absurdity of lusting for the Lady of Shalott. When he calls her that, Yasha Jones says, "What does that make you? Lancelot?" and Brad says, "It was the Queen he was getting it off." But though he says it, he does not see it. Driven by his incongruous desire to possess what has become for him what it is precisely because it cannot be physically possessed, he takes Leontine to the Seven Dwarfs Motel, to the spot where he had once before rejected himself by rejecting Lettice. He is now sure that what he thinks was the promise of his boyhood, the promise of a simple, happy, innocent life, is about to be fulfilled—until he feels the diaphragm Leontine is wearing and she is saying, "Oh, slower, slower, oh, slow." With practiced ease, Brad slides back into his protective irony. "Who the hell is running this show, girlie?" he says. When they leave, Mortimer Sparlin, "grinning at him, not idiotically now," whispers, "Tell me, Mac, how do you like blind tail?" "You bastard," Brad says, "You bla—" and Mortimer, a Golden Gloves boxer, knocks him down. "Sure," he says, "everybody knows Miss Purtle. Lots of boys, it would seem, like blind tail. And you, Mr. Tolliver...." A man like the rest, Brad has fooled himself so badly that not even finding himself with Leontine in the Candy Cottage of the Seven Dwarfs Motel could awaken him from his dream of her as the Lady of Shalott. It is not Leontine's fault; "shy and hesitant like a child asking for praise," she says afterwards, "Brad—I sort of fooled you didn't I?" She is, without false shame, herself. It is Brad who is not, who has been asking something both impossible and inferior of life in order to avoid being himself.

For Mr. Warren, uncorrupted consciousness is the "awareness of evanescense," a grasp of the precious "human moment" when one has "the past and the future in a present vision." To live in this knowledge is to live so that the incommensurables of the imagination with its tempting promises and of history with its recalcitrant actualities become commensurable. The novelist who tries to realize this consciousness must recognize "the story of someone who had no story," not try to create and enact a story. Good fiction documents a vision; it does not lose itself in the way things happen, in documenting the multiplicity of the world. That is why *Flood* is not a realistic novel with a carefully articulated plot, minutely lifelike characters, and a deadly serious system of motives. You have to document the vision, and therefore Mr. Warren provides the necessary amount of facts but he does not "depend on the documentation." *Flood* is a complex metaphor with the vision I have been crudely paraphrasing as its tenor. "Life," as Yasha Jones says, "is so logical—superficially, that is—therefore so plotty.... But...don't we [writers] have to violate life? To stylize life?"

Instead, then, of being a "realistic" picture of life, *Flood* is an image; instead of appealing to our interest in "what happens next," it appeals to us as a poem does. It is an action, arranged, "stylized," with wonderful skill to bring a very large number of events into the best possible order for documenting a vision—"like those long strands of lights for Christmas trees you take out on Christmas Eve and can't for hell's sake untangle." One may or may not share Mr. Warren's vision, but one ought to recognize its depth and inclusiveness. Nearly every important American way-station of the spirit is here with all its self-deception—complacent or suffering—and all its human pathos: our nostalgia for the imagined past; our earnest dreams of a sensible, school-lunch future; our longings for the nirvanas of manly lust and pastoral love and romantic disillusion; our delight in gadgetry and mere skillfulness; our desire for the release of war's respectable violence or of political dogma's solemn irresponsibility. The vision projected in *Flood* is large and relevant, and the form Mr. Warren uses for it—whether, again, one approves of its kind or not—is used with a sureness of control that gives the documentation of his vision a marvelous, eloquent coherence.

Meet Me in the Green Glen

by Barnett Guttenberg

Beginning with *All the King's Men,* Warren's novels present the true love which arises only with selfhood; the description of false love begins even earlier, with *Night Rider* and Mr. Munn's interest in Lucille. The central concern of *Meet Me in the Green Glen* is love, both true and false, but particularly the romantic dream of love. This love, the idyllic conclusion to countless novels and films, the love of "and they lived happily ever after," is the green glen, the place of enthrallment.

The glen is, literally, Spottwood Valley, and its inhabitants—Cassie Killigrew Spottwood, Sunderland Spottwood, Cy Grinder, and Murray Guilfort—are spiritual as well as literal residents. Cassie's early, unconsummated romance with Cy Grinder, revealed through flashback, is chronologically the first representation of the green glen. Cy is in flight from his origins, so that for him the romance is a dream of courtly love. He treats Cassie as object of adoration, beyond reach until he can transcend the contamination of his family. He plans to rise to the level of his lady by completing a correspondence course in engineering; he cannot have her, he thinks, until he is "translated out of himself, no longer the son of Old Budge, but an untarnished Adam walking the new earth with the breath of the Worldwide Correspondence School blown into him."[1]

Cy's new self dies aborning when Mrs. Killigrew, spiritual counterpart of Matilda Bingham in *The Cave,* discovers the romance and delivers a merciless tongue-lashing, in which the shortcomings of his family figure prominently and in which she suggests that Gladys Peegrum—whose inelegant surname attests to her flaccid unattractiveness—is the appropriate mate for such a degenerate as he. Her diatribe is galvanic; he listens in silence, for he "knew that he had lived among shadows and delusions and that the words that fell from that bony apocalyptic face were the blaze of truth.

"Meet Me in the Green Glen." From Barnett Guttenberg, *Web of Being: The Novels of Robert Penn Warren* (Nashville, Tenn.: Vanderbilt University Press, 1975), pp. 139-55. © 1975 by Barnett Guttenberg. Reprinted by permission of Vanderbilt University Press.

[1][*Meet Me in the Green Glen* (New York: Random House; London: Martin Secker & Warburg Limited, 1971), p. 77. Subsequent quotations from this edition will be identified in the text.—Ed.]

Nothing he had done, or could ever do, would change the truth." (79) In that "blaze of truth" he leaves Cassie with neither a word nor a backward glance, for he has a new vision of unreality to replace the old; "he would ferociously act out his destiny, which, as he now saw, was to need nothing." (80) He drops his study guides down the privy hole and leaves Spottwood Valley to fulfill his nihilistic destiny. After eight years of wandering, he returns only to prove that his destiny is complete and that Spottwood Valley now means nothing to him. "He could move through it, now, spit on its earth, and not see it." (80) Sitting over the privy hole which Budge had used and which houses the study guides of the Worldwide Correspondence School, he sees the way to "crown his destiny"; he marries Gladys Peegrum.

The end of the romance has a similarly destructive effect on Cassie, who lives from that time on "with the sense of having no role in the world, no identity." (81-82) Less than a year after Cy's departure, she fulfills her mother's dream by marrying Sunderland Spottwood, who, as roaring sensualist, views her only as sexual object; she, in turn, detests him. She gives herself to him initially in an unreal daze, in which she sees him as Cy Grinder. After four years of such unreality, she has a nervous breakdown— or a sudden access of awareness—when she bursts out laughing at her mother's funeral, and is institutionalized from 1942 to 1946. During this period, Cy returns to Spottwood Valley and marries Gladys Peegrum. Imagining them together, Cassie articulates the fragmentation which has claimed him, and her as well. "In her intuited understanding of the vengeful alienation of Cy Grinder from himself implicit in the act performed upon Gladys Peegrum, she found confirmation of her own rejection of that other Cassie who had been her then-self, and who had once quivered under his touch. What a little fool that then-self of Cassie had been!" (81) In 1946, Sunderland has a brain stroke which leaves him paralyzed and speechless, and Cassie is released to serve as his nurse in the decaying house.

The house is sustained by another figure of the void, Murray Guilfort. Murray is haunted by nothingness, as an early visit to the Spottwood house dramatically reveals. Looking about the house and thinking how little change has occurred, he suddenly realizes that "everything, even as he looked, was changing. The shreds of the carpet raveled under his eyes, writhed like worms in anguish, burning in their lightless combustion. The leather of the Bible disintegrated and fell, like pollen, on the white marble of the table top. The paint scaled off the eyes of old Sunderland Spottwood, the arrogance fell away from those painted eyes in minuscule pale flakes that lay on the dark brick of the hearth, like dandruff. Everything was nothing." (35).

In his flight from nothingness, Murray becomes a master of false love. As a young man he marries Bessie solely to further his career, and through his cold indifference he kills her. His relationship with Cassie involves a different form of false love. He meets her at the Spottwood house while she is still there in the capacity of nurse; "out of the shadows, shyness, and distance, the face had floated at Murray Guilfort, who, in that instant, twenty years ago, had inarticulately, but with an angry wrenching of the heart, recognized his destiny." (33) He makes this instant the substance of an enduring dream, which, as his impossible "destiny," leaves him the victim of an unkind world. Even as this dream continues, Murray enters a new phase of false love under the tutelage of Alfred Milbank, who advocates the sensual life. Describing the performance of his call girls as art, he instructs Murray that "'illusion...is the only truth.'" (23)

In the attempt to gain that truth, Murray assumes the role of sensualist. Sophie is a success, and Murray, like Jack Harrick in *The Cave*, feels "strong and immortal." (25) The replacement of Sophie by Mildred troubles Murray only slightly, but the news of Milbank's sordid death in a hotel room checks his sense of immortality, and he contracts "a severe gastric disturbance." The sexual realm receives still another shock when Murray learns that Mildred has married, and the new girl is to be Charlotte. "But at the thought of Charlotte, a nameless fear has gripped him, and the strange discomfort which the doctor had said was a symptom of pancreatitis again began." (27) Although Murray does not realize it, he is experiencing anguish as the dream proves inadequate to fill the emptiness of his life. With the sexual domain discredited, his need to dominate the void takes a new form; he decides to become a justice of the Tennessee Supreme Court.

Murray's dream of Cassie and his dream of sexual immortality have common origin in his idolization of the young Sunderland, which stems in turn from his conception of Sunderland's indomitable sensuality mastering the void. To Murray, "the flushed face, the blazing glance, the ruthless selffulness had been...its own confirmation, the fulfilment of life beyond all the deceptions and niggling of the world." (133) His "image of Sunderland Spottwood was that of an angry, laughing self clamped astride a great beast that reared triumphantly against a world of nothingness." (34) Milbank in his sensuality is simply a Sunderland surrogate, as the animal imagery indicates; he is "horsy" and has a "raw, neighing laugh" (21, 23). Cassie, in turn, is Sunderland's, to Murray, and his fancied feeling for her can only be explained as an extension of his envy for Sunderland.

It is that envy which forms the basis of Murray's financial support for Sunderland and Cassie. Just as Murray sees in the image of Sunderland's vitality the measure of his own failure, so he sees in the fact of Sunderland's paralysis the measure of his own triumph. Looking at his old friend, Murray experiences a "burst of cold, justifying joy. He had felt the moment that justified all. It was Sunderland Spottwood who lay there." (44) In a later visit, as he looks into Sunderland's eyes, once "like the flame of a Bunsen burner," now "the sad sick blue of skimmed milk," he feels "a surge of dizzying elation…as if justice had, at last, been achieved." (134) Out of this friendship which is hatred, Murray embarks both on the love which is sexual mastery and on the love—the adoration of Cassie, spiritual nurse—which is total surrender of being, imagining himself in Sunderland's place receiving Cassie's ministrations.

Cassie, Sunderland, Cy, and Murray, then, all represent the green glen-valley and its unreality. At the symbolic heart of the valley's unreality lies Sunderland, paralyzed, like Jack Harrick in his wheelchair; both are symbolically stricken. Cassie, too, is paralyzed; Sunderland says, "'You—you're bottled-up crazy.'" (92) The decaying Spottwood manse completes the symbolic pattern; in its "dark hollowness" (4), it is another version of the cave. The narrator makes the analogy between the house and the void explicit when he notes that "it is not possible to caulk every crack, nail up every rat-hole, seal every window casing and perfectly defend the dark inner nothingness." (51) Cassie and Sunderland live in the house, Cy lives in a poorer version of the house, and Murray assumes the protectorship of the house and feels drawn to it because all have lost themselves in the void. Angelo, looking down into Sunderland's eyes, feels that "they were looking up at him, they were alive, they were sucking him in. It was like losing your balance, falling into a deep hole." (157)

The action of the novel begins with the arrival of Angelo, who, although a stranger to Spottwood Valley and the Spottwood house, has found his spiritual home. While Cassie is sitting in the house staring at the window, so lost in the void that she cannot distinguish inside from outside, memory from fact, and her face, "very white, seemed to be floating there, bodiless" (8), Angelo—another of Warren's angels—appears, coming down the road "trying not to think of anything." (6) In flight from Sicilian revenge and, more important, from his own sense of guilt, he settles into the emptiness of the house with a certain amount of satisfaction, happy "to hide himself…in this unreality." (46) For "if certain thoughts or images came into his head he would start sweating or shaking. Therefore, it was wise to cultivate the blankness of being." (51)

Although Angelo finds his new life of unreality comforting, he is also troubled by it, so that he makes abortive attempts at flight. One such escape is his pursuit of Charlene. As he watches her move up the path, "she flamed into reality." (53) Walking with her, he is surprised to find "that she was real. Not a dream." (60) Another escape is the day's labor; "every morning was, in its own way, a flight into occupation." (49) Perhaps most revealing is the escape which occurs in the early weeks of his stay, when he literally flees the farm and the task of hog-butchering which he and Cassie perform.

> Then, all of a sudden, the woman straightened up from the big pan of en-
> trails, fixed her gaze upon him in a moment of recognition that became, in a

flash, nonrecognition, and moved toward the house. He straightened up too, saw the bulk of the house floating dark and motionless in the chill brightness of air, saw the figure moving away from him, saw the darker spot where the earth had soaked the blood, saw the scraped baby-pink of the carcass.
He turned and fled. (48)

Angelo's subsequent reflections on his flight indicate that he does not merely flee blood, entrails, and carcass: "it shook him because he became aware that he had fled from something just discovered in himself that he did not know the name of. Something had stirred in the depth of black water, for an instant glimmering white like the belly of a fish, as it turns. Something had breathed in the dark." (49) The imagery itself is conclusive; the dark, watery, inner cavern is clearly the void, as is "the house floating dark." Angelo flees "the chill brightness of air" and its indifference, which is Cassie's, in her "recognition that became, in a flash, non-recognition," in her "moving away from him," and his own as well, in his seeing her only as "the woman." Insofar as he runs from the carcass, it is, like the chill air, a sign of his spiritual death.

These flights, however, all lead back to the house. Angelo's literal flight ends with the realization that he has nowhere to go. The relationship with Charlene, although—like all the relationships in Warren's novels—rich with the possibility of discovering another, of an 'I' encountering a 'Thou,' is stunted by Angelo's unreality. Even the day's work leads Angelo back to the house, for with that work he becomes its custodian. The house increasingly claims him, and he begins to feel curious about it. As he explores the master bedroom, imagery of water and darkness once again defines the atmosphere of unreality. "His own shadow, cast by the candle held breast-high before him, made the darkness darker behind him. There his shadow filled the air, enormous, hovering over him. ... Out of the darkness, the furniture swayed slowly at him, swaying into the light of the candle like clumps of waterweed in the backwash of a sluggish current." (106) His major project during this phase of false being is, appropriately enough, repairing the plumbing of the house. As he lies in the crawlway beneath the house tracing the pipes, "he felt a lassitude creep over him, rising from the earth beneath him, like water rising, and then, as the deliberate flood seemed to close over him in the dark, he knew that it was peace, a nothingness that was, strangely, a kind of sweetness." (116) His ritual morning rape of Cassie is no more than an affirmation of this nothingness. He is occasionally troubled by the emptiness of their contact, at one point crying out in frustration, "'Who you?...*Porca Madonna!* Who are you?'" (103) But their relationship in this first phase remains mechanical. Readying himself for the sexual attack, in his deepened alienation from self he thinks of himself as "*the man,*" and of Cassie as "*quella cretina.*" (69) The orgasm itself is empty;

"the spasm seemed impersonal in its automatism, not involving him, as though it were not even happening to him." (71) Later, he thinks, "It was like she was not real. No—…it was like you, you yourself, were not real." (113)

For Cassie, too, this phase of their relationship is unreality. When Angelo returns to the house after his flight, "In her sight he seemed to sway and swim there, as though the darkness from which he had come were a medium like water sustaining him. It was as though the pressure of all that darkness flooding down the hills and woods had just pushed the door open, and in one second more, would come pouring in, filling up the room, washing him at her." (98) When she hears the sounds of Angelo exploring upstairs, she thinks, "him." *"Him,* for he didn't have a name, at least not in her mind. Even if he had told her his name, as she knew he had, she never called him by it. He was no name, he was the shape with no name: *him."* (109)

The second phase of their relationship begins when, with Murray having jealously informed Cassie of Angelo's past, she goes for the first time to Angelo's room in the evening and says, "'Tell me your name.'" (130) In the story of his imprisonment, she has seen her own void. She tells him, "'I thought how all my own life, it was like that, like being locked up, and lying in the dark—'" (148) As Cassie realizes that her life has been "like being locked up" and "lying in the dark," she realizes that the void is shared. She goes on to tell Angelo, "'It was all of a sudden then that I knew—I really knew—how you felt. It wasn't till I knew how I had been always locked up that I knew how you felt—'" (148) Cassie has gained the reality of selfhood. Awakening the next morning in Angelo's bed, she tells him, "'I feel I just got born.'" (153) Like all of Warren's reborn, she has a new vision of the world. "'You look different,'" she tells Angelo. "Maybe it's because I never saw you before.'" She then adds, "'Maybe I never saw anything in the world before.'" (154)

Although Angelo resists Cassie's offer of reality, it finally seems to affect him. When Cassie first enters his room to share her new vision, he feels angry, and pictures himself provoking her into sending him away; he pictures himself once again walking the road alone. "He felt a kind of angry joy in that image, a sense of being himself again, free again." (129) In her altered attitude he senses some coming change which he dreads, for it comes "just when he had found a way to live in that changelessness." (129) Cassie, trying to draw him into her new vision of context, places a hand on his forehead. What touches him, however, in his continued flight from context and the betrayal of his countryman Guido, is Cassie's repeated assertion that it was "'not your fault—not your fault—oh, no—it wasn't—'" (140) Cassie offers him involvement, but what he hears is the promise of continued freedom from his past; in his mind he cries out, *"Senti, Guido—listen— non è colpa mia—she say not my fault—she say me innocente—inno-*

cente—" (140) Yet the love which Cassie offers finally seems to convey its
reality to Angelo as, while Cassie talks, he feels his protective walls—which
Warren has built of wood this time, to accord with the house—collapsing,
"as though something inside had cracked like a piece of dry, dusty wood
under a great slow pressure." (149)

Even this crumbling of the walls, however, is not unambiguous, for they
crumble when Cassie assures Angelo of his freedom to leave the house;
although this is symbolically the freedom to join Jack Burden and emerge
from the closet of history into the creation of history, to Angelo, Cassie offers only the freedom from himself. Whereas the new phase of their relationship is, for Cassie, an escape from illusion into reality, for Angelo it is
a new form of dream, to be carefully nurtured. He molds Cassie into a
sexual plaything, buying her a whore's outfit of scarlet and black and
teaching her the technique of love-making, together with its forbidden
words. In this act of creation he finds the sense of power with which to fill
the void. In the narrator's words, "In the end it was her ignorance that
possessed him. It was the emptiness that he had to fill up. ... Filling it up,
molding it, breathing it, eating it—that was his way of being alive. He lived
by her ignorance. When he taught her something, he felt the thrill of his
own knowledge, her own power." (177)

Once again, this dream world, while insulating Angelo from his past,
frightens him in its abstraction from the world and from time, so that he
enlarges his sphere of false being by absorbing himself in the objective reality of an alternate, daytime life involving farm tasks. "He was dimly aware
of some need to grasp first one project, then another, as some new image of
the future. ... To get through the day, he had to pack it with moments that
seemed to be stolen from the future, that seemed to promise a world that
would have a future." (181) In his fragmentation, he rigorously separates
the worlds of day and night. Thus, he conquers the impulse to tell Cassie
of his plans for the farm, because "the tractor was real, the field to be plowed
was real, the cows would be real, and deeply, darkly—in something like
despair—he knew that you could never carry what was real, and belonged to
the day, over the secret line into the world that was a dream and belonged
to the night." (171)

Angelo nearly gains the awareness that would unite these two worlds
when, having mastered the tractor, he comes to the house early for a drink
of water and, for the first time in weeks, sees Cassie in her baggy brown
sweater and brogans. With that sight, "he realized that everything else—the
red dress, the black patent-leather slippers, the black lace of the panties
and brassiere on her white skin, the bottle of whiskey held to her lips, the
wrenchings and contrived tensions, the forbidden words she had humbly
learned to utter, the calculated frenzy—all had been a lie...a lie he had
told to himself." (190) He begins to see anew. "He looked across at her and

thought, marveling, how he had never really seen her before." (190) For the first time, he calls her by her given name. But then he catches the scent of her perfume, which reminds him of a girl in his guilt-ridden past, and this much reality proves more than he can bear; he flees to the dairy house and Charlene.

The major event of the novel, which, like Jasper's misadventure in *The Cave,* affects each of the characters in different ways, is the murder; following that, in what is perhaps a weakness of *Meet Me in the Green Glen,* Angelo and Cassie are no longer central as they move in different directions. Angelo's letter to Cassie from prison seems to indicate that he has finally gained selfhood; he awaits death fearlessly. Cassie, on the other hand, draws back into her unreality. Several years after the execution, when Cy talks to Murray about her, he says, "'The truth has done gone and changed on her. She's got a whole new kind of truth.'" (355) To investigate, Murray goes to the sanatorium, where a robin outside "would not stop its mellow, drowsy, petulant note: *gluck,* silence, then *gluck,* like water dropping." (356) Cassie offers her hand, which seems "dry, cool, boneless. To his pressure the hand was as unresponsive as a small rubber glove filled with sawdust." (355) Her new kind of truth, Murray finds, is the belief that Angelo has not been executed, but rather, as she tells Murray, "'has gone away. ... Somewhere far away, and he is happy.'" (359)

Murray moves to center stage after the murder, to become the primary example of absorption into unreality. The imagery surrounding that immersion is explicit. When Cassie informs him that Charlene is Sunderland's daughter, he responds by "gaping like a fish." (216) When he returns to the Spottwood house, he takes pleasure in the thought that "soon, when the land lay under the dark suffocation of water, there would be nothing to remember." (351) As he goes through the house for the last time, "his body drifted from room to room, slowly, weightlessly, as though floating through that medium." (351) After Miss Edwina censures him and he hears that Angelo has been executed, "he stood there, and in his interior darkness a tide, black, thick as slime, and nameless, was sluggishly flooding upward. ... All night the viscous, lightless tide would be slowly rising in him. It would be like an internal drowning." (333)

Fleeing from Cassie's happiness, Murray goes to spend the night at his wife's house, where his sense of the void pursues him and finally forces itself on his consciousness. Cassie has spoken to him of love, and, as he sits in the study, "the word rang hollowly in his head as in a great cave." (365) He goes out of the study into the hall; "the walls of the house seemed to be slowly constricting," and the high chandelier "was hanging above him like ice in a dark cave." (366) He thinks, "He was in himself and could not get out." (366) He recalls Cassie's question, "'Did you ever love anybody, Murray Guilfort?'" and "For a moment, frozen on the stair, in the darkness, he started to cry out: 'You!'" Then a ray of recognition comes: "he knew it was a lie." He thinks how "long ago, the door of the old Spottwood house had opened and there was the white face of a girl floating toward him in the shadows...and that was all he had ever known: a dream. It was the dream he had been forced to dream." (367)

Awareness strikes still deeper as he goes to his bedroom and thinks of Bessie, and of how she had loved him even knowing that he had married her only for money and status. "Well, if she loved him—and he tested the edge of the thought like sliding your thumb down the honed edge of a knife —her love was the mark of her inferiority, her failure." (369) Then he begins to see the situation whole. *"And of mine,* he thought, even as he desperately tried to stop the thought: *of mine!"* (369) He manages to stop the thought with another: that Bessie's love, going unrewarded, was no more than an illusion. *"Love,* he thought, *so that is love.* To dream a fool dream like that fool Bessie Guilfort, to dream a fool lie like that fool Cassie Spottwood, to dream a lie and call it truth." (369) His next thought, that they have in fact experienced truth as he never has, overwhelms him by confirming his sense of his own unreality. In a daze, he gets into bed, downs an overdose of sleeping pills, and falls away from reality completely; "he sank deeper, sinking into truth, into the truth that was himself, whatever his self was, as into joy, sinking there at last." (372) Like Ikey in *The Cave,* he is fully at one with his false self in its void.

The development of the true self is shown primarily through the characters of Angelo's defense attorney, Leroy Lancaster, and Cy Grinder. Leroy, unlike the other characters whose thoughts the reader shares (Cassie, Angelo, Murray, Cy), is not literally a product of Spottwood Valley, but he is a victim of unreality nonetheless. He dreams, as a young man, that Corinne will prove sexually tempestuous; on their wedding night he is only partially disillusioned when "she gave herself to him sweetly, gravely, graciously." (270) Nearly twenty years later, after Cassie's courtroom confession, he imagines himself spying on Corinne, and suddenly feels the abstraction of his life from reality. "He wondered where life had gone. He thought: *When will I be done with illusion?"* (272) He goes to his office, where his musings explain his unwillingness to go home; within the framework of his dream, he is a failure. At first he does not see that his dream is his failure; he wonders whether Corinne married him because he had the smell of failure and would therefore serve as object of charity, or whether her charity had made him a failure. As he sits there feeling "demeaned, outraged, emasculated," he has a startling revelation: "blazing in the darkness of his head," he sees Corinne in the old sexual fantasy, this time with Angelo as her partner. "After a moment, sitting, he knew that that afternoon, in the courtroom, his own eyes had fixed upon Angelo Passetto as unforgivingly as those of the juryman from the hills. He had wanted Angelo

Passetto to die." (277) He realizes that he has been one with those who "stared unforgiving" at Angelo "from the thorny shadow of their own deprivations, yearnings, and envies" (275): that he shares in the dream and its destructiveness. *"Me too,* he thought, sitting there, shivering. *Me."* (277) With a new vision of unity, Leroy thinks, "God forgive me—I have blasphemed against my own life." (278) By dreaming his dream he had hated himself for his inadequacy, hated Corinne as the source of his inadequacy, hated Angelo as the measure of his inadequacy. Leroy, then, is ready to go back to Corinne and a new life; "slowly he became aware that he wanted to go home. That was what he wanted to do. Somehow, he felt that he could go home now." (278)

Cy Grinder also emerges from his unreality. The process begins when he stops with Cassie in a roadhouse after their unsuccessful attempt to see the Governor. She tells him what might have been: how they might be an old married couple returning from a visit to their son at the University. His response is to lurch from the table and bolt for the restroom. Staring into the mirror, he begins to discover his place in the context of the world and time. Stricken with that glimpse of true being, unable to face himself or anybody else, he locks himself in a stall. "Cy Grinder stood and thought how his whole damned life had been working to bring him here to stand shivering, locked in a can like he was afraid, saying *now, now,* for if you could just live now, no backwards and no forwards, you could live through anything. But a man can't. He was finding out that a man can't." (324) Alone with that knowledge, Cy experiences a moment of anguish. "Something was like a big hand reaching through his ribs, a hand big enough to grab his heart like a wet washrag and squeeze it into a wad, and then that hand was tearing his heart out by the roots while he stood there in that atrocity of anguish and could not breathe." (325)

After the trial, as Game Warden of the new Reservation whose lake is to cover most of Spottwood Valley, he comes to an accommodation with reality which results in a limited contentment. As Game Warden, like Angelo, he tries to absorb himself in the world of fact. "He had learned the trick of thinking, every night before trying to sleep, of what he could do the next day, what task he could turn his hand to, where he would go on the Reservation. So he almost never thought of the past." (340) The thought of the prospective lake pleases him. "Cy began to feel that the past itself would be flooded...that part of his being was already under water, and he thought of the shadowy depths with a kind of cold contentment." (341)

Several years later, however, as he sits up sleeplessly, the past forces itself upon him through the television news and its report of Murray's apparently successful attempt at suicide. This intrusion of his context fills him with a loneliness which draws him to the bedside of his daughter, whom he adores, and then to the bedside of his wife, whom he does not adore.

"Before he turned away to undress, he realized that the face on the pillow was very much like the face of the little girl who lay in the next room. He had never before observed that fact." (374) For the first time, Cy sees the web of being, with its physical and temporal relationships. "Then he was wondering if there would ever come a time when the little girl in the other room would be heavy and slow-footed and short of breath and would lie sleeping...beside a stranger who, wakeful, was listening to her breath and did not know or care who she was. The thought was too terrible to bear." (375) Momentarily, he flees to the void; "he closed his eyes and tried to think of nothing, nothing at all." (376) In spite of himself, his wife's face comes into his mind. "Yes, that was like the face of the little girl. All those years, and how had he failed to see it?" This time, the thought leads Cy to the matrix of involvement, and he sees his wife for the first time. "With the image of the woman's face so clear in the darkness of his head, he began to wonder what she thought, what she felt; and his wondering was mysterious to him. He wondered what she had ever thought, what she had ever felt. He realized, slowly, that never, in all the years, had he wondered that before." (376)

The novel begins and ends on a distinctly Coleridgean note. The opening scene, in which Cy kills a deer with bow and arrow, presents an *Ancient Mariner* tableau. Cy's act, like the ancient mariner's, conceivably blameless, is morally defined (according to Warren's analysis of the poem)[2] by the spirit in which it is performed. Cy exults, "'The bastard—did you see me snag that big white-bellied bastard!'" (8) The narrator emphasizes the immorality of the act by terming the deer "the creature," and Angelo adds to the implication of sanctity by responding to the deer with a mental short-circuit in the thought, "Sandy Claws!" Cy has re-enacted his destruction of Cassie and his violation of the great web of being. Angelo, by imagining Santa Claus's sleigh "with the fat little, red-nosed, red-dressed son-of-a-bitch grinning out" (7), shares in the crime, as he does more concretely by lying about the circumstances; with his vision of unreality, he is a false witness. Cassie in her turn also shares in the crime of firing her shotgun at Cy.

The final scene of Cy's conversion takes its Coleridgean tone largely from Warren's use of light and water imagery. Warren notes, in his essay on Coleridge, how *The Ancient Mariner* ends with a reversal of light-dark imagery, with darkness suddenly become beneficent, and says, "Coleridge's reversal is, I take it, quite deliberate—an ironic reversal which, in effect, says that the rational and conventional view...seeks truth by the wrong light."[3] A similar reversal occurs in this last scene. Cy comes to aware-

[2]Robert Penn Warren, "A Poem of Pure Imagination: An Experiment in Reading," in *Selected Essays* (New York: 1958), p. 229.
[3]Warren, "A Poem of Pure Imagination," p. 234.

ness late at night, and the moonlight in the scene is repeatedly described in terms of water. The moon is "swimming high" (376), its light was "leaking into the room" (374), "seeped" into the room, and "washed" across the face of his wife (375). This flood differs profoundly from that drowning out Spottwood Valley and the town of Fiddlersburg in *Flood.* The moon is antithetical, on the one hand, to the sun of the merely objective world, and, on the other hand, to the naked light bulb of the Spottwood kitchen and Cy's television tube, both of which, as artifacts of man, illuminate only "the world he has made" (373).

The flood of moonlight, as it "spill[s]" out of the sky "to fill the vastness of the world" (376), is the source of a new vision. At first, Cy resists it and stands under an oak; "the tree was only leafing now, but he felt the need for the protection of what shadow it gave." (375) As he realizes in anguish that he has never before wondered what his wife thinks and feels, as he sees that that realization is "what he had to stand there and suffer" (376), he leaves his darkness and enters the great awakening light. "When the time came, he stepped out of the shadow of the tree. He looked up. There was the moon, with the sky, and the whole world, in its light." (376) This light is the redeeming light of what Warren, again speaking of Coleridge, calls the sacramental vision,[4] according to which the world is indeed "whole." The religious nature of the conversion represented in the scene helps to define Cy's transgression in the opening scene as well as the transgressions of all those who have lived false lives, unable to step out of their shadows.

In *Meet Me in the Green Glen,* then, Warren provides his most explicit statement about true being; he also focusses on love more closely than in his other novels. True love appears unchanged, revealing itself in the symbolic touch. When Leroy, after having reached awareness, lies awake with his thoughts of the injustice threatening Angelo, he takes Corinne's hand. (295) When Angelo, having violated Cassie daily, finds her reborn and feels the walls crumble within him, he reaches out for her—and she gives him her hand. (150) When he writes to her from jail, he comments on her smile when he kissed her hand in leaving, and concludes, "'You try save me and now I kiss your hand, I thank you.'" (365)

In addition, Warren further articulates his view of false love, which appears in two forms, the love of exploitation and the love of idealization. Cy and Murray both adore Cassie in the love of idealization, which is like Manty's submissive self-denial in *Band of Angels,* particularly as she turns Tobias into a white statue. On the other hand, Murray marries Bessie for wealth and status, while Cy marries Gladys Peegrum to "crown his destiny" of loving life at the very bottom; the two marriages are clear versions of exploitation. But perhaps the clearest is sexual, as it has appeared before in

[4]Warren, "A Poem of Pure Imagination," p. 214.

The Cave. Thus Angelo turns Cassie to scarlet and black, Murray dallies with his call girls, and Leroy fantasizes about Corinne. These loves of exploitation and idealization involve, in Sartrean terms, the lover's conceiving himself as object or subject:[5] within Warren's terminology, choosing the world of fact or the world of idea. The two forms of love are finally the same, for both are the dreams which result from individual fragmentation. The two epigraphs are germane here. Whether, in John Clare's vision of innocence, the green glen of love is viewed as attainable in a pastoral idyl, or whether, in the darker vision of Andrew Marvell, it is viewed as beyond reach, in each case it is equally abstract and unreal.

True love, like false love, is an ideal, and as such, may prove a dream. But, as Warren says of Conrad's fiction, "the last wisdom is for man to realize that though his values are illusions, the illusion is necessary, is infinitely precious, is the mark of his human achievement, and is, in the end, his only truth."[6] This is precisely Murray's discovery, when, having condemned Cassie and Bessie for living their lies, he realizes that "the dream is a lie, but the dreaming is truth." (370) Loving is redemptive, whether or not returned. As Cassie tells Murray, even if the gift of the heart is rejected, "It doesn't matter....because it...belongs to them anyway. Even if they just drop it and walk away, you're happy." (358) Of primary importance is the individual's rebirth, stemming from a sense of the ravaged face in the mirror, together with a sense of relationship, of *caritas,* which is, in Manty's words, "a charity deeper than what is love because it is the dark depth of the fountain from which love leaps but as the flashing spray." The state of caring is both a condition and a mark of the reintegration which is true being; as in Buber's formulation, the 'I' becomes a true 'I' only in caring.

[5]Jean-Paul Sartre, *Being and Nothingness,* trans. Hazel E. Barnes, (New York: 1957), Part Three: "Being-For-Others."

[6]Warren, "'The Great Mirage': Conrad and *Nostromo,"* in *Selected Essays,* p. 45.

A Place to Come To

by Tjebbe Westendorp

I

Robert Penn Warren's tenth novel is a fine achievement and deserves to be ranked as the most important of his novels about the contemporary world since *All the King's Men*. It is very much a novel about one man and it is actually narrated by him as the true history of his life. Jediah Tewksbury is a middle-aged professor of medieval history at the University of Chicago, whose memory is overwhelmed by the flood of his past experiences as he sits down to record his life. He has previously denied the connection between himself and the image of him which the past presents. His youth was spent in Dugton, Claxford County, Alabama, where his father had died ignominiously after a fall from a wagon, drunk, in the middle of the night, and "holding his dong." After that there was the humiliating poverty of his mother who went out to work in the local canning factory. Many years afterwards Jed still has nightmares of being exposed to the contempt of the other boys in town:

> The faces all had enormous eyes that seemed to whirl in their sockets, and great mouths, too big for the faces, with great rubbery lips that were twisting and slickly convolving in laughter, and fingers that pointed at me and were swelling enormously at the thrusting tips — at least, that was what the scene became in my nightmare.[1]

The "Fugitive prose" works well here. The sense of being hunted down by his past was impressed on Jed at an early age, and is associated with the larger issue of the crisis in Western culture and the prevalent sense of doom in a vision which is intimated to him by Dr. Stahlmann, a German refugee, who is Jed's supervisor at the University of Chicago. Stahlmann tells him how once in Switzerland he had observed through his binoculars the begin-

"A Place to Come To" by Tjebbe Westendorp. This article appears for the first time in this volume.

[1] *A Place to Come To* (New York: Random House; London: Martin Secker & Warburg Limited, 1977), p. 20.

ning of a landslide. He had seen a hare sitting on a slope, undisturbed by the first loosening boulders and rocks, but as the landslide increased in speed, the hare suddenly turned and ran. Dr. Stahlmann had watched with growing excitement how the hare was eventually caught by it. He had identified with the hare as well as with the birds which had attracted his attention to the impending disaster.

This image of a landslide is psychologically significant for Jed. He has always felt threatened by the fearful nightmare of his past experiences:

> Some massive concurrence of forces had been working, all my life, in darkness, to bring me to this spot and instance. All sense of my own force, even of identity, seemed to flee from me. ...[2]

It is through a confrontation with his past that he tries to establish "a continuity" and "an integrity of self." What kind of individual emerges?

II

When one looks at the bare facts of his life (Professor Jediah Tewksbury calls them "facts inert" as opposed to "facts operative," as he explains in the novel[3]) one finds that taken by themselves they are hardly calculated to enlist the reader's sympathy. As a boy he is thoroughly ashamed of his father and he comes to hate him. He is embarrassed by his mother's embittered poverty, though it is her hard work which enables him to go to college. Once he has left Dugton, he does not return until after his mother's death. As an intelligence-officer in World War II he kills a German prisoner-of-war, in violation of the Geneva Convention as he well knows. In Chicago he comes close to assaulting his own wife, Agnes, on a rainy Sunday afternoon "out of cold-blooded lust, boredom, and frustration." When she is dying of cancer in hospital, he uses her experiences as his laboratory findings for a dissertation entitled *Dante and the Metaphysics of Death*. In a later episode he deceives a friend with his wife over a long period. His second marriage ends in a separation: his wife rightly accuses him of refusing to participate emotionally in their relationship. Thus presented the story of his life does little to endear him to us.

Yet Jed Tewksbury comes off well with the reader in the end, I would argue. He tells the story of his life with some embarrassment (when things get really disgraceful, he switches to "he" and "him"), and with a great deal of honesty. A healthy earthiness (some readers might prefer to call it crudity), which has its roots in the small-town South of his younger days, is coupled with an erudition which is brought into play unobtrusively, but

[2]Ibid., p. 193.
[3]Ibid., p. 19.

interestingly. Central to his narration is the sense of guilt which Jed Tewksbury has taken upon himself and which he displays in his self-analysis. It
would appear that he fills perfectly the role that St.-John Perse claims for
himself: "It is enough for the poet to be the guilty conscience of his time".[4]
Jed himself uses a similar terminology when at the end of his story he declares himself prepared to confess to anything, "even to sonhood." This
awareness of guilt affects his memories of others in retrospect, and after
many years he revisits the scene of his father's death. He now shows a compassionate understanding of his "wild nobility." It was his father's tragedy
that he was born "out of phase," Jed realizes; he really belonged to the era
of the Civil War.

He redeems his guilt towards his mother, too. Though he never sees her
again after he leaves Dugton, he always cherishes her semi-literate letters.
In the end his guilt towards her is expiated in two separate scenes, both
equally ritualistic. In a Chicago hospital the gesture of reconciliation involves an elderly lady who has mistakenly identified Jed as her son. (Both
are in the hospital after Jed has been knifed on coming to her rescue in a
street robbery.) Jed accepts the part assigned to him by fate—it is here that
he "confesses to sonhood"—and he pays for her funeral.

The second gesture of expiation to his mother's memory is his return to
Dugton where he revisits the old house. He is received ceremonially by
Perk, his mother's second husband. This homecoming scene might easily
have become sentimental or melodramatic (Jed sleeps in his old bed again),
but such a tendency is counteracted by its ritualistic quality and by the old
man's sincere affection for Jed which is comic at the same time. Jed is gen-
uinely touched: Perk is more "real" to him than most people he has met in
the arty or academic worlds of Nashville or Chicago. In the old days it was
his mother whose sense of reality had made her tell him: "You git stuck
here [in Dugton], and I'll kill ye." The same forthrightness had impressed
Perk (she always made him feel like a man) and both Perk and Jed have
reason to be grateful to her.

With this visit to Dugton the wheel has come full circle: as the novel
is about to end, Jed shows himself to be concerned about the ease with which
he has come to accept solitude after his separation from his second wife.
Where Jack Burden at the end of *All the King's Men* goes "into the awful
responsibility of time" Jed Tewksbury, a mellower man, walks to the mail-
box with a letter to his former wife Dauphine: "I ask you for your company
for what blessedness it is."[5] Now Jed is willing to participate in the expe-

---

[4]Used as the motto in Robert Penn Warren's *Democracy and Poetry,* Cambridge, Mass.:
Harvard University Press, 1975. The meaning of terms in the present essay like "continuity of
self" and "de-selved" correlate with Warren's use of them in *Democracy and Poetry.* The general concerns of these two lectures are closely related to the issues dramatized in the novel.

[5]*A Place to Come To,* p. 401.

rience of others and to have others participate in his: he is ready to return to the human community.

Jed Tewksbury, then, is a good historian of his own life, just as he is a sound scholar of medieval history. It is worth pointing out here that Tewksbury, like Jack Burden, is a professional historian, that he tells us explicitly that he is not an artist, and that there is a noticeable lack of references to the narrative strategy to be followed by him. In *Democracy and Poetry*[6] Warren expresses his disagreement with Henry James's view that art is the justification of life. For Warren, history, in the Crocean sense, subsumes all other disciplines and all art: it is on the strength of this conviction that he has chosen, once again, a historian as his center of consciousness rather than an artist.

III

There are several mutually supporting patterns which express Jed Tewksbury's progress through life as well as the development of his insights into the true nature of "his continuity of self." There are first of all the places where he lives and which he visits. All of these places are revisited and the rhythm of visiting and revisiting runs parallel with that of meeting friends and losing sight of them. Often there is, many years later, a revaluation of their common experiences. This pattern is brought out in the narrative strategy: the earliest experiences are related in a flood of words. Afterwards there is a retreat from the scene and a revaluation: the tone becomes detached and ironic, but never cynical. Tewksbury shows himself capable of perceptive analysis.

There is, also, the alternating pattern of joy and depression, hope and despair, promise and frustration. In every new episode a promise of joy (the word is used a great deal) is held out to him. The promises are never fulfilled and Jed's disenchantment is linked each time with an acute commentary on contemporary society. The most impressive of these visions is that communicated to him by Dr. Stahlmann who presents the young aspiring scholar with his dream of an *imperium intellectũs*. In his beautiful house (called the Castle of Otranto) and surrounded by Dresden porcelain and other *objets d'art* he relates his dream of an international community of scholars:

> I dreamed of a timeless and placeless, sunlit lawn, like that of Dante's vision, where the poets and philosophers and sages sit, and where we who are none of those things may come to make obeisance and listen.[7]

[6]*Democracy and Poetry*, p. 91.
[7]*A Place to Come To*, p. 69.

The words *imperium intellectūs* are to Jed "like the slow commanding tones of a great bell and, on the instant, a joy suffused my being."[8] Dr. Stahlmann himself, however, tells Jed that he considers his dream more and more gratuitous. On the very day of his newly acquired American citizenship his memories lead him back to "the swill of München": he can never permit himself to forget that he is implicated forever in the bestiality of German attitudes towards the Jews. The abstract beauty of a community of scholars loses out to his deeply felt sense of guilt and complicity, which overtakes him in the same way that the hare was overtaken in his vision of the landslide. That very night he commits suicide.

In the war against Germany which Jed joins in reaction to Dr. Stahlmann's death his daily reading of Dante and the total meaningfulness of events in the medieval world contrast sharply with the blankness of spirit which is induced in Jed by the meaningless violence of the war. There is one incident in particular that is an ironic comment on the dream of an *imperium intellectūs*. As intelligence officer he kills, in an interrogation, a German prisoner of war, an SS lieutenant, who is a classical scholar. He acts out of solidarity with the Italian partisans, and on account of a sudden feeling of jealousy of the man's poise and self-assurance. The incident is to haunt him for the rest of his life.

Back in America he continues his studies at the University of Chicago. His dissertation analyzes the notion that Dante defines the meaning of life by his definition of death: it is after his wife's death by cancer that he comes to the tragic conclusion that he has really and truly loved her. Paradoxically, without her death he would never have discovered this. From this he derives his conclusions about Dante's vision of life and death which are to make his reputation in the world of medieval scholarship. In the circumstances he finds it impossible to accept "the golden promises" of an academic career based on observations made at his wife's deathbed. So he flees and takes up a teaching post at Nashville.

In Nashville, "a thriving city of the Buttermilk Belt," the promises held out to the newcomer are of two kinds: there is "the communal joy" of the gracious living and friendly hospitality of old Nashville, with its dinner parties, horse riding, and its whiskey—but he is never fully able to participate in this world, though he has a sympathetic appreciation of its charm. The other promise is the complete submission to him of Rozelle Hardcastle, a former Dugton girl. She is married to the sculptor and socialite Lawford Carrington ("Mr. Nashville") whose local reputation is unrelated to any true achievement. His only worthwhile piece of sculpture is the head of Rozelle in orgasm. Carrington is a fine addition to Warren's gallery of abstract men who are absolutely "nothing."

It is Rozelle who takes all the initiatives in the affair with Jed and frees

[8]Ibid., p. 70.

him from all the scruples he has vis-à-vis her husband. It is Jed who after a long and passionate affair proposes that they give up their irresponsible *liaison* as it is, and plan a future together: he has come to understand that "the orgasm was like the black hole of the physicists—a devouring negativity into which all the nags and positives of life may simply disappear."[9] At one stage he had thought: *Debatuo ergo sum* (I copulate therefore I am).[10] He now knows that it is necessary to turn away from "negativity" back into the fever and the fret of the world. She, however, is incapable of thinking in terms of a future at all.

When many years later Jed meets her again, she is married to an Indian guru who had made a big impression on the ladies at Nashville parties, but who had turned out to be a Southern black. They now live in Morocco on the money he made peddling dope. Rozelle is the archetypal example of the "deselved individual," for whom the moment is all, and who has no attachment to either place or history.

It is an attractive feature of the novel that Jed Tewksbury arrives in Nashville as a keen observer who has no previous acquaintance with the city. Thus he provides Warren with a unique opportunity for a penetrating, almost Swiftian satire on the sophisticated world of the New South, with its *maisons de tolerance*, and its intrigues and scandals.

But Jed Tewksbury's diagnosis of cultural crisis—a crisis that he, clearly, is in the middle of—goes beyond Nashville and its environs, beyond even the South and the American continent, to take in the entire Western world. Not long ago, Warren quoted with approval Daniel Callahan's statement that "it is now trivial to say that Western culture is undergoing a crisis, but it is not trivial to live it".[11] *A Place to Come To* presents us, finally, with a vivid illustration of this remark, one representative attempt to "live it."

IV

More than ever before Warren has been willing to test his own values and ideas in this novel, which is certainly his most autobiographical work.[12] With Jediah Tewksbury Warren shares a Southern upbringing in a small town, a successful academic career in the North and occasional returns to the South, a thorough acquaintance with Nashville, the role of being an academic celebrity with all its trappings, and an involvement with teaching

[9]Ibid., p. 220.

[10]Ibid., p. 218.

[11]*Democracy and Poetry*, p. 41. The statement is in Daniel Callahan, *The Tyranny of Survival* (New York: Macmillan, 1973, p. 23).

[12]The dedication of the novel to his brother and his sister may be relevant here.

for many years. A great deal of what we know about Robert Penn Warren's own life is, in fact, successfully integrated into the dramatic monologue of this, the most recent of his protagonists. Conversely, the consistency and integrity of vision displayed by Jed indicates that Warren has achieved the creation of "an organized self." If a novel is, what he has said about poetry in *Democracy and Poetry,* "a vital emblem of the integrity of self," the creation of this novel, and more particularly the creation of the character of Jed Tewksbury, shows that Robert Penn Warren still holds at least one idea with passion: in a world of non-selves, the man who tries to establish his individual identity through art need not fear that "all was for naught."

Warren Selected: An American
Poetry, 1923-1975

by Stanley Plumly

I

I *in the lyric arsenical meadow*

A man is lucky, in a lifetime, to manage a single selected poems, that chance to go back for rescue if not revision. To have had three chances suggests more than luck: in Robert Penn Warren's case it confirms a profound capacity for growth. Each of the three *Selected Poems* has started in the present and returned, in reverse chronology, to the past; and each has reselected and often rearranged the patterns of the poems. This latest, and likely the last, selection[1] represents more than fifty years of an American poetry. Indeed, it represents American poetry, as a history, better than any other comparable collection of our period. The perception is paradoxical because at the same time that Warren offers our poetry its most complete retrospective, he remains what he has always been— unique, unfashionable, and underrated. He can still write terrifically bad lines—"The heel of the sun's foot smites horridly the hill."—but in the sum, poem by selected poem, he has become our great poet.

That Warren is a Southerner, that he began writing poems in the context of the Fugitive movement, that he has written some of the most judicious prose of the New Critical period is to merely identify sources. He has too often been labeled by and limited to those sources by readers and reviewers. "Bearded Oaks," for example, threatens to survive as a kind of antebellum anthem—proud, subtle, and marine. It symbolizes a form of perfection, in

"Warren Selected: An American Poetry, 1923-1975" by Stanley Plumly. From *The Ohio Review.* (Winter 1977), pp. 37-48. © 1977 by *The Ohio Review.* Reprinted by permission of *The Ohio Review,* Ohio University, Athens, Ohio.

[1][*Selected Poems: 1923-1975* (New York; Random House; London: Martin Secker & Warburg Limited, 1976).—Ed.]

both art and attitude, better left to its period. Warren's entire career is written into the juxtaposition of the formal assumptions of this early meta-physical poem with the free-fall abilities of a new, transcendental one, "Trying to Tell You Something." The humid sensuality of the older piece— "So, waiting, we in the grass now lie/Beneath the languorous tread of light:/ The grasses, kelp-like, satisfy/The nameless motions of the air."—is light years away from the bone-chilling isolation of the new poem. Warren, confronting a huge iron-ringed, cable-hooped oak ("older than James-town or God, splitting/With its own weight), in dead winter, late at night, and listening to the "thin-honed and disinfectant purity" of the siren sound the wind makes through metal, discovers that this tree wants to tell him something, something

> Of truth, and its beauty. The oak
> Wants to declare this to you, so that you
>
> Will not be unprepared when, some December night
> You stand on a hill, in a world of whiteness, and
>
> Stare into the crackling absoluteness of the sky. The oak
> Wants to tell you because, at that moment
>
> In your own head, the cables will sing
> With a thin-honed and disinfectant purity.
>
> And no one can predict the consequences.

Aside from the obvious and important difference of the abstracted pas-sion of the one poem and the passionate inquiry of the other, it is clear that "Bearded Oaks" ruminates its philosophical position, while "Trying to Tell You Something" directly dramatizes its position. The older poem suffers its premeditation well, too well perhaps; the newer poem provides for the imperfections and possibilities of a man thinking out loud. Ironically, "Bearded Oaks" is the least typical of Warren's original *Selected.* Warren is never as young nor as old as he is supposed to be. "Late Subterfuge," from this same beginning period, a poem of accent and declared rhyme, is much more like the Warren who will follow. Like a lot of the early stuff, it is a hard-bitten love poem, and concludes:

> Our feet in the sopping woods will make no sound,
> The winter's rot begun, the fox in ground,
> The snake cold-coiled, secret in cane the weasel.
> In pairs we walk, heads bowed to the long drizzle—
> With women some, and take their rain-cold kiss;
> We say to ourselves we learn some strength from this.

We say to ourselves we learn some strength from this: the fact of the longer, enjambed line is almost enough in itself to suggest the advantage to the brooding, Kentucky-bourbon voice of the poet. We need no slide-rule to measure the length of the *e*'s and *a*'s or the repetition of *s* sounds. This is Warren's considering voice. The well-wrought urn strategy of a "Bearded Oaks" would have split or clipped an already tight line such as "The snake cold-coiled, secret in cane the weasel." The hyphen and the syntactical inversion help free the energy of the line, they do not conserve it. Warren's tone of voice depends on its drawl, not on a seventeenth-century speech of good manners.

No good poem can afford to have its tone conferred upon it; good poems, of course, earn their speaking parts. Warren was to learn quickly that he needed *time*, time across as well as down the page, in order to accommodate the pace and size of his statement. "Original Sin: A Short Story," also from the first selection, is one of his finest poems because the form is as fluid and flexible as the content.

> Nodding, its great head rattling like a gourd,
> And locks like seaweed strung on the stinking stone,
> The nightmare stumbles past, and you have heard
> It fumble your door before it whimpers and is gone:
> It acts like the old hound that used to snuffle your door and moan.

Here the variation of line length accentuates the "variation" of the slant rhyme, while the rhyme, unpredictable, never impedes the destination of the line and sentence, particularly the sentence. This quality of complexity, and soliloquy, continues for eight more full stanzas—a thorough story, if "short"—with the nightmare, as recurring as it is kaleidoscopic, manifesting itself everywhere, from Omaha to Harvard Yard to "the lyric arsenical meadow."

> You have moved often and rarely left an address,
> And hear of the deaths of friends with a sly pleasure,
> A sense of cleansing and hope which blooms from distress.

This "original sin" is Warren's first encounter with his deepest subject, a subject less defined by the popular critical assignations of Time or Self and more by the intimations of a common guilt—the weight and wages of the past. It is at once a mythic and a personal haunting. The best of the early selection, and re-selection, either magnify this theme of pursuit or are burdened with it, poems as different in tone as "Revelation" and "To a Face in the Crowd." It is no idea ingratiated into the material; it is a center of gravity, both a locus and local. It can be the past personified, whether as a "mother who rises at night to seek a childhood picture" or as something that "goes to the backyard and stands like an old horse cold in the pasture." It can be birthplace or home place, the place you take with you. It certainly is the present tense of the past, the dream re-enacted and paid for, again and again, a little like folk history and folk wisdom—deadly, fierce, and all illuminating.

II *geometric, circular, gold*

Warren's second *Selected Poems*—occupying in the latest selection central position—proposes the next double decade, 1943-1966. If we include the
transitional book, *Incarnations, Poems, 1966-1968,* we are dealing with a
full quarter century of the poet's career. That is a long time in the life of
any writer; for Warren it is crucial. For the ten years following the Second
War he did not write poems. Then, in the late fifties, under the general
title *Promises,* Warren published two sequences, dedicated respectively to
his daughter and son. These two poems-within-a-poem mark the maturation
of his poetic line. He will not write as well again until the end of the twenty-
five-year period in another sequence called "Island of Summer," the first
of four in *Incarnations.*

The daughter and son sequences are just that: poems in series, in outline,
placed in parallel in a space suggesting time, dedicated to making promises.
The first grouping, "To a Little Girl, One Year Old, In a Ruined Fortress,"
consists of five individual poems addressed to the daughter's instruction
("This is the world.") by way of building around her an actual, a real context—in this local instance, the southern coast of Italy.

> Sun blaze and cloud tatter, now the sirocco, the dust is swirled
> Over the bay face, mounts air like gold gauze whirled;
> > it traverses the blaze blue of water.
> We have brought you where geometry of a military rigor survives
> > its own ruined world,
> And sun regilds your gilt hair, in the midst of your laughter.

> All night, next door, the defective child cried; now squats in
> > the dust where the lizard goes.
> The wife of the *gobbo* sits under the vine leaves, she suffers,
> > her eyes glare.
> The engaged ones sit in the privacy of bemusement, heads bent:
> > the classic pose.
> Let the beetle work, the gull comment the irrelevant anguish
> > of air...

Both of these examples—both are third quatrains—come from what are
essentially sonnets. The formal point is worth making because Warren has
not only exploded the idea of the familiar pentameter line, he has also
altered the position of the speaker in such poetry. The line simply will
not quit; the speaker simply will not stay on the sidelines, looking on, commenting, essaying. The speaker here is also the primary participant, actor,
"at the center of what he creates." The decisions of language are those of
discovery, of perception as opposed to conception. Finding what will suffice in such circumstances can take a line as long as the arm. But beyond the

extended music and perspective, there is likewise the insistence that the language pay its way, whether by the illusion of *completed* action or by means of the extra, delayed adjective and delayed verb. One of the problems with a poetry of four-square formality is that too often it calls attention to its decor at the expense of other issues. What is so exceptional in the above examples is that Warren has sacrificed none of the dimensions of his truth for any of the possibilities of beauty. The rhythms are rich, their needs inevitable: Warren is working with, not against, the silences that surround any poem; he has confused, as does Whitman in his own ragtime, the white space. He is testing what a line can hold, how much it can support. Later he will drop the rubber-stamp of the rhyme.

The promises to his son—"In first darkness hydrangeas float white in their spectral precinct."—require more poems, eighteen, as the issues require more room. The promises in this sequence provide for the emphasis of theme over the experience of form. "We died only that every promise might be fulfilled," says the parental voice to a title question, "What Was the Promise That Smiled From the Maples at Evening?" The parents here are grandparents, with Warren as go-between. Throughout the entire sequence Warren balances the witness of his own boyhood against the wisdom he offers his son. Death, it seems, is the real parent. We remember what we remember for a reason, and that reason pulls at us like the earth. Gravity: grave: guilt: the associations are predictable enough. What distinguishes them in Warren's case is the density and the relentlessness with which he pursues his losses. Three books from now it will be called love, but for the moment one more name for such memory, the dream and the daydream, is knowledge.

> Long since, in a cold and coagulate evening, I've stood
> Where they slept, the long dead, and the farms and the far
> > woods fled away.
> And a gray light prevailed and both landscape and heart
> > were subdued.
> Then sudden, the ground at my feet was like glass, and I say
> What I saw, saw deep down—with their fleshly habiliments rent,
> But their bones in a phosphorus of glory agleam, there they lay,
> Side by side, Ruth and Robert. But quickly that light was spent.

"Their fleshly habiliments rent/But their bones in a phosphorus of glory agleam"—the resonant power of Warren's language, that eccentric, acute diction, those long, Biblical rhythms, is the genius of his evolving vision. He looks at the thing straight on before he changes it, transforms it. And his cold eye consistently looks into the fire rather than at the light. "Truth's glare-glory," he calls it…or "the quantum glare of the sum." The fact that nearly all of the poems in a sequence for his son are about his own boyhood indicates how much he intends to teach by example rather than by instruction. Even the three lullabies are stays against his own insomnia. The teacher, though, as always, has outlearned the pupil. At the end of *Promises,* the year and setting shift suddenly back to nineteen-eighteen and the farm: if in dreams begin responsibilities, then in memory begins perspective.

> In the cedar dark a white moth drifts.
> The mule's head, at the barn-lot bar,
> Droops sad and saurian under night's splendor.
> In the star-pale field, the propped pitchfork lifts
> Its burden, hung black, to the white star...

After *Promises* there is a considerable period of trying-out. First, in *You, Emperors, and Others,* Warren tries repeating his recent success in form—the extended and variable iambic line and rhyme—but without repeating the successes of subject. Most of the poems in *Emperors* depend on idea rather than image, on speculation rather than the specification of a life. The book that follows, *Tale of Time,* tries out more vital material, death of the mother, but is too often discursive ("insistent assiduity") or didactic—"Death is only a technical correction of the market/Death is only the transfer of energy to a new form." The content of the situation here begins to sound, as the lines pile up, more and more like a postulation than a possible poetry. Both of these books contain fine moments ("Two Pieces After Suetonius" and "One Drunk Allegory," as instances). On the whole, however, they depend on Warren's previous achievement and invention, hence their clichéd ring.

Incarnations, Poems 1966-1968 marks the end of a rhetorical bind and offers Warren an insight into the means he will use thereafter. The text is made, again, of sequences, the second and largest of which, "Internal Injuries," is more the journalistic jazz of popular fiction, complete with melodrama. "Island of Summer," the initial sequence, in thirteen parts with subparts, indicates a newer approach to total form, corporate form, and what such form can free. Warren has, of course, fiddled with the sequence format most of his poetry writing life. The fact of his fiction is evidence enough of his interest in the sustained story. In the past he has largely juxtaposed poems, carried over images, and enforced a spatial order to create the impression of a unity. In the island sequence he observes two central Aristotelian unities, those of place and purpose, and suggests movement through time, as in a narrative, and thereby sets up expectations of a coherent story. The story's problem is clear: "I sit and meditate the/Nature of the soul." The method of meditation, and mediation, is to introduce the reader to the history, "The Mediterranean flotsam," of his island (exposition) and to illustrate how that particular past bears on the speaker's immediate situation—"My mind is intact, but the shapes/ Of the world change" —(complication) and to show a way out—"The world is a metaphor"—

(resolution). Roughly, a beginning, a middle, and an end, as if Warren's work could be reduced to structure.

> All day, cicadas,
> At the foot of infinity, like
> A tree, saw. The sawdust
> Of that incessant effort,
> Like filings of brass, sun-brilliant,
> Heaps up at the tree-foot. That
> Is what day is.
>
> Do not
> Look too long at the sea, for
> That brightness will rinse out your eyeballs.
>
> They will go gray as dead moons.

What is remarkable in this small example, beyond the characteristic delays of verb and modifier, is the cleaner rhythm. The language is "purer" and the pace down the page takes its own good time. Warren is in no rhetorical rush, since, obviously, there is no apparent rhetoric to embellish the music with. He works the space as if it were time, which it is. The stanzas do not so much proceed as they suspend in a cause-and-effect relationship. The individual poems in this whole group grow in a similar way, by hanging together in the total, common space of the sequence, the silence. "Island in Summer" is indeed an island sequence, organized as an archipelago, supported and connected by implication. At the proper distance the poem looks like a paradigm—

> He sways high against the blue sky,
>   While in the bright intricacies
>   Of wind, his mind, like a leaf,
>   Turns. In the sun, it glitters.

As is true generally of Warren's newest poetry, the real matter is not debated in the major portion of the story, in the individual issues of the individual poems/parts; instead it is held at the back of the mind until more pressing problems have been exhausted. "I have been in a place where/ Nothing is," says the poet near the finish of the sequence, "The world means only itself." How typical of Warren to look out, at "the furious energies of nature," in order to see in. His island poem stratifies its subject by continually enlarging its dimensions, by providing, part by growing part, for the inevitability of Warren reading himself back into the world. "The world," says the poet,

> Is fruitful, and I, too,
> In that I am the father
> Of my father's father's father. I,"

Of my father, have set the teeth on edge. But
By what grape? I have cried out in night.

From a further garden, from the shade of another tree,
My father's voice, in the moment when the cicada
                                    ceases, has called to me.

III   *sound passing northward*

This third *Selected Poems,* placing as it does the most recent work in the foreground, and fixing, as it must, the labor of a lifetime as a backdrop, reveals at once a career as remarkable as it is restorative. *Career* itself comes from a long list of starts, back to the Medieval Latin *carraria,* referring to a road, and the old Latin *carrus,* meaning a vehicle, a cart—that is, both the way and the way of the way. There is no better metaphor for what we call a story than that: the way and the way of the way. The means as means, the cart because of the cartroad. In *Audubon: A Vision,* Warren's famous good-bye to the sixties, he finds the vehicle, the career, by which and through which he can express his version of the sublime.

Tell me a story.

In this century, and moment, of mania,
Tell me a story.

Make it a story of great distances, and starlight.

The name of the story will be Time,
But you must not pronounce its name.

Tell me a story of deep delight.

A story of deep delight. What Warren discovers in his Audubon figure is the superiority of a story over a sequence, the difference between explicating as opposed to implicating order. The novelist in the poet has begun to think in plot instead of pattern. Except for overt gestures in that direction, such as "The Ballad of Billie Potts," so much of his early and middle poetry is organized pieces, outlines of materials only half willing to cooperate. Even the separate poems can sound under pressure to cohere, to contain, to check the outbound energy—"Just once we look back./On sunset, a white gull is black./It hangs over the mountain crest./It hangs on that saffron west./It makes its outcry./It slides down the sky." But in *Audubon* Warren comes to a complete rest. The rhythms relax, the imagination penetrates. This poem about a painter of birds—"He put them where they are, and there we see them:/In our imagination"—about a man who named what he saw, this first man, in the act of becoming a man—

> He slew them, at surprising distances, with his gun.
> Over a body held in his hand, his head was bowed low,
> But not in grief...
>
> What is love?
>
> One name for it is knowledge—

this dreamer of "a season past all seasons," this New World witness, this poem about a killer and painter of birds is Warren's way back, back to his boyhood, back to being "an ignorant man again," back to the dream out of time, the sound of the geese passing northward. Audubon's story is more than a vision of the mind's eye and the mind; it is Warren's acknowledgment to himself of having come to terms with the deep past. It is story telling in which the hero is the teller.

If *Audubon* is finally about knowledge, *Or Else,* published just a year before the present selection, is first and finally about wisdom. "Have I learned how to live?" asks the poet at one point. He concludes another piece with:

> All items listed above belong in the world
> In which all things are continuous,
> And are parts of the original dream which
> I am now trying to discover the logic of. This
> Is the process whereby pain of the past in its pastness
> May be converted into the future tense
>
> Of joy.

Joy is a good gloss of deep delight. This post-*Audubon* book refers to itself as a *Poem/Poems,* an attempt at having it both ways. Actually, its twenty-three "parts" do compel the complications of a plot, not just by repeating certain themes and images, but by creating a continuum of their interrelations. The book ends the way *Audubon* began, with a bird—this time a hawk rather than a heron—posed "on the topmost, indicative tip of/The bough's sharp black and skinny jag skyward." Of course: "The hawk, in an eye-blink, is gone." *Or Else* takes place in New England, mostly Vermont, save for sidetrips with writers in other climes (Dreiser in the Midwest, Flaubert in Egypt, and James Dickey in "Rattlesnake Country") and takes time in real winter, inevitably in snow, save for a moment or two in fall. The narrative line follows from a statement of the problem ("All day, I had wandered in the glittering metaphor/For which I could find no referent.") to conflict ("But remember//What I remember, but do not/Know what it all means, unless the meaning inheres in/The compulsion to try to convert what now is *was*/Back into what was *is*.") to a return if not a resolution ("What we know, we know, and/Sun now down, flame, above blue, dies up-ward forever in/Saffron."). It is a book-length poem about how to die, having made a difficult passage; it is the poet's first book in the seventies, his year and the century's. He began his career, his way, by writing lines like "the waves' implacable monotone." Now he simply remembers how

> once I, a boy, crouching at creekside,
> Watched, in sunlight, a handful of water
> Drip, drip, from my hand. The drops—they were bright!
>
> But you believe nothing, with the evidence lost.

IV   *a shell, a dry flower, a worn stone, a toy*

Poems are a lot of things, but before anything else they are memory memorized. Robert Penn Warren's poems, deeply flawed, patently ambitious as many of them are, restore poetry to its sometime place as something primary. *Selected Poems,* fifty-two-years worth, is a book of life, total in its attempt to embrace all the evidence. It is without peer as a living history of the art in our time.

Some while ago, in a Jefferson lecture, Warren spoke of "the capacity of man to face the deep, dark inwardness of his nature and his fate." He was certainly talking about himself. His capacity for such confrontation is in the record. He is our tragic poet, an appellation that applies as much to the quality of the struggle as to the size of the stage on which it is acted out. The issues are not new, but the terms of the issues—the moral equivalent of technique—are especially his. His singular power is to risk the combination of passion and philosophical inquiry, a burden his language, or anybody's is not always up to. He is still a metaphysical poet, one who replaces light with incandescence. The broad, sometimes sweeping nature of his poems tends to obscure the smaller, brilliant moments. But be the vision wide-angled or close-up, his most evocative passages have about them the hallucinatory, surreal sense of the dream. "The texture of the dream," he calls it. He hates rooms, even when the out-of-doors is unspecified.

> Of old I know that shore, that dim terrain,
> And know how black and turbulent the blood
> Will beat through iron chambers of the brain
>
> When at your back the taciturn tall stone,
> Which is your fathers' monument and mark,
> Repeats the waves' implacable monotone,
> Ascends the night and propagates the dark.

This throw-back is from the last, and therefore, earliest poem in the new selection. How wonderful and assured it sounds, sober without being somber, like finely polished mahogany. We must remember that it was written by one of the singing-masters. Fifty years later the issue is the same; the rhythm, however, has appropriated the free speech of a more democratic voice.

> ...will you be with me when
> I arrive and leave my own cart of junk
> Unfended from the storm of starlight and
> The howl, like wind, of the world's monstrous blessedness,
> To enter, by a bare field, a shack unlit?
> Entering into that darkness to fumble
> My way to a place to lie down, but holding,
> I trust, in my hand a name—
> Like a shell, a dry flower, a worn stone, a toy—merely
> A hard-worn something...

Inside that room, in the dark, he still asks, "Can I see Arcturus from where I stand?" It is a rare moment, that room. Invariably, Warren is outside, under stars, or standing in the dusk, the sun going down.

Some poets belong to the Psalms, some to Proverbs, others still to the Book of Job or the Songs of Solomon. The Genesis poets all speak in the third person. Warren is an Ecclesiastes poet, all wisdom and wandering. He may belong to some of the other books too. At any rate, he is Old Testament—angry, alluvial, *there*. His presence is unmistakable. It allows for the latitude and liberties he is so fond of taking. "In the lyrical logic and nightmare astuteness that/Is God's name, by what magnet, I demand,/Are the iron and out-flung filings of our lives..." And so on. We have been taught that the art of the poem is that which intervenes between the raw material and the reader, like a third thing. But there is that poetry of poetry where the promises are enough.

Taproots of a Poem: The Long Foreground of "Old Nigger on One-Mule Cart"

by Victor Strandberg

In *All the King's Men,* Jack Burden makes witty use of Tennyson's "flower-in-the-crannied-wall theory," discovering that the "delicate little root" of a local corporation "ran all the way to New York City, where it tapped the lush dung heap called the Madison Corporation."[1] While stopping short of the dung heap image, we may say that Robert Penn Warren's poems generally bear out the same theory. When plucked up for closer inspection, they display a root system often tracing back through decades of earlier verse-writing, so that we may witness the evolution of certain recurring motifs, themes, or images over upwards of half a century's poetic handiwork. Perhaps, with Jack Burden, we may feel unprepared to say we know what God and man are, but we may reasonably hope to gain a stronger grasp of Warren's total poetic design by a close study of one representative root system. The poem I have chosen for this purpose is one of Warren's finest in his remarkably fertile most recent decade, "Old Nigger on One-Mule Cart Encountered Late at Night When Driving Home from Party in the Back Country"—the longest and terminal poem in the 1975 collection, *Can I see Arcturus From Where I Stand?*

As we approach the poem, a brief definition of Warren's poetic theory seems desirable, beginning with his concept of the image or symbol. "Man lives by images," Warren has said; "They/Lean at us from the world's wall, and Time's." That assertion, from "Reading Late at Night, Thermometer Falling" (in *Or Else,* 1974), makes clear not only the supreme importance of the image in Warren's poetics, but also the manner in which images come to him, leaning at him from "the world's wall" as though he were a connoisseur being arrested and absorbed by one painting after another while moving down the corridors of Time. From this process a set of master images

---

"Taproots of a Poem: The Long Foreground of 'Old Nigger on One-Mule Cart'" by Victor Strandberg. This article appears for the first time in this volume.

[1] *All the King's Men* (New York: Modern Library, 1953), pp. 234-35. Published in Great Britain by Martin Secker & Warburg Limited.

may gradually emerge into definition, images that ascend to the status of symbols by reason of their numerous recurrences, their largeness of meaning, and their insistent emotional urgency. When functioning in this fashion, Warren says, the image or symbol imparts design and coherence to a poet's work as a whole:

> The symbol affirms the unity of mind in the welter of experience; it is a device for making that welter of experience manageable for the mind—graspable. ... It does not "stand for" a single idea, and a system of symbols is not to be taken as a mere translation of a discursive sequence. Rather, a symbol implies a body of ideas which may be said to be fused in it. This means that the symbol itself may be developed into a discursive sequence as we intellectually explore its potential.[2]

A bit later in the same essay, he adds a codicil describing the consistency of meaning that an image will maintain throughout the repetitions and variations of its recurring usage. Warren is speaking here of a single poem, *The Ancient Mariner,* but we shall find good reason to extend the principle beyond the framework of the single poem into its long foreground of earlier poems by the same author: "My reasoning is this: Once the import of an image is established for our minds, that image cannot in its workings upon us elsewhere in the poem be disencumbered, whether or not we are consciously defining it."[3] Our final precept from Warren's poetic theory is his assertion, in his essay on Conrad, that "The philosophical novelist, or poet, is one for whom...the image strives to rise to symbol, [and] for whom images always fall into a dialectical configuration."[4]

In "Old Nigger on One-Mule Cart," the central taproot is the epiphanic encounter with a stranger—perhaps *alien* would be closer to Warren's meaning—who turns out to be a spiritual guide or even an alter ego for the Warren persona: a "Brother, Rebuker,...Philosopher past all/Casuistry," as the old Nigger comes to be in the afterlight of Time. A decade ago, in *Audubon: A Vision* a similar encounter between the great ornithologist and a haglike old woman formed the crux of that major poem; and a decade before that, in *Promises,* the motif surfaced hauntingly in the meeting between Warren's boy-persona and the tragically rootless wandering bum of "Dark Night of the Soul" (originally titled "Dark Night of"). That poem, in turn, drew upon Warren's short story of a decade earlier still (the 1940's) —Warren's finest short story, by general consensus—"Blackberry Winter," whose closing vignette indicates the strength of the motif's grip upon the artist's imagination:

---

[2]"A Poem of Pure Imagination," in *Selected Essays by Robert Penn Warren* (New York: Vintage Books, 1966), p. 218.
[3]*Selected Essays,* p. 237.
[4]*Selected Essays,* p. 58.

...the tramp leaned his face down at me and showed his teeth and said: "Stop following me. You don't stop following me and I cut yore throat, you little son-of-a-bitch." That was what he said, for me not to follow him. But I did follow him, all the years.

Ultimately the encounter with the stranger-brother traces all the way back to Warren's earliest entry in all three of his *Selected Poems* collections, "To a Face in a Crowd," which was published in the June, 1925 *Fugitive* magazine when the signatures were hardly dry on Warren's college diploma. Its opening line, "Brother, brother, whither do you pass?" could—perhaps with a bit of stylistic enhancement—find easy lodging as a theme statement in any of the subsequent poems I have cited, including, at a half-century's distance, "Old Nigger on One-Mule Cart."

Correlating with Warren's critical pronouncements, his own images typically fall into a "dialectical configuration." To the figure of the stranger he therefore ascribes characteristics that accentuate the stranger's alienation from the Warren persona: differences in race ("Old Nigger on One-Mule Cart"), age and family connections ("Dark Night of the Soul"), or sex, nationality, and social position (*Audubon*). Further emphasizing their alienation is the nature of their momentary interaction, which ranges from the anonymous and ephemeral in "To A Face in a Crowd" to the hostile in "Dark Night of the Soul," and on to the near-homicidal in *Audubon* and "Old Nigger on One-Mule Cart." Much in the fashion of Melville's Ishmael and Queequeg, Warren's encountering figures must therefore transcend formidable interpersonal barriers before any human bond may develop between them. "Old Nigger on One-Mule Cart" comprises practically a tour-de-force in this respect, its juxtaposition of opposites being extensive enough to form the essential structure of this poem: white youth vs. old Negro; speed/dance/automobile vs. slow-motion/stasis/mule cart; winter/snow/cold/Vermont vs. summer/dust/heat/Louisiana; namelessness (opening lines) vs. "holding,...in my hand, a name" (closing lines); earthly limitations—dirt, sweat, flesh, time—vs. "the high stars" ("Can I see Arcturus from where I stand?"). To reconcile these contraries would for a fact be a task for "the philosophical poet," demanding very considerable resources in both poetry and philosophy.

What makes those resources available, for Warren, is his lifetime's work in the thought and craft of his poetic calling, giving any particular poem in his canon its indispensable infrastructure of meanings. Behind the freshly imagined material that gives each poem its individual integrity is the larger integrity of the poet's career as a whole, stamping the poem with the authority of his signature. So far as "ideas" or "philosophy" is concerned, "Old Nigger on One-Mule Cart" manifests the Warren signature first of all in the dualities we have noted, secondly in the problems of identity they pose, and finally in the (tentative) resolution of these problems via the Osmosis of Being concept. So far as "poetry" is concerned, Warren's signature discloses itself most significantly in the symbols and images that, embodying these conceptions, trace back in taproot fashion to earlier stages of evolution within the poet's developing canon.

Identity—to begin with Warren's master theme—is for him a split-level concept. *Ultimate* identity, as defined in his seminal essay "Knowledge and the Image of Man," subsists in the individual's union with the whole of reality, the "continual and intimate interpenetration, an inevitable osmosis of being, which in the end does not deny, but affirms, his identity."[5] A man wholly absorbed in Nature, like Audubon or "you" at the end of "Billie Potts," may experience this cosmic consciousness; or a person who simply falls asleep may attain it, like the woman in "Lullaby: Exercise in Human Charity and Self-Knowledge" (in *You, Emperors, and Others*): "Galactic milk spills down light years./ ... And your sweet identity/Fills like vapor, pale in moonlight, all the infinite night sky." In this latter instance, the woman's namelessness in sleep—"what I now bless/Is your namelessness" are the poem's closing lines—indicates her overcoming of separateness. But in the same essay, Warren goes on to describe the awareness of separateness as the basis of our conscious identities as human beings: "Despite this osmosis of being to which I have referred, man's process of self-definition means that he distinguishes himself from the world and from other men. He...discovers separateness."

Bridging the gap between Warren's two modes of identity is the experience of the epiphany, the moment when—as Warren describes it in *Democracy and Poetry*—"a glorious *klang* of being awakens to unify mind and body, to repair, if even for a moment, what Martin Buber has called 'the injured wholeness of man.'"[6] At the outset of "Old Nigger on One-Mule Cart," that experience is evoked by the rhythm of the dance, which—in the opening line—has already absorbed the separate identities of the dancers into that larger pulse of being indicated by their "nameless" condition:

> Flesh, of a sudden, gone nameless in music, flesh
> Of the dancer, under your hand, flowing to music, girl-
> Flesh sliding, flesh flowing, sweeter than
> Honey, slicker than Essolube, over
> The music-swayed, delicate trellis of bone
> That is white in secret flesh-darkness. What
> The music, it says: *no name, no name!*—only
> That movement under your hand, what
> It is, and no name, and you shut your eyes, but
> The music, it stops....

---

[5]"Knowledge and the Image of Man," in *Robert Penn Warren: A Collection of Critical Essays,* ed. John L. Longley, (New York: New York University Press, 1965), pp. 241-42.
[6]*Democracy and Poetry* (Cambridge: Harvard University Press, 1975), p. 74.

In the sound texture of these lines—the five-fold recurrence of "flesh" and "music," the pattern of recurring consonants, the strong insistent thrust of the rhythm—Warren clearly is approximating his poetic form to the motif of the dance; but more than that, he is illustrating the aesthetic principle whereby, according to *Democracy and Poetry,* the rhythm of an art form—of both poetry and music, in this instance—may lead toward the osmotic insight: "I must insist that even in literature rhythm—not mere meter, but all the pulse of movement, density, and shadings of intensity of feeling—is the most intimate and compelling factor. ... [It] binds our very physiological being to it in the context of the rhythms of the universe."[7]

In Warren's earlier poems, the dance has similarly figured as a motif of cosmic unity, evolving from a mere wish that "everything/Take hands with us and pace the music in a ring" in "The Mango on the Mango Tree" (1943) to a "moment of possibility" in "Gull's Cry" (1955): "But at your laughter let the molecular dance of the stone-dark glimmer like joy in the stone's dream,/ And in that moment of possibility, let *gobbo, gobbo's* wife, and us, and all, take hands and sing: *redeem, redeem!*" In their "nameless" condition, we may say that the dancers of "Old Nigger on One-Mule Cart" have realized their "moment of possibility," submerging their singular beings in a larger consciousness. But, as T. S. Eliot ruefully observed concerning the evanescence of the epiphany experience, "And after this our exile"—which is to say, in Warren's phrasing, "The music, it stops." In "Old Nigger on One-Mule Cart," Warren eases his persona's return to ordinary consciousness by allowing him to linger a bit in an intermediate stage, with "Booze in the blood," but the main part of the poem is now given over to the individual ego that, soberly conscious of its separateness, must earn its way back toward unity with others not by recourse to psychedelic stimulants but through developing an expanded perspective. Not the quick fix of alcohol and music but a slow lifelong toil of thought, art, and imagination would be the agency through which the world's fragmentation might be transcended, the dualities gathered, identity affirmed.

The artist at work is therefore the persona that unifies the rest of the poem, moving from "the urgency of experience"—as Warren's essay on Conrad puts it—to "the urgency to know the meaning of experience."[8] Warren himself is clearly the artist-persona who is conducting that search, following the pattern he established when he installed "R.P.W.: The Maker of this poem" as the presiding figure in *Brother to Dragons* (1953). Apparently encouraged to some degree by the Confessional movement of the 1950's, he intensified the personal presence in collections like *Promises* (1957), *Tale of Time* (1966), and *Or Else* (1974); and his latest volume, *Now and Then* (1978), I would judge his most poignantly personal volume of

[7]*Democracy and Poetry,* p. 74.
[8]*Selected Essays,* p. 58.

them all. In all these works, Warren bears out his thesis that "it is not only the objective characters that serve as 'models' of selfhood; the work itself represents the author's adventure in selfhood"; and further, that "the self is a style of being, continually expanding in a vital process of definition, affirmation, revision, and growth."[9]

As a paradigm in miniature of this intensely personal thrust toward meaning, "Old Nigger on One-Mule Cart" moves rapidly toward its center of meaning, the encounter that is this poem's version of Warren's most profound insight: the intuition of One Flesh. That doctrine was implicit in the gathering of creatures at the end of "Billie Potts" ("The bee knows and the eel's cold ganglia burn..."), became explicit in *Promises* ("all Time is a dream, and we're all one Flesh, at last"), and found increased eminence in the epigraph to *Incarnations* ("Yet now our flesh is as the flesh of our brethren"). "Old Nigger on One-Mule Cart" strikes up the theme in its first word—"Flesh"—which in its five-fold repetition underscores the "one Flesh" experienced by the dancing partners swaying to music. That experience in turn leads to the One Flesh of sexual intercourse ("sweat-grapple in darkness"), but this mode of self-transcendence, like that associated with the dance and the music, proves so fleetingly evanescent that "I can't now even remember the name" of the dancer-sexual partner. Again, the quick fix of sensual experience, though it has an undeniable integrity of its own, will not suffice as a substitute for philosophical insight.

In the encounter that does evoke permanent insight, we find two motifs of long and noble pedigree within Warren's total literary canon, both sustaining the One Flesh ideology. The first of these, in the poem, is the apparition of the mule's head, which recalls the "judgment of the cows" motif —one of the book's great charms, in my response to it—in *All the King's Men*. There in the novel, as here in the poem, the automobile—symbol of modernity, speed, the mechanical and inhuman (Warren was a charter-member Agrarian, we remember)—is periodically reduced to an image in an animal's eye. As Jack Burden describes a typical instance, "Now and then a pair of eyes would burn at us out of the dark ahead. I knew that they were the eyes of a cow—a poor dear stoic old cow with a cud, standing on the highway shoulder...but her eyes burned at us out of the dark.... We were something slow happening inside the cold brain of a cow."[10] Elsewhere in the novel a woman throwing water out the door of a shack or a Negro looking up from his cotton field at a car accident—"Lawd God, hit's a-nudder one done hit!"—comprises a variation of the theme. In the poem, the mule-head caught in the headlights conveys that sense of ageless, patient, all-enduring biological identity, held in common by man and beast. "From darkness and the saurian stew of pre-Time," Warren writes, "They blaze

[9]*Democracy and Poetry*, pp. 71, 89.
[10]*All the King's Men*, p. 53.

from the incandescent magma/Of mule-brain. Thus mule-eyes." Immediately there follows the most significant of all those images that lean from the world's wall, the image of the human face—which in this case manifests both individual human identity and the One Flesh doctrine.

That the human face manifests individual identity is a truism that Warren has often exploited skillfully in his fiction—we recall vivid verbal paintings of Sadie Burke's face, or Tom Stark's, in *All the King's Men*, for example, as well as Nick Pappy's encounter (in *The Cave*) with "the first human face...he had ever looked into. Really looked into, just for its humanness. At that, some bone-shaking happiness broke over him...."[11] In his poetry, the extension of the face motif toward the Osmosis of Being (or One Flesh) concept appears—for one example—in "Homage to Emerson" (1966), a seven-poem sequence that ends with the image of "a face half in shadow, tears...in the/ Eyes, but/...about to smile?" This is the poem's answer to the question, "What constitutes the human bond?" But Warren's most compelling conjunction of the face motif with the One Flesh ideology occurs in the context of the human creature confronting its imminent extinction; for in that moment of transition, when the individual yields back his separate identity to the biological continuum that created him, the One Flesh becomes manifest. This acceptance of personal mortality in deference to some larger collective Being first claimed major importance at the end of "Billie Potts," where the wanderer returns, after his journey in Time, to eternity's border: "To kneel/Here in the evening empty of wind or bird,/ To kneel in the sacramental silence of evening." It recurs in "Night Is Personal" *(Incarnations)*, where the deathwatch for the dying convict evokes the Osmosis of Being motif—"for we are all/One flesh"; and it converges with the face imagery in "Interim," one of the poems about the deaths of the poet's mother and black mammy in *Tale of Time*. Most importantly, the image of the human face confronting personal extinction comprises the central episode in *Audubon: A Vision* (1969). Here the dying woman's personal identity, as expressed in her will to die bravely, emanates from her face with the force of a solar flare, drawing Audubon's own identity into her last pulse of being:

> The face,
> Eyes a-glare, jaws clenched, now glowing black with congestion,
> Like a plum, had achieved,
> It seemed to him, a new dimension of beauty.
>
> There are tears in his eyes.
> He tries to remember his childhood.
> He tries to remember his wife.
> He can remember nothing.

[11]*The Cave* (New York: Signet Books, 1959), p. 291.

In "Old Nigger on One-Mule Cart," the parallel to this scene is another face that also, by reason of the impending car-accident, confronts its mortality: "Man-eyes, not blazing, white-bulging/In black face, in black night, and man-mouth/Wide open, the shape of an O, for the scream/That does not come." Later, having barely avoided the collision, the poem's speaker reconsiders that last detail: "Perhaps he had screamed, after all." As a spontaneous expression from the innermost citadel of self, the scream has figured importantly in Warren's identity-psychology. The scream of his mother upon learning of her lover's suicide gave Jack Burden, as well as the mother, a new identity in *All the King's Men,* for example; the motif also appears within the *Arcturus* poems in "Midnight Outcry," where "The depths that cry rose from might shrivel a heart, or member," in the listener-husband. And in "Ballad: Between the Boxcars" (1960) the cry of the crushed youth evokes the One Flesh theme: "And [when] our own lips utter the crazed organism's cry,/We may know the poor self not alone, but with all who are cast/To that clobber and slobber and grunt, between the boxcars."

In the self-portrait of the artist motif that now assumes predominance in the poem—a motif we have already traced to Warren's "Confessional" tendency of the 1950's—the artist's "urgency to know the meaning of experience" rises into immediate action. On the same night that the encounter takes place, the artist begins his work, waking in the insomniac fashion long typical of the Warren persona, at "the hour when the downy/Throat of the swamp owl vibrates to the last/Predawn cry, the hour/...[when] some/Recollection of childhood brings tears/To dark-wide eyes." This time, however, those usual night-images are displaced by the urgency of his artistic calling: "and I wake to see/Floating in darkness above the bed the/Black face, eyes white-bulging, mouth shaped like an O, and so/Get up, get paper and pencil, and whittle away at/The poem." The art-work, initially, fails embarrassingly—"[I] remember/Now only the couplet of what/Had aimed to be—Jesus Christ—a sonnet." But now, having evolved into "Old Nigger on One-Mule Cart," it reaches toward that concept of design which has often appeared to be Warren's chief objective as a philosophical poet: "[In] God's name, by what magnet, I demand,/Are the iron and out-flung filings of our lives, on/A sheet of paper, blind-blank as Time, snapped/Into a polarized pattern."

The polarized pattern, in this case, consists of the two journeys in Time that have separated the two wayfarers ever since the moment of their encounter. One wayfarer journeyed home to his shack to lapse into quiet sleep, while the other—the Warren persona—"Moved on through the years" to a faraway land, where he cannot sleep because of his hunger for meaning: "having risen/In darkness, feet bare to cold boards, [I] stare ...into/The white night and star-crackling sky over/The snow mountain." That hunger mounts to unappeasable proportions in the ensuing passage, where the speaker longs to immerse himself in the nightscape so as to extract its inner meaning by the main force of his desire, as it were:

> ...Have you ever,
> At night, stared into the snow-filled forest and felt
> The impulse to flee there? Enter there? Be
> There and plunge naked
> Through snow, through drifts floundering...
>
> Upward and toward the glacial assertion that
> The mountain is? Have you ever
> Had the impulse to stretch forth your hand over
> The bulge of forest and seize trees like the hair
> Of a head you would master?....

What answers that deep hunger for meaning is the completion of the "polarized pattern" whereby the two wayfarers attain psychic reunion despite their vast separation in time, distance, and worldly circumstance. Seen now as the speaker's alter ego or secret sharer, the Old Nigger provides a model of how to live and how to accept mortality. In so doing he reconciles the poem's dualities, gathering its images into the concluding phase of their "dialectical configuration" and thereby subsuming the speaker's restless hunger into his own final serenity. His face, just moments ago confronting death "with eyes white-bulging, mouth shaped like an O," is now "calm as prayer." Urinating with "soft, plopping sound in deep dust" while his face "Is lifted into starlight," he epitomizes in that stance the range and the reach of human identity, from animal need to infinite aspirations. In the end, he reconciles individual with collective identity, passing easily from his life's work into death's sleep, from his cart of junk into the shack to lie down in darkness: "The last glow is reflected on the petal-pink/And dark horn-crust of the thumbnail."

So the two wayfarers walk their last journey together: "Brother,...will you be with me when/I arrive and leave my own cart of junk/...To enter, by a bare field, a shack unlit?" Pending that moment, the Old Nigger has shown how to live, by answering a question raised in the "Homage to Emerson" poems (in *Tale of Time*): "there must be/A way by which the process of living can become Truth." The way "to convert life into truth"—to use Emerson's original phrase[12]—inheres in the cart of junk, the image of every man's life-work which is the truth that will go attesting to the life he lived after the life itself has ended. In the closing dozen pages of *Democracy and Poetry,* published the same year as the *Arcturus* collection (1975), Warren speaks of work (in this context, art-work) as the truest expression of identity, "an activity fulfilling the doer in the doing...in which the doer pursues

[12]Emerson uses this phrase in "The Divinity School Address."

the doing as a projection of his own nature upon objective nature." "What …would be created in the process of work would be a self," he goes on to say—an increasingly difficult achievement in our technocratic-commercialized world characterized either by too much "free" (which is to say, vacuous) time or by work in which no personal fulfillment can be realized.[13]

The old Nigger with his mule and cart of junk is the antithesis of this unhappy futuristic vision. He fulfills the definition of work that Warren traces back to the Garden of Eden myth:

> Even in this realm [after the Fall], he [Adam] might, however, still catch some painful and glorious glimpse of the old activity of the Garden—of the possibility of work as inner fulfillment.... First, by work he might sometimes impose his conception of himself—his self—upon nature in that he humanized his world. Second, what he achieved in this process—object, image, deed, or utterance—gave promise of being durable past his natural span. It was his redemption from death, the Horatian boast: *Non omnis moriar.* It was also a redemption into the fulfilled self.[14]

As against the fast-paced search for pleasure at the beginning of the poem, immersing the speaker "nameless" in the dance, booze, and sex, this concluding mode of identity—which yields "a name," "A hard-won something," a "trophy of truth"—is the Old Nigger's final legacy to his secret sharer, enabling him to accept his mortality with his hunger for meaning satisfied:

> Entering into that darkness to fumble
> My way to a place to lie down, but holding,
> I trust, in my hand, a name—
> Like a shell, a dry flower, a worn stone, a toy—merely
> A hard-won something that may, while Time
> Backward unblooms out of time toward peace, utter
> Its small, sober, and inestimable
> Glow, trophy of truth.

In the poem's terminal line, "Can I see Arcturus from where I stand?," the Warren persona adopts the stance earlier taken by the Old Nigger with face "lifted into starlight, calm as prayer." In these latter two phrases, Warren evokes both the extreme dualities he wants to reconcile—the human face beholding infinity—and the subtle but essential religious attitude ("calm as prayer") that alone can reconcile the human creature to his limitations as a finite particle within the incalculable whole of reality. Both the star imagery and the posture of humility have a long ancestry in Warren's verse, their earlier manifestations comprising two vital taproots for the present poem. A star reflected in dark water remarks the deaths of Billie

---

[13]*Democracy and Poetry,* pp. 84-85, 89.
[14]*Democracy and Poetry,* pp. 82-83.

Potts and Audubon; more generally, the stars are only "a backdrop for/The human condition" in "Star-gazing" (1966), but they instill fear of too much reality: "And the girl is saying, 'You do not look/At the stars,' for I did not look at/The stars. ..." *Brother to Dragons*—both the 1953 and the forthcoming re-written versions—expresses that fear of the universe with compelling force: "The stars are arctic, and/Their gleam comes earthward down uncounted light-years of disdain"; "the huddled stones of ruin/...say the human had been here and gone,/And never would come back, though the bright stars/Shall weary not in their appointed watch."[15]

Mediating between this cosmic immensity and the finite creature is the posture of humility that dates back, in Warren's verse, to "The Last Metaphor" (1931), where the denuded trees of autumn "rear not up in strength and pride/But lift unto the gradual dark in prayer." The kneeling posture, at death, of both Billie Potts and "you, wanderer" at the end of "Billie Potts" confirms the archetype, as does Audubon's attitude toward the birds he has killed in "Love and Knowledge": "Over a body held in his hand, his head was bowed low,/But not in grief." Rather than a meaningless waste, death now becomes sacramentally rendered, a sacrifice to the One Flesh continuum as Warren's deceased parents, speaking "with the calm of a night field, or far star," declare it in *Promises* (Poem I, To Gabriel): "We died only that every promise might be fulfilled." In *Or Else* (1974), this sacramental acceptance of mortality pervades poems like "Natural History," about two spectral parents gladly absorbed into nature, and "Sunset Walk in Thaw-Time in Vermont," about the Warren persona's own forthcoming entry into "the loving vigilance of death." And here, in "Interjection #6: What you Sometimes Feel on Your Face at Night," the mist—which is Warren's metaphor for the state of being dead (see "Fog" in *Incarnations*, for example)—is God's touch upon the face: "Out of mist, God's/...fingers/Want to memorize your face. ... God/Wants only to love you, perhaps."

The opening poem of the *Arcturus* collection, "A Way to Love God," ramifies this theme, its images of mortality—"your father's death-rattle," the severed head of Queen Mary of Scots, sheep staring blankly into mist—indicating anew that submission to one's death is a way to love God. In "Old Nigger on One-Mule Cart" the face "lifted into starlight, calm as prayer" effects that poem's statement of the theme, which is further sustained by religious diction elsewhere in the poem: the twice-stated "in God's name" and "the world's monstrous blessedness." Transmitted to the secret sharer in the terminal line of the poem, which in turn acts as the title image for the entire *Arcturus* collection, the face under starlight becomes the chief unifying, reconciling symbol for both "Old Nigger on One-Mule Cart" and the

---

[15]*Brother to Dragons* (New York: Random House; London: Martin Secker & Warburg Limited, 1953), pp. 95, 32.

sequence as a whole. In so doing, it performs the ultimate function of poetry as Warren conceived it at the end of his essay on *The Ancient Mariner:* "If poetry does anything for us, it reconciles, by its symbolical reading of experience (for by its very nature it is in itself a myth of the unity of being). ..."[16]

Elsewhere in the same essay, Mr. Warren raises the question, "on what basis may a poem be interpreted?," and answers that one must look for, among other things, "internal consistency" in the poem itself and "external consistency" in "the over-all pattern of other artistic work by the author in question."[17] Although "all critics must fail in some degree, for the simple reason that...the discursive activity cannot render the symbolical," his use of this approach produced a masterpiece of criticism for our modern appreciation of Coleridge. Our analysis of "Old Nigger on One-Mule Cart," while falling far short of that achievement, indicates that these critical principles furnish perhaps the best way to approach Warren's own poems. As we recall the prevalent images in this one poem—the dance, the encounter, the cart of junk, the scream, the polarized patterns, the face under starlight—and as we relate them to Warren's larger themes—the One Flesh motif, the *no name!*/name dichotomy, the artist's urgent hunger for meaning, the converting of life into truth, the acceptance of mortality—we find both "internal consistency" and connection with "the over-all pattern of other artistic work by the author in question." In this connection we also find a key reason why "Warren's greatness has been palpable"[18] in his recent volumes, to cite Harold Bloom's judgment. As our flower in the crannied wall has clearly shown, this poet's late-blooming garden of verse has been nourished by the growth, in previous decades, of a dense and deep-thrusting root-system.

[16]*Selected Essays*, p. 272.
[17]*Selected Essays*, pp. 269-71.
[18]Harold Bloom, "The Year's Books," *The New Republic*, November 20, 1976.

Psychology and Theme in
Brother to Dragons

by Frederick P. W. McDowell

Warren's novel in verse, *Brother to Dragons*, is most notable in its philosophy and psychology and summarizes vividly his continuing metaphysical and ethical themes. Aware in his moralist's zeal "that poetry is more than fantasy and is committed to the obligation of trying to say something about the human condition," Warren is in this work more than ever haunted by an anguished sense of the disparity in man between recurrent beatific vision and the ubiquitous evil which blights it. Accounting for the force of the book are Warren's realization of character, his flair for the arresting image and apt phrase, his evocation of situation and atmosphere, and his instinct for the telling structural contrast. Indispensable as are these aspects of literary talent to the precise rendition of value through form, they are all subordinate to Warren's tense brooding over human motivation and human destiny.

Despite his cavils against oversimplified abstract thinking in his critique of "The Ancient Mariner" and elsewhere, abstract speculation has come to absorb Warren. He has, however, eschewed the dangers he warns against— the abstract, the general, the universal is always related forcibly, even violently, to the concrete, the particular, the local. Warren achieves a sensible, sometimes drily pragmatic balance, then, between the relative and the absolute, the mutable and the permanent, the fact and the archetype. In *Brother to Dragons*, the combined reflections of the several interested persons, including the author as R. P. W., yield a valid disinterested truth, since its roots are in their immediate experience. The localizing of his narratives in history achieves a similar purpose. Viewing dispassionately the dilemmas of individuals in history, Warren has a specific perspective upon which to focus his ranging intelligence. To reach exact definitions of elusive moral and metaphysical values, to reach befitting conclusions as to the provenance of good and evil, Warren also utilizes in *Brother to Dragons* an incident from out of the past, one drawn from the annals of the Jefferson family.

The central figure in this episode is Jefferson's nephew, Lilburn Lewis, who, after his mother's death, butchers his Negro valet, George, when the latter breaks a pitcher once belonging to the mother. Since a maniacal self-love and a maniacal Oedipus complex consume him, Lilburn must at all costs secure vengeance for an imputed spiteful violation of his mother's memory by George and the other household Negroes. The senselessness of Lilburn's crime and the sinister forces it epitomizes all but overwhelm the hapless idealist, Thomas Jefferson, who had not, in his aspiration, fully considered the evil in all men. With his eventual if somewhat reluctant attainment of a more valid knowledge—presupposing right reason, infused by the spirit, or else creative imagination, informed by the sense of fact— he is then able to effect a fruitful reconciliation between aspiration and reality, between the disparities, in general, of his experience. As a result, he achieves wholeness of spirit.

Warren is even more insistent in *Brother to Dragons* than in his other work upon the transforming influence of the true spiritual principle and the nefarious influence of perverted spirituality. Both Lilburn and the early Jefferson illustrate a familiar pattern in Warren's work: the individual's search for spiritual peace by side-stepping his inner difficulties and by subservience to an abstract ideal only indirectly related to them. Unable to find peace within, through his lack of internal resources and through his too easy disregard of the truths to be found in religious tradition, such an individual searches for it too aggressively outside the self—in the empirically derived configurations of his experience or in nature. From these sources, he seeks some kind of absolute which can always command allegiance, but an absolute personally defined and designed to further his own interested motives, whether he will admit to this tacit hypocrisy or not. Such anodyne for inner insecurity is only temporary since too much is expected from it. Unless conversion to a different mode of being has finally occurred, disillusionment and violence rather than meaningful insights into reality result from a quest thus histrionically self-centered and self-sufficiently pursued. The aborted spirituality which may derive from such activity often has dire consequences, since if prideful man alone provides the measure for all values there is nothing to prevent him from going to any length, even to crime, to make his vision prevail. Barring a conversion from such self-righteousness, the typical Warren character is unable—or unwilling—to lose his soul to find it.

In purport *Brother to Dragons* does not depart markedly from Warren's previous work, but its exacerbated tone and persistent undercurrents of violence reveal Warren's increasingly urgent sense that the provenance of original sin is universal and that it is inescapable. The potential acedia of spirit resulting from our possible despair at such a prospect Warren condemns, however, at the same time that he shows how little room there can be for complacent acceptance of human nature as it is. If human nature in itself is seen to be ultimately monstrous, and if we are lost in its labyrinthine fastnesses, there can also transpire, through the accession of Grace, an enlargement of our possibilities beyond those predicated by any superficially optimistic philosophy. The succinct definition of these possibilities and of the positive values that man, in his fallen condition, may yet embrace is Warren's most distinctive achievement in *Brother to Dragons*.

I

A psychology which distorts the facts of experience by assimilating them into a self-generated obsession betrays Lilburn Lewis. Consumed by Oedipal attraction, he idealizes Lucy Lewis and makes of mother-love a worshipful abstraction, to be put forward regardless of the consequences. This intense, abstract benevolence ultimately leads to crime, enforcing Warren's judgment that this is a tragedy of "our sad virtues." In Lilburn we see the most frightening aspect of our moral history, that all too often "evil's done for good, and in good's name" and that a single-faceted idealism can be tragic. Lilburn has made no compact with the devil, Warren says—he has not had to go that far afield. He has only had to follow the good impulse, love of his mother, to be corrupted. If, after his mother's death, Lilburn had been humble in his sufferings, he might have escaped the degradation which ensues when he insists that all others revere his mother's memory as he does. When the household Negroes, in particular, seem to forget Lucy Lewis, Lilburn's fury works at odds with the affection that prompts it. He finds to his horror that love diminishes to the degree that he asserts it strenuously and desires to preserve it intact. In its place, injured pride and fear lest the organizing principle of his life be destroyed now fanatically motivate him. Like the Ancient Mariner in Warren's interpretation, Lilburn is the victim of self-deception as to his own motives, judging the morality in an act in terms of its advantage to him while pretending to be dispassionate. The good impulse, conceived in self-interest apart from Christian restraints, can become through its induced intensity more uncontrollable than calculated evil and eventually more destructive. When self-knowledge or "definition" eludes Lilburn, he adheres to his mistaken idea of the good and does the worst. Following a reductive principle, Lilburn tries, with fearful results, to define the human, to give order, violently, to chaotic flux. In such wrenching of the spirit to preconceived ends, all hint of humility evaporates. Such eager defense of his self-locked love for his mother from contamination in the outside world blinds Lilburn to his mother's greatness of soul and causes him more and more to fix upon the letter of his affection for her.

To implement this ruling devotion to his mother's memory, Lilburn develops a passion for the pure act motivated by the pure idea and untouched by embarrassing reality. Afraid that the facts might rout his cherished ideal, he raises it above them to an absolute and assures himself that its importance justifies his realization of it beyond the limits of the ethically permissible. "The dear redemption of simplicity" in such abstracted activity becomes his solace despite its untruth and the anguish it fosters. To others, the gratuitous act inspired by unreasoned fervor is forcible but not ethically justifiable. When they then react sharply against it, Lilburn is only the more confirmed in his self-righteous vision.

Lilburn's desire for others to meet his impossible standards prevents, first of all, a normal sexual relationship with Laetitia. Something she describes as "awful" transpires in their relationship shortly after their marriage. Though we are not told definitely what has happened, some sort of sexual violence has undoubtedly occurred. Lilburn seems to force the apparently inexperienced Laetitia against her will and then holds this fact against her, particularly after he compels her the next night to tell what she thinks has happened. Irrationally, he resents the fact that she is spoiled at his own hands and would not remain "pure" despite her helplessness before his violence. His "angelic" Laetitia is an ordinary mortal after all; she has, he is sure, liked stepping in "dung." Shock from her violent experience deepens in Laetitia to frigidity, so that, after the mockery of their marriage, she cannot respond to the husband whose contempt for her increases nor help him when he most needs her.

Because obsessive love for his mother excludes the possibility of other emotional commitments, Lilburn uproots the love that might have steadied him after her death. After he spurns Laetitia, he becomes yet more tortured, more unfeeling, more inhumane. He beats his servant George, whom Lucy sent out to bring him home following a three-day drunk when Laetitia had disappointed him. Having resisted the affection of Laetitia and George before Lucy's death, he is led, in his overwrought fixation upon his mother, to repudiate, after her death, both Aunt Cat and his hound. Since these two love him most unquestioningly, he derives sadistic pleasure from senselessly repulsing them. Poetic justice is served when they betray him after his crime—though such betrayal is paradoxically also Lilburn's "deepest will"—the dog unwittingly, Aunt Cat by clever design. By killing love, Lilburn attains "the desiderated and ice-locked anguish of isolation" which then frightens him, a security breeding insecurity. He asks love, yet he cannot bear to be loved, since it magnifies his guilt; he must then destroy what disturbs him. Symbolic of his confusion and incipient degradation is Lilburn's hatred at his mother's grave for the encroaching grass which destroys her memory among men. In view of the raw, cold, cruel, pure fact of his love, he wishes her grave to remain bare and open as a fresh wound, to be a perpetual reminder to him of his loss.

In order to break through to a reality whose force, however, diminishes in proportion to his frantic efforts to reach it, Lilburn is led, Macbeth-like, from one crime against man and nature to others still more harrowing. Now that any other love except that for his mother seems desecration to him, he instinctively kicks the hound which comes fawning to him at the grave. The resulting rapture of conflicting joy and sorrow brings catharsis in cruelty for his festering grief. When he kicks the hound the second time, Lilburn is not surprised but soothed. Distraught by his mother's image, he feels no joy "of the soul's restoration" in reconciliation with the hound. Terror and violence besiege the homestead, while the Negro victims counter with supernal cunning. He rages inwardly and broods upon insatiate revenge, trusting that inward force will vindicate the self by vindicating what the self most reveres.

At no time does Lilburn question the rightness of his acts, since their absolute rationale forbids any vacillation. The only necessity he now feels is to remain true to the light within, to a self-appointed destiny. Defining thus expeditiously his own necessity, Lilburn resembles Warren's other uncritically self-confident characters like Slim Sarrett in *At Heaven's Gate,* Willie Stark and Adam Stanton in *All the King's Men,* and Jeremiah Beaumont in *World Enough and Time.* Like them, once Lilburn tastes the spiritual security inherent in a self-generated absolute principle, he has no power to remain aloof from its demands. To compensate for deficient inner resources, which had earlier made him discontented with the frontier, he now enshrines at all costs the ideal which orders his life. In contrast with his previous states of incertitude, Lilburn is now perfectly adjusted, if occasionally still unsure of himself. As he waits for the "thrilling absoluteness / Of the pure act to come," Lilburn is unaware of the price he has paid for this assurance, the snuffing out of intervening benevolent instincts. Forcible and self-willed, he abrogates the intelligence and attains to a ruminative peace like that which any monster might feel, sunk deep in nature, such peace as Warren depicts in his poem "Crime" as "past despair and past the uncouth / Violation." Linked to Lilburn's superhuman surety is the motionless, insensate catfish with its brute face and complacent adaptation to the channel-mud as it hibernates under the Mississippi ice. In his complete harmony with amoral nature, of Lilburn as well as of the catfish it might be said, "How can there be / Sensation where there is perfect adjustment?" The result is that Lilburn is unconscious of the barbarity of his crime, since his own nature justifies it.

His crime moves him one step nearer a more perfect realization of self as he has been able, delusively, to define it. The fact that he has now completely left the world of actuality behind him is implied in his inability to kill a huge moth which comes in the window and which distracts him only momentarily from concentrating upon his vision of his self-imagined destiny. With the help of Isham after the crime, he awaits then, in his half-joyful abandonment to the currents of the self, the grand hour when he can still more completely fulfill his nature, "the hour of the Pentecostal intuition." In his impatience, he moves to bring this time about more quickly when he gets Isham to agree to a mutual death pact. Because Lilburn savors the full pleasure of this abstracted moment—the grandest of moments because the farthest removed from the distracting realities of life—and because he wishes to enjoy to the full his "sweet alienation" and the sense of injustice done him previously, he counts slowly while Isham stands before him with a pistol. He then betrays Isham by himself not firing, since he knows that the law will take care of Isham. Monomania induces the "death of the heart," despite the fact that a heart too sensitive to confront the reality had induced the monomania.

II

At a more intellectual level, Thomas Jefferson in Warren's view is also initially motivated by the oversimplified abstraction. His ruling passion is the idealistic destiny he foresees for man, for he grasps the fact that man in his median position between God and beast aspires to the God-like. He is too anxious, however, to believe this aspiration exists pure, and he discounts too readily and vehemently the beast-like within man, as he himself admits later. Subscribing to this self-defined "rational hope" and leaping beyond man's "natural bourne and constitution" to envisage his glorious future, Jefferson denies, until too late, the discomfiting reality. At first, he looks upon the evil in man as a blot upon his shining nature, which the centuries have all but erased. With its clean lines and simple harmonies, the Romanesque cathedral at Nîmes is a symbol of ideal human fulfillment and of Jefferson's noble vision. If man would but strike off his shackles, his divine innocence would then "dance" amid the oppressive realities of the world which tend to stifle it. Because one must struggle with some of the realities of the world to attain to inner integrity, one cannot, as Jefferson tends to do, deny them all. "The eternal / Light of just proportion and the heart's harmony," which Jefferson so insatiably hungers for, is, accordingly, ironically extinguished in his fanatical craving to achieve it. As Warren presents him, Jefferson is, in his early phase, as fervent in his idealism and as insensitive to pragmatic realities as Jeremiah Beaumont in *World Enough and Time*. As a result, Jefferson cannot see that he desires too unmixed a good, impossible under the imperfect conditions of this world, just as Jeremiah Beaumont cannot see that if his antagonist, Cassius Fort, once did evil he might yet be, on the whole, a good man. Neither character realizes until he has been inexorably reoriented by tragedy that beatitude for man— a partial realization at best of all that he aspires to—is possible only through humble contrition and dispassionate love. Such a transcendence of reality must be earned through suffering, through divine Grace, instead of merely being asserted by the intellect as a cherished aim.

Warren shows how close Jefferson's psychology is to Lilburn's, despite their different purposes in life. Both seek to define the human through the self-determined abstraction, and both wish to assert an innocence consonant with it. Both lack in large part a sense for tangible realities, and both become enslaved to an overpowering vision. Both are romantic in that they tend to transform by wishful thinking things as they are into what they are not. As with so many of Warren's misguided characters, they both wish a too easily attained coherent explanation for an essentially incoherent world. Hate, the result of a naive emotionalism in Lilburn's case, and nobility, the result of a misguided intellectuality in Jefferson's, are, as Warren explains, but different "thrust[s] toward Timelessness, in Time." The only valid motivation, Warren implies, is just the opposite: with one's intuited sense of the eternal, one must work toward time, the actual, the objective, and bring one's sense of the ideal always back to the reality. Life without saving illusion is a mockery, but a life given over to furthering at all costs the self-righteous illusion can be calamitous. Neither Jefferson of the early hopeful stage nor Lilburn could realize that the "impalpable" is not the ideal and that the ideal, in becoming too nebulous and disembodied, is in danger of being distorted.

The difference between Jefferson and Lilburn is in sensitivity, the contrast Warren had made memorable in *World Enough and Time* between Jeremiah Beaumont and Skrogg. Despite the fact that he meets a violent death, Jeremiah could ultimately be saved in a spiritual sense after a wasted life because he had spiritual receptivity, whereas Skrogg had deliberately snuffed out his soul. This kind of sensitivity also underlies the bluff exterior of Jack Burden in *All the King's Men* and allows him finally to decide between the conflicting claims of the illusion and the reality, of the self and the world of other men. The education of a misguided protagonist to the truth is thus a constant theme in Warren. In *Brother to Dragons* both Lucy Lewis and Jefferson are educated by tragedy, Jefferson the more slowly because his mistaken vision is so inflexible. Jefferson's conversion from a restrictive idealism to a more integral view of life is the chief situation explored in this verse-novel. It is significant that Lucy Lewis, reborn through her death—the result of her inability to cope with reality—redeems Jefferson by making him aware of realities outside those apparent to the intellect when it perceives only what it is interested in perceiving. For most of the novel, Jefferson is in the first period of his redemption—when he has become disillusioned with his earlier ideals and has come to realize the universality of evil in men. Only at its end, through Lucy's intervention, does he reach a decisive spiritual poise and the second period of his redemption —when he can acknowledge original sin without recrimination.

In the first stage, Jefferson is haunted by the fact that human nature too often turns its back upon the glories of which it is capable to revel instead in the evil act. Like Lilburn, Jefferson lacks to a large degree the spiritual reserves, the stabilizing philosophy he needs to combat the evil which destroys his perfectibilist vision. Heartfelt joy in his vision leads to Jefferson's sense of betrayal, then, when one of his own blood, through the absolutely evil act, extinguishes it. Trying to order reality according to his own ideals, Jefferson continually fails to grasp the circumstances under which it may be ordered. Like Jeremiah Beaumont or Adam Stanton, Jefferson at this point both overemphasizes and underplays the intellect: he worships an intellectualized abstraction while disregarding the critical function of reason except as it reinforces his interested idealism. Jefferson becomes bewildered, disillusioned, almost cynical in outlook. In this phase, this induced pessimism is so powerful as to becloud his earlier humanism. In a world where evil is apparently supreme and obliterates by greater force the serene good, Jefferson even comes to feel that violence alone gives truth. He now assumes that "all values are abrogated in blankness," and he reproves his sister for not having struck George after he had returned from Lilburn's beating. At this stage, Jefferson does not understand how close this counsel is to that suggested to Lilburn by his own unleashed nature before the crime. From Lilburn's brand of violence Jefferson had, indeed, recoiled in loathing. The fact that redemption often derives from violence through the polar connection existing between a strongly negative evil and a strongly positive good does not justify this counsel of Jefferson's to Lucy, although he is right in feeling that the violence he recommends is preferable to the inertia of Charles Lewis, for example. Jefferson does not perceive, moreover, that Lucy's inability at this point to conquer pride and assert the love which inwardly prompts her is her real sin and the ultimate cause for her son's tragedy.

In his first stage of regeneration, Jefferson cannot see past the fact of human evil, which has paralyzed his soul. In his obsession with its prevalence, he is as unreasoning in his denial of aspiration as he had been devoted to it previously. At a time of crisis, the inflexible philosophy of life, whether it stresses demonic pride in Lilburn or angelic aspiration in Jefferson, fails to comprehend the complexities of experience. In recoil from the reality he misunderstood, Jefferson now condemns love as "but a mask to hide the brute face of fact, / And that face is the immitigable ferocity of self." Unrealistic also is his present despair over humanity itself: "I'd said there's no defense of the human definition." This agonized pessimism is actually as intense and as uncritical as the optimism of his unregenerate days had been.

Since he has had to relinquish the perfectionist enthusiasm which motivated him at the First Continental Congress, Jefferson now recognizes "the darkness of the self" and its labyrinthine wilderness. At the height of his dreams, he had been realist enough to acknowledge the fact of evil, but he had tried to minimize it. He knew from his reading of history, for instance, that there lurked horror in its "farther room" and that the act and the motive are not always ballasted by the good deed and the good intention respectively. He also had known that all men are not innocent despite his belief in Innocence as an ideal. His disillusion, however, makes him perceptive where he had been merely suspicious. Correctly but reluctantly gauging evil, even if unnerved by it to an unreasoned denial of the good, he now sees that it can be passive, since all things come to it and seek it out in magnetic attraction. He sees the lurking beast within us all, a minotaur to be found at the last turn of the spirit's labyrinth. This beast, "our brother, our darling brother," is not, in Warren's view, to be denied by any mere effort of the will; his insidious promptings can be finally overcome only by effort of the will if one can force himself to make it. Like Pasiphaë with her unnatural lust, we can become enamored of our evil. This Jefferson now sees. At the height of indulgence, we catch, like her, in the same sneaking way, a glimpse of our beatific innocence in childhood, and thereby rationalize our evil acts. Except for the reductive premises in each case, Jefferson's initial vision of man's preternatural innocence was the obverse of Pasiphaë's. She was evil but rationalized her evil by the fleeting vision of the innocent good, while Jefferson thought of man as innocent only to find him besmirched with evil. Thus the lie was given to Jefferson's earlier "towering definition, angelic, arrogant, abstract, / Greaved in glory, thewed with light." That earth's monsters are innocent in their lack of knowledge Jefferson had always realized; but that man, capable of knowledge and self-definition, could be a "master-monster" and exhibit only a blank, ignorant innocence Jefferson had not realized. Neither had his nephew, Meriwether Lewis, comprehended "the tracklessness of the human heart" until the facts of experience forced him to do so.

Now that his original conception of man has been proved wrong, Jefferson would have stressed the truth about man at all costs, he asserts, had he known then what he knows now: he would have run with "the hot coals" of that truth till they had burned through his flesh to the bone. That evil is progressive, that one deed of horror can poison all else, is Jefferson's sickening conclusion. When he still tries to cling tenaciously to "the general human fulfilment," he finds that violent evil obtrudes in his thoughts and proliferates emotionally. In his near-hysteria, therefore, Jefferson looks upon Lilburn's deed as the reigning archetype of human psychology, as the microcosm of the evil which infects all hope and which lies like a cloud and curse over the land he had once loved. To Jefferson, all social injustice and all crime are, in fact, somehow inherent in the fall of the meat-axe, in the fact that his nephew could commit his crime and that other people might commit similar crimes. That one must not only shudder at evil but try actively to understand it Jefferson doesn't realize until later, nor the fact that suffering, in some degree, atones for it. He is impatient at its persistence, failing to see that it can be only partly overcome and that one must not shirk the struggle to master it.

The second stage of Jefferson's education provides the poem with its central meaning. Under the guidance of Lucy Lewis, Jefferson accommodates his original resplendent vision of man's nobility to the actual facts of human existence, especially to the cardinal fact of original sin, and mitigates the harsh abstractness of this ideal with the exertion of his sensibility. A grander nobility than Jefferson's initial conception consists, Lucy claims, in testing that conception in the world. His redemption is assured when his faith in the Idea is renewed, once a "deep distress" has humanized it and once he relates it to mankind. The dream—or idea—of the future, Jefferson concludes, requires for complement the fact of the past:

> Now I should hope to find the courage to say
> That the dream of the future is not
> Better than the fact of the past, no matter how terrible
> For without the fact of the past we cannot dream the future.

Since lack of self-knowledge is original sin in either Lilburn or Jefferson, and since complete self-knowledge is impossible, original sin is universal, and we are all implicated in it and with each other. As a gesture indicating he now understands that he and all men are involved in Lilburn's crime, Lucy insists that Jefferson take his hand. Evasion will no longer do, for Jefferson can't escape our universal complicity in sin, "our common crime," as Warren phrases it in "End of Summer." As commentator on the action, "R.P.W." stresses throughout our complicity in the tragedy. It contains us, he says, and it "is contained by us," for we in our fallen condition are all guilty of it in being human. We are guilty, furthermore, in being too complacent about evil, since we are only too anxious to adjust ourselves comfortably and snugly to it. As to the crime which so unnerves Jefferson, R.P.W. explains that it is not so special as he thinks. It is but one episode in the long pageant of man's sinfulness down the ages and is "impressive chiefly for its senselessness" as all evil acts tend to be. The earthquake which followed the crime struck fear into the hearts of guilty men who had had no knowledge of Kilburn's act—they were simply guilty of it by extension, by being human, and by being capable in their worst moments of kindred atrocity. Guilt is common enough, therefore, to make any one day appropriate for the Judgment, even as this present hour would be. R.P.W. expresses, however, the ironical fear that the modern age might be too "advanced" to pray for deliverance from its guilt or to fear God's wrath, just as men in 1811 had got used both to the repeated quakes and to the "horror" of being men. In any event, Jefferson's complicity in original sin through his use of black labor to build that citadel of freedom, Monticello, is real, if at first unacknowledged by him. The fact that evil exists should not attract us nor repel us, but should interest us since we all are, for better or worse, involved in it. When the evil is done is the question R.P.W. would explore, for all who face up bravely to life must solve that question, must analyze the anguish and the agony involved in bringing the evil act to its full birth. Unless we have that curiosity, we can never attain to saving knowledge, R.P.W. would insist.

In a noble speech Lucy tells Jefferson that she in her love brought disaster to her son, just as he in his aspiration brought disaster to Meriwether Lewis. "Our best gifts," she says, carry some ineradicable taint, and we corrupt even as we freely give—Jefferson like Lilburn has done evil in the name of good by interfusing his altruism with pride of self. This burden of our shame should always confront us, and while it should not inhibit us, it should make us bestow our gifts with humility. Lilburn's face, Jefferson must realize, is but a "mirror of your possibilities." To the criminal we are linked by the terror we all must feel at our own demonic propensities which, without our careful scrutiny, will project outward into the evil act: Lilburn's last indefensible hour is simply "the sum of all the defensible hours / We have lived through." Jefferson has squelched his fear that he, too, might be capable of all evil in being capable of any evil. As R.P.W. expresses it, Jefferson had forgotten that even the wicked man seeks God according to his own lights and fulfillment as he can find it. Along with his disillusion and his cynicism, Jefferson is forced to see that his rejection of Lilburn is too summary. Now that his confidence in himself and in his Utopian dreams has been shaken through Lilburn's crime, Jefferson rejects his nephew principally out of pique. There is some truth, then, to Meriwether's charge that Jefferson had originally contrived his "noble lie" for his own comfort and to feed his own vanity. Jefferson has a sure sense for the horror of Lilburn's crime, but hardly sees, in his revulsion, its application to himself:

> For Lilburn is an absolute of our essential
> Condition, and as such, would ingurgitate
> All, and all you'd give, all hope, all heart,
> Would only be disbursed down that rat hole
>   of the ultimate horror.

In commenting upon the action and characters, R.P.W. insists that evil—at least its germ—is universal. Modern Smithland, a village near the site of decayed Rocky Hill, is to Warren a symbol for universal sin and universal suffering, by virtue of the sin and suffering it does contain. The minotaur-in-labyrinth image, so forcibly presented by Jefferson early in the poem, also becomes a symbol which dominates the poem in vividly suggesting the lurking evil in the dark heart of man. In greater or less degree, all the characters in the poem sin, and they all suffer because they cannot transcend their failings and emerge completely from the darkness of their inner selves. None of them are as wholly innocent and glorious as Jefferson had initially imagined the men at the First Continental Congress to be; rather they all resemble his colleagues as Jefferson describes them in a revised estimate:

> lost
> Each man lost in some blind lobby, hall, enclave,
> Crank cul-de-sac, couloir, or corridor of Time.
> Of Time. Or self: and in that dark no thread…

Lucy Lewis, radiant as she is, is prevented by pride from making toward George in his suffering the spontaneous gesture which would alleviate it and result in her own fulfilment: "the small / Obligation fulfilled had swayed the weight of the world." Similarly, Laetitia is prevented from making toward Lilburn at Lucy's death the gesture which would gain his love forever through her willingness to forgive his past violence to her. Actually, Laetitia had in part willed Kilburn's violation of her, and in one sense, therefore, merits the scorn of her husband for imputed impurity—at least she could not, and hardly wanted to, tell Lilburn to stop. Betrayed by her innocence into a fascination with the evil she shrinks from, Laetitia in her psychology at the time of her defilement by Lilburn is not unlike Pasiphaë, as Warren describes her, at the time of her submission to the plunging bull.

Our common complicity in evil Warren elaborates upon still further in his analysis of Laetitia's brother, of Isham, of Aunt Cat, and of George. Laetitia's brother is indignant when he learns that Lilburn had forcibly used Laetitia, and he proclaims loudly how sweeping would have been his revenge if he had known. Laetitia acutely says that he would not have avenged her out of love, but out of pride at accomplishing the deed—at best, out of desire to protect the family honor. Aunt Cat, Lilburn's colored mammy, really loves him, but in her love there is calculation too, manifested for years in the silent but tense struggle between her and Lucy Lewis for Lilburn's affection. To a degree she also merits what she gets when Lilburn, in a fit of fury at the time of his mother's death, pretends to disgorge the black milk he had been nursed upon. Isham, too, is as guilty of George's butchering as his brother, for Isham knew instinctively what was going to happen and did nothing to prevent it. In that he seemed half-willing to meet his fate, George was, in some part, an accomplice in the deed. He almost wills, with obscene pleasure, the fatal stroke, and seems more in love with the "sweet injustice to himself" than fearful of death. Even though he keeps running away, George is also drawn back hypnotically again and again to Lilburn in a continuing attraction-repulsion pattern. R.P.W. admits this notion of George's complicity is, in some degree, fantastical, since nothing can really excuse Lilburn's crime. But R.P.W.'s observations are true, he would assert, to the extent that "we're all each other's victim. / Potentially, at least."

III

Jefferson has failed to see, in short, that positive good presupposes positive evil, that the two are closely related, and that Lilburn's motivation is really the need, as R.P.W. maintains, "to name his evil good." That moral and psychological values are complex Jefferson is unwilling to admit, because of his zeal to preserve the integrity of his vision. That ambiguity is the indispensable feature of the moral life, that philosophical truth is to be measured in terms of an adjustment of the discordancies of experience, that illusion must be squared with a multiform actuality has somehow escaped Jefferson, as it had also escaped the unintellectual Lilburn. In describing the crime, R.P.W. had addressed the night as a symbol of the absoluteness of vision that Lilburn—and Jefferson—aspired toward. The night would obliterate in its uniform blackness "the impudent daylight's velleities," that is, the concrete actualities of our experience. Once they are obscured, it is tempting to define the Absolute by an interested exertion of the will alone rather than by the vigorous reconciliation of the Many to the One. The mixture of good and evil in humanity is something that Jefferson had realized in his intellect, but he had not given the concept his emotional assent. Jefferson's psychology is essentially too simple—in his disillusion he rejects, for instance, the innocence of the newborn babe because of the evil that human nature can also perpetrate. He then denies the generous act because it can never exist pure, because it is always tainted inescapably by the self. The omnipresence of malignant evil disturbs his inner poise to the extent that he all but denies the worth of the ideals he had once cherished. Though love, for example, has an admixture of pride in it and is scarcely ever disinterested, Jefferson fails to see, notwithstanding, that it is truly estimable. The all-or-none point of view is thus pernicious in overlooking the truth that every act and emotion carries within it not only its own impulsions but its contrary possibility. A fervently accepted good, therefore, has more possible evil in it than a lukewarm virtue, while an unabashed evil carries within it latent violences that augur the possibility of heartfelt conversion.

Every act, moreover, implies a choice among motives for it to become the act, implies a resolving of "the essential polarity of possibility" contained within it. The act has a finality "in the mere fact of achieved definition," therefore, a degree of purity and simplification at variance with its confused intent. Even though such choice among motives is made and a large degree of purity is thereby attained, the act still carries within its secret core other latent impulsions. If it represents a simplification of our swarming experience, the origins of the act are never clearcut, but rather a "hell-broth of paradox and internecine / Complex of motive." It must, accordingly, be exhaustively analyzed, not merely accepted at its apparent value for the relief it brings the doer. Lilburn's evil deed, for instance, must be judged not only for its destructiveness but also as misguided creation. The wicked man, says R.P.W., is, after all, but seeking for his crimes some outward rationale which the good man would term God.

The paradoxical substratum underlying all our acts is variously emphasized in the poem. One aspect of the tangled nature of reality is suggested by Charles Lewis—though Warren shows more contempt for him than for anyone else—the fact that madness is "the cancer of truth" and has more affinity with the actuality than has a deadened complacency. For this same reason, Warren values violence more highly than timid conformity to convention. Even Jefferson realizes this truth when in his disillusion he says that "all truth is bought with blood," except that he then is too much obsessed with the blood to realize that violence is only one avenue to renewal. At the very least, violence will exorcize unreality, will expose the fraudulence of "the pious mind" to whom "our history's nothing if not refined." Only when violence is pursued with self-interest, as with Lilburn, does it become the supreme evil. Since reality is thus elusive and multiple, R.P.W. maintains that a balance of qualities, educed by the supple intelligence, is the essential of wisdom. Grace, pity, and charity we all need from God, but that does not mean that free-will can be set aside. The glorious possibility acknowledges the despair which hems it round, and derives its strength from that honesty. But it does not give in to this pessimism. The complexity of existence is again emphasized when R.P.W. asserts that it is through isolation that we grasp "the human bond" and at length define the self—in "separateness," Warren has declared in his poem "Revelation," "does love learn definition"—while at our peril we reject our fellow man completely. If we withdraw from society to gain a greater inner irradiation, we must, thus fortified, return to it and seek our place in it. Failure to see that a personally determined moral code has weight only when it comprehends the self in relation to other men was, after all, Jefferson's original mistake as it had also been Lilburn's.

Of the many ambiguities explored in the poem, the most striking concerns the natural world. On the one hand, Warren stresses the malignancy and impersonality of nature. The fact that the white inhabitants have unfairly wrested the land from the Indians places a curse upon it, so that moral unhealth hangs like miasma over the wilderness, and its shadows enter the souls of the pioneers. Both sons of Lucy Lewis come under its dark spell; both have become victims of "the ignorant torpor / That breathed from the dark land." After his crime, moreover, Lilburn feels only at home in "the unredeemed dark of the wild land." Raised on the edge of the wilderness, Jefferson had also come to feel over and through him "the shadow of the forest," sinister and foreboding. Even then, he had felt that man must redeem nature, for nature is too harsh and unfeeling for it to serve as moral ministrant to erring, aspiring man. As she did in 1811, nature will likely as not visit mankind with earthquakes, floods, and sickness to add to his discomfort and perplexity. As measure of her hostility to living creatures, she causes the dog-fox to drown in protracted agony in a flood, or she causes the oak tree, like Jacob, to struggle all night in anguish with "the incessant / And pitiless angel of air." In a perfect adjustment to nature, there is either overplus of misdirected feeling or inability to feel at all. In its "idiot-ignorance" nature obliterates the purely human and the moral law which alone can educe the human. Feeling strongly this need for other than naturalistic values in their undiluted form, Warren asserted in his poem "Monologue at Midnight" that "Our mathematic yet has use / For the integers of blessedness." The grandeur of nature, Warren maintains in the concluding lines of the verse-novel, can give us an "image" only for our destiny, but can in no sense give us a "confirmation" of it. That must be sought from within the soul itself.

If nature "as an image of lethal purity" is a symbol of evil, it is also a symbol of reality and truth; it is both malignant and beautiful, soul-be-numbing and life-inspiriting, giving rise to heartfelt joy despite the infinite darkness at its heart, as Warren also tells us in "Picnic Remembered." The beauty of the springtide upon the untracked forest, its "heart-breaking new delicacy of green," is an emblem of such ambiguity. If we follow the promptings of nature too closely, we can lose our humanity; but, paradoxically, it can also assuage our sufferings deriving from the evils which follow the loss in others of that humanity. By making such men contemptible and insignificant in comparison with its power, it can comfort us for the violence and cruelty they may instigate. It can bedwarf even the monstrous and endow us with the vital energy that can alone enable us to transcend the "human trauma." Lilburn is as if driven onward by the raging wind, as if in the whirlwind of senseless force. Yet if he is so closely part of nature, it is only by escaping from him out into "the glimmering night scene" that we can regain proportion and sanity. After his crime Lilburn, so much a part of nature in his unrestrained violence, can no longer respond to its spiritual influence. He inhabits then a somber inner landscape "of forms fixed and hieratic," and abjures the promiscuous promise of joy in newly wakening nature.

Nature is in essence spiritual and a source for deep reality provided its power is used to strengthen the innately spiritual and not substituted for it. Warren can say, therefore, that in spite of "all naturalistic considerations" or because of them, we must believe in virtue—nature can both extinguish the human impulse and reinforce it. We ought not to regard nature abstractly by naming its objects out of their context, for they are more than mere names: they are symbols of inner spiritual facts, so that a snake is really a symbol of evil, violence, darkness, and terror, though science would call it only "Elaphe obsoleta obsoleta." Such a rationalist approach to nature impoverishes it, yet Warren's earlier emotional fervor for it, as recounted in the poem, is also unreal. The joy he had felt as a boy in holding tight the objects of the sense provides an easy faith that cannot last. Neither an easy nor an exclusive faith in nature is tenable, yet Warren does quote Lucretius to the effect that the order underlying nature, the ranging of natural phenomena under natural law, may dispel the "darkness of the mind" and lead to inner light. A true knowledge of nature, fortified by our sense of the human, can dispel our morbid fears and the darkness and terror that haunt the innermost soul of man, while an unconditioned emotional response to its promptings can intensify those fears and that darkness and terror. Man is at once part of nature and above it, and should, in his adjustments to it, be mindful of this paradox. A security or joy obtained, like Jefferson's, by a denial of inconvenient natural fact is as reprehensible as Lilburn's blind immersion in nature.

IV

More than any of his other poems, *Brother to Dragons* represents a mature if sometimes muted statement of Warren's own values. From his narrative Warren elicits certain conclusions about human life which he is always careful to clothe, however, in the specific symbol or to educe from the concrete situation. While for Warren the absolutes of tradition have an independent existence, he avoids sentimentality and provides for their inevitable definition by allowing them to emerge from a specific milieu.

Chief among these positive values is glory, which alone makes life worthwhile, fearful as the experience of it may become. It is a dynamic spiritual harmony, the exaltation attendant upon salvation, the sense of being attuned to both the natural and the supernatural. Failing to cultivate such a mystique as it illuminates his experiences, man fails to live as deeply as he could, Warren asserts. Despite this truth, it is with reluctance that we face the necessity of being saved, of surrendering ourselves to the radiance of glory and permitting it to determine the quality of our lives. As the chief reality in our lives to be reverenced, glory will, once its provenance is admitted, reorient us positively: "for it knocks society's values to a cocked hat." Glory is what the soul is best capable of, contrasting with the abstract idealism which becomes hardened to formula and withers rather than elicits the potentialities of the soul. If we are identified with all other men in guilt, we are also identified with them in their troubled aspirations after glory.

To know the farthest reaches of the spirit demands an emotional sensitivity toward others, a realization that it is fatal only to love and to love well, and not to love well enough. In these terms Lucy Lewis describes her own failure with respect to the family tragedy. Unable because of fear to extend her hand to George in kindness and love, she soon collapses physically and morally. Her death retributively follows her inability to live the life her instincts countenance. Because she fails in love toward George, she fails in love toward her son. She learns that love is the most valuable human trait and represents "definition"; once expressed it can never again be denied, unless one would die spiritually, the same point that Warren had made in his poem "Love's Parable." As we have seen, Laetitia does not love Lilburn enough, either, to minister to him at the time of Lucy's death. She is right in feeling that a change of heart in herself would have availed her husband; in her pride, however, she is unregenerate and cannot attain to selfless love. Lilburn is in a sense betrayed by the women who love him—Lucy, Laetitia, and Aunt Cat—because they do not love him strongly enough to stand by him when he needs them most and to instruct him in "the mystery of the heart." In the modern age, we also deny ourselves too often to others. As we speed down the highway, we can too easily forget, for instance, the loveless eye, which glares at us from a hovel and reminds us of our inhumanity; we merely press the accelerator "and quick you're gone/Beyond forgiveness, pity, hope, hate, love."

Closely allied to Warren's reverence for both love and glory is that for virtue and its concomitant, humility. There is no possibility of our not believing in virtue, for our conscience is always with us and will not be silenced, Warren asserts. Virtue is tougher and more "remorseless" than any of our other attributes, for it isolates the human amongst the other forms of life. Virtue, if disregarded, will lie in wait murderously, like "the lethal mantis at his prayer," to pounce upon the heart that denies it. It is also the necessary rationale for all human anguish. Without anguish, virtue could not be so clearly delimited as to command our absolute allegiance: anguish gives to virtue its local habitation so that it does not become intolerably abstracted from reality:

I think I begin to see the forging of the future.
It will be forged beneath the hammer of truth
On the anvil of our anguish. We shall be forged
Beneath the hammer of truth on the anvil of anguish.
It would be terrible to think that truth is lost.
It would be worse to think that anguish is lost, ever.

Virtue purifies from pride and induces in the more sensitive characters of the poem needed humility, a sacramental vision of the universe such as the regenerate Ancient Mariner also embraces in Warren's interpretation of the poem. Through thus dying to the self, real selfhood alone will be achieved, says Warren in his own poem. As to Jefferson, he remains cynical until Lucy can prevail upon him to cease dwelling upon the outrage of Lilburn's crime and to accept him. When he finally acknowledges Lilburn, the pride inseparable from the judging of another by one's own standards disappears. Jefferson then attains the humility needed for the inner balance his near-hysteria had heretofore destroyed. The other chief characters, Laetitia, Lucy, and Aunt Cat, are, as we have seen, all prevented by varying kinds of pride from being true to their instinctive sympathies. Only when they accept in humility rather than reject in pride are they serene. The forms of pride, Warren argues, are many and treacherous. Even the act of forgiveness stems in large part from injured self-esteem, and allows us to placate the wounded self. Heroism, declares the knowledgeful Jefferson, this time speaking for Warren, is more often motivated by pride in putting down the monster than by any altruism. The usual hero is potentially more evil than the monsters he vanquishes, because vainglory encourages him to reject normal human limitations in an aggrandizement of self: "man puts down the bad and then feels good," says Warren. The black snake that R.P.W. sees outside at Rocky Hill is not only the traditional symbol for the evil and violence that have brooded there, but it is conversely a symbol of the fact that forgiveness for such evil is necessary, of the fact that by humility and love we gain wisdom to oppose the influence of furtive evil. Like man at his ideal moral and spiritual fulfillment, the snake both forgives and asks forgiveness.

An activist cluster of values also informs the poem. As members of the human race, Warren insists, we must be morally responsible—our connections with other men are so subtle and so pervasive that we deny them at our peril. Because we are all in some degree the victims of history and of our environment, we have no right, Warren alleges, to disavow responsibility:

For if responsibility is not
The thing given but the thing to be achieved,

> There is still no way out of the responsibility
> Of trying to achieve responsibility
> So like it or lump it, you are stuck.

Jefferson's rejection of Lilburn is simply his rejection of what is unpleasant, says Lucy, Warren's mouthpiece. In his presentation of Charles Lewis, Warren even more directly inculcates the need to assume gratefully and without evasion our responsibilities. Lewis had fled his moral obligations in Virginia in the hope of finding peace in a new land; but since he brought his inner weakness and hollowness with him, he is, if anything, more at loose ends on the frontier than he had been in Virginia. By his repudiation of family responsibility, his descendants are left, without light, to degenerate on the frontier.

Coming to Kentucky to seek reality, to become once more "part of human effort and man's hope," Charles does not find it because his soul is shrivelled. After Lucy's death, Charles in fact sometimes thinks he is empty so that he is surprised to find his footprint in the earth. At that time he feels relief, as well as sorrow, that he need no longer seek reality. It demands too much uncomfortable effort now that the one person to whom he was in any way real has gone. He hopes that her remains will rot quickly "into the absolute oblivion" and that she may soon be the nothingness he has already become. He goes back to Virginia to fulfill a barren, hollow destiny amid the artifices of civilization where the reality—as well as the stark evil—of the dark land will not so rudely challenge him, where he will be safe from disturbing violence, and where he can pursue, unimpeded, a materialist "success." Like his nephew Meriwether, Charles Lewis had also found that the foulness of savage men had more vitality than the artifice of "civilized" man, but Charles lacks the vigor to break out of his moral torpor. He cannot escape the lie he lives because he brings it with him from Virginia to the Kentucky wilderness. The milieu he fled, he sees, is intolerable simply because it had nothing intolerable in it. His desire to find some new "tension and test, perhaps terror" in the West is thwarted because he tells the only lie that a man cannot embrace and still live, "the lie that justifies." Lilburn and Jefferson—and in his wake, Meriwether Lewis—also tell the lie that justifies. Tragic violence, disheartening disillusion, and suicide are the respective results. This kind of lie is simply a rationale for irresponsibility: in each case, the critical sense, or, as R.P.W. calls it, "a certain pragmatic perspective," is lacking.

The effort of the will to achieve definition is ultimately necessary if the individual is to attain spiritual clarity. One cannot arrive at the reasons for George's anguish and Lilburn's degradation by thought alone, says the reborn Jefferson, but one must create the possibility for such a reason by a directed resolution, wherein strength is modulated by charity. This, the only knowledge worth possessing, is so elusive as to be almost impossible to possess fully. Understanding—even understanding a crime—requires an active exertion of the will, not merely a passive analysis by the intellect. One cannot define abstractly the inscrutable, but one must participate, at least vicariously, in its manifestations: "what is any knowledge / Without the intrinsic mediation of the heart?" Above all, we have to realize that such intuitive sympathy demands that we also acknowledge, unflinchingly, the worst that can happen:

> We must strike the steel of wrath on the stone of guilt,
> And hope to provoke, thus, in the midst of our coiling darkness
> The incandescence of the heart's great flare.
> And in that illumination I should hope to see
> How all creation validates itself,
> For whatever you create, you create yourself by it,
> And in creating yourself you will create
> The whole wide world and gleaming West anew.

To translate idea into action demands a courage which Warren's characters do not usually possess, though they may recognize its desirability. Lucy and Laetitia, for example, are unable to realize in actuality what their hearts tell them is right. Warren says that bravery is the quality which counts most, for only those who meet moral tests without cowering have a true knowledge of life. The reasons which prompt the Lilburns to evil will become apparent alone to those who have striven, for they alone will be aware of the suffering involved in translating the evil impulse into the actual evil act. Warren, as we have seen, quotes Lucretius to the effect that, in dispelling the "darkness of mind," the law and aspect of nature is needed: this implies a patient perusal and endurance of the tests it offers. Stoic endurance is also necessary for the expunging of vanities: it is needed, for example, says Warren, in accepting our fathers' reconciliations to experience, which we can do only when we do not set ourselves above our fathers and when we can accept our own failure to achieve their triumphs. Recounting his experiences in the West, Meriwether Lewis stresses how greatly fortitude was required, a quality, moreover, which eluded him in his own adjustments to life. His sentiment that "pride in endurance is one pride that shall not be denied men" is surely, in its clear emphasis, Warren's own. Aunt Cat also illustrates the tenacious fortitude that Warren values so highly, for she has the stability which permits her to survive to a ripe old age, to outlast the rest of the people at Rocky Hill who are either physically dead or blighted inwardly.

Warren is poised in his general view of things between an outright pessimism, which is most intense when due to self-dramatized frustrations, and a too easy optimism, which feels it can control to its own advantage the conditions of life. Warren is pessimistic to the degree that he feels life is possible only because we do not have to face realities too often. He condemns both Lilburn and the earlier Jefferson for not facing them at all, yet he knows also that mankind cannot stand too much reality. Life is possible only because of its "discontinuity." A partial glimpse of the truth is about all that we can ordinarily endure. Otherwise the pressures upon us might cause us to go mad. In the conduct of life, discretion is all-important, for it is an outward sign of inner balance. Jefferson's ultimate reasoned position and, by extension, Warren's own is a qualified optimism or a meliorative pessimism: "we are condemned to some hope," says Jefferson at the last to contrast with the fulsomeness of his earlier utterances and with the blackness of his intervening despair. The fact that Grace is possible, that a modicum of knowledge may be attained, that tentative definition is possible implies that a constructive point of view is, in part, valid. Extreme optimism [and] extreme pessimism are both false since they both falsify the facts. Warren is not sure, however, how far he ought to stand from either pole. Lucy Lewis is his avatar: the spaciousness of her personality, superior to both transient enthusiasm and soured despair, induced in the slaves under her control an enthusiastic loyalty which to them—and to Warren— represented a serenity that transcended in value their love for her and her love for them.

Exploration of Value:
Warren's Criticism

by John Hicks

Let me confess at once that I speak with a friendly voice of the critical writings of Robert Penn Warren. It is not fair to approach, or to reproach, him with clichés of expectation drawn from the fact that he is often labeled a "New Critic." He is both apt, and a bit plaintive, when he says: "Even the 'New Critics,' who are so often referred to as a group, and at least are corralled together with the barbed wire of a label, are more remarkable for differences in fundamental principles than for anything they have in common."[1] Those of us who remember the New Humanists might very well call Warren a new New Humanist. The values which he embodies in his criticism are humane and humanistic.

> Intelligence, tact, discipline, honesty, sensitivity—those are the things we have to depend on, after all, to give us what we prize in criticism, the insight. Insight into what? Into many different kinds of things, for those qualities may function in many different perspectives. Those qualities may give an insight into the nature and meaning of the thing being criticized, into the process by which it came to exist, into its relation to the world it came from and now exists in, into its value as a celebration of life.

Matthew Arnold would have said "criticism of life," rather than "celebration"; but with the same intention. The insight that Warren strives for is a moral one, and the end to which all his critical writing moves is moral—not didactic nor moralistic, but a search for moral value: ordered, symbolized, but not abstracted.

There is no real development in a collection of Warren's critical essays, only expansion. The choice of terminology may shift a little. But we do no

"Exploration of Value: Warren's Criticism" by John Hicks. From *South Atlantic Quarterly,* LXII (1963), 508-15. Copyright 1963 by Duke University Press. Reprinted by permission of the publisher.

[1]All quotations are from Robert Penn Warren's *Selected Essays* (New York: Random House, 1958).

injustice in taking the body of Warren criticism as one extended discourse, from any part of which we may justly derive a hint or a word of a quotation to fill out the following exposition. Equally in treating fiction or poetry, Warren's end is to discover, to unfold, or to reconstruct the thematic center around which a work has unity and symbolic validity. He seeks to hold clearly before himself and his reader the operative symbol by means of which a story or a poem illuminates for the reader some vital awareness: not a set of abstractions or allegories, but an immediate intuition with massive and multiple implications—in other words, "the value as a celebration of life." What he means thereby will be clarified by noticing his beliefs concerning the process of literary creation.

Warren insists upon an organic creative process. He refuses to think of a poet as a contriver of verses and images and impressive lines; or of the fiction writer as a deviser of plots and scenes and descriptions. Both have value only as explorers into hints of meaning implicit in life and personal experience. They are solvers of human problems, discoverers of vital symbols that will hold in imaginative suspension the most significant aspects of life itself.

> Actually, the creation of a poem is as much a process of discovery as a process of making. A poem may, in fact, start from an idea—and may involve any number of ideas—but the process for the poet is the process of discovering what the idea...means...to him in the light of his total being and his total experience. Or a poem may start from a phrase, a scene, an image, or an incident which has a suggestive quality...the symbolic potential. Then the process of the poet is the process of discovering why the item has caught his attention in the first place—which is simply another way of saying that he is trying to develop the symbolic potential. ... What comes unbidden from the depth at the moment of creation may be the result of the most conscious and narrowly rational effort in the past. In any case, the poet always retains the right of rejecting whatever seems to violate his nature and his developing conception of the poem. And the process of rejection and self-criticism may be working continually during the composition of a poem.

The principle of composition as search and discovery applies equally to fiction. Of Katherine Ann Porter, for example, Warren speculates as to her habits of composition:

> a section here and a section there have been written—little germinal scenes explored and developed. Or scenes or sketches of character which were never intended to be incorporated in the finished work have been developed in the process of trying to understand the full potentiality of the material. One might guess at an approach something like this: a special, local excitement provoked by the material—character or incident; an attempt to define the

nature of that local excitement, as local—to squeeze it and not to lose a drop; an attempt to understand the relationships of the local excitements and to define the implications—to arrive at theme; the struggle to reduce theme to pattern.

The work done in creative revery, the discoveries, the rejections, the choices and the dead ends, are stages of the constant search for the "meaning" which was intuited or guessed at in the germinal ideas or sounds or words or scenes with which an artist embarked. "In this state of concentration certain things float into his mind; but these things are *unwilled,* for he cannot deliberately summon up any particular item; if he knew what to summon up, his work would already be done....He can, however, reject by *will* whatever items are unsatisfactory, and he continues this process in the gradual envisagement of what he is creating."

In a superficial sense, what the author searches for is his story or poem or novel. But how will the author know that he has achieved it? Here we return to Warren's persistent test question: What is the integrating center? What is the moral and structural focus?

Imaginative writing should achieve complete integration about a center. The center is variously described; each writer has his own peculiar methods, forms, and achievements. The writer may so enrich a character that he becomes a massive symbol, toward which the significance of all other characters, actions, and motives is oriented. He may work about a theme or an idea which, placed in the creative context, reveals a potential for illuminating significant areas of human experience and human need: "The philosophical novelist, or poet, is one for whom the documentation of the world is constantly striving to rise to the level of generalization about values... for whom images always fall into a dialectical configuration, for whom the urgency of experience, no matter how vividly and strongly experience may enchant, is the urgency to know the meaning of experience."

The grandeur or impact of the imaginative creation is not superficial. "We do not get any considerable emotional impact unless we sense, at the same time, some principle of organization, some view, some meaning. This does not go to say that we have to give an abstract formulation to the principle or view or meaning before we can experience the impact of the work, but it does go to say that it is implicit in the work and is having its effect upon us in immediate aesthetic terms." To rest short of the vital symbol, to substitute for it the inadequacies of specific allegory, is to fail imaginatively: "When we read a poem merely in terms of a particular application of the attitude involved in it, we almost always read it as a kind of cramped and mechanical allegory. [A good work, rightly read, defines, on the contrary,] an attitude, a basic view, which can have many applications. It defines, if it is a good poem, a sort of strategic point for the spirit from which experience of all sorts may be freshly viewed." "Grandeur inheres in the fact that the artistic work shows us a parable of meaning—how idea is felt and how passion becomes idea through order."

Warren does not make a split between literature and life, between material and form. So far as I know, he never chooses to discuss either poetry or fiction as an isolated construction having its meaning in self-oriented aesthethic values. The end toward which he moves is always: What are the human values, and how are they made the controlling center by use of symbol or image or theme? Questions of technique are a small but integral part of his literary criticism, and then only because form and style and structure are rooted in the total or symbolic meaning. Style or form or structure have value only as parts of the whole expressive creation: "It is, of course, just and proper for us to praise Miss Porter for her English and her artistry, but we should remind ourselves that we prize those things because she uses them to create vivid and significant images of life....we would balance praise for the special with praise for the general, praise for subtlety with praise for strength, praise for sensibility with praise for intellect."

The obverse is equally bad—to praise content at the expense of form: "This is a dangerous distinction in practice, for it tends to lead to an arbitrary definition of form, to a conception corresponding to Coleridge's notion of 'superimposed form' as opposed to 'organic form' or Blake's notion of mathematical form as opposed to living form. ... And it is a very dangerous and narrow conception of form that would equate it with mere syllogistic deployment of argument in a poem, with neatness of point and antithesis, or consecutiveness or realism or action."

An inadequate writer is not in command of all his resources, not sufficiently scrupulous to follow his germinal idea to its full development, fully rounded, and refined of irrelevancies, however rich may be separable elements and parts. Thomas Wolfe most clearly exemplifies for Warren an inadequacy as to centrality of idea or symbolic concentration. The failure does not remain one of subject matter only; it must inevitably become a failure of form and style as well.

> It is possible sometimes that a novel possessing no structure in the ordinary sense of the word, or not properly dominated by its hero's personality or fortunes, may be given a focus by the concrete incorporation of an idea, or related ideas. Now, *Of Time and the River* has such a leading idea, but an idea insufficient in its operation. The leading symbol of the father, old Gant...is not the total expression of the idea.... [Wolfe] attempts to bolster, or as it were, to prove, the mystical and poetic vision by fusing it with a body of everyday experiences of which the novelist ordinarily treats. But there is scarcely a fusion or a correlation; rather, an oscillation.... Mr. Wolfe is astonishingly diffuse, astonishingly loose in his rhetoric. ... Mr. Wolfe has not been able to compensate for the lack of a fable....

Since, as I said before, Warren does not make a split between literature and life, "value as a celebration of life" does not arise from simplicity, but from clarity wrought of complexity. The terms *irony* and *paradox* are especially meaningful to Warren. As he insists in "Pure and Impure Poetry," the writer must earn his imaginative discovery and wholeness by submitting his symbol and his vision to the destructive trials of dialectic, of irony and logic and paradox. The values which can not only endure a context of difficulty, but in the process even illuminate that context, are the values to be cherished. "The poet is like the jujitsu expert: he wins by utilizing the resistance of his opponent—the materials of the poem. In other words, a poem, to be good, must earn itself. It is a motion toward a point of rest, but if it is not a resisted motion, it is motion of no consequence. ... the good poem must, in some way, involve the resistances; it must carry something of the context of its own creation; it must come to terms with Mercutio." His praise of Katherine Ann Porter carries this same burden:

> There is the same paradoxical problem of definition, the same delicate balancing of rival considerations, the same scrupulous development of competing claims to attention and action, the same interplay of the humorous and the serious, the same refusal to take the straight line, the formula, through the material at hand. ... her irony is an irony with a center, never an irony for irony's sake. ... It affirms...the arduous obligation of the intellect in the face of conflicting dogma, the need for a dialectical approach to matters of definition, the need for exercising as much of the human faculty as possible.

Significant life itself, he holds, is a "concern with the fundamental ironical dualities of existence."

As I read Warren's *Selected Essays* in chronological order, I realize how powerfully one human value problem dominates his thinking: the existentialist problem of alienation and communion. His concern may be typified most succinctly in his praise of Conrad's *Nostromo* in its image of man's precarious "balance between the black abyss of himself and the black outward abyss of nature."

> Wisdom, then, is the recognition of man's condition, the condition of the creature made without gills or fins but dropped into the sea, the necessity of living with the ever renewing dilemma of idea as opposed to nature, morality to action, "utopianism" to "secular logic"...justice to material interests. Man must make his life somehow in the dialectical process of these terms, and in so far as he is to achieve redemption he must do so through an awareness of his condition that identifies him with the general human communion, not in abstraction, not in mere doctrine, but immediately. The victory is never won, the redemption must be continually re-earned.

The same theme, sometimes less obtrusive but still the same, will be found in discussion of the work of Welty or Hemingway, Faulkner or Coleridge.

The most exhaustive, if not the most impressive, examination of this problem of human alienation and communion is Warren's search for Coleridge's integrating symbols in "The Rime of the Ancient Mariner," in his essay "A Poem of Pure Imagination." For Warren, ultimate value lies in an artist's achievement of adequate symbolization and realized idea in this moral realm: man's human predicament, poised between self-loss or alienation, and self-gain or human (and perhaps natural) communion.

Herein lies the "value of the celebration of life" which the artist finally shapes when he is most powerful. "What good fiction gives us is the stimulation of a powerful image of human nature trying to fulfill itself, and not instruction in an abstract sense." This symbolization need not take the form of realistic writing, though most of Warren's chosen subjects could be broadly classed as realistic. Rather, the spiritual reality of the symbols and the ideas are all that Warren demands in this dimension.

Has my exposition so far failed to fulfil your expectations? You may have supposed that I would tell you how Warren goes about practicing criticism, what machinery he calls into action, or what program of procedure he follows. Instead, I have tried to clarify his criterion of artistic achievement in poetry or fiction.

But criticism in Warren's hands is neither programmatic nor mechanical. It is protean—or to be more artistically precise, it is plastic: he thinks of the evolution of a work of art as plastic. Starting from a germinal idea, scene, or suggestion, the artist evolves a creation out of himself, his world, his dreams, chance materials. The creative mind could not drive straight to its goal as to an X on a map; the goal itself is what the imagination has to search for. To follow the artist, through his workings to his end, is the task of the critic. Beginning naïvely, simply opening himself to any effect whatever that the poem or fiction has to offer, the critic tries also to follow plastically.

Warren's methodology, if we call it that, consists of moving back and forth inside the poetry or the fiction, picking up this detail, this phrase, this rhythm or character, and putting it with that one—all with the aim of achieving the "immediate and intuitive awareness" in which integrating ideas and symbols have their imaginative impact, without having first to be sliced into concepts and precepts. "Every new work is in some degree, however modest, wrenching our definition, straining its seams, driving us back from the formalistic definition to the principles on which the definition was based." "The perfect intuitive and immediate grasp of a poem in the totality of its meaning and structure—the thing we desire— may come late rather than early—on the fiftieth reading rather than on the first. Perhaps we must be able to look forward as well as back as we move through the poem—be able to sense the complex of relationships and implications—before we can truly have that immediate grasp."

Perhaps, after all, Warren's method is mere haphazard? If one finds himself puzzled in a Warren essay—especially in his long essay on "The Ancient Mariner"—has one, or has Warren, become lost in Warren's restless moving back and forth within a work or in a writer's body of work? As he moves, he feels free to pick up any instrument or material that helps the penetration at any point. In his search he utilizes logic, biographical information, context in history or society, stylistic and formal analyses. He calls to witness writings other than the one under examination, or he has resort to ideas current at a time relevant to his subject.

I do not think this is haphazard. I regard his criticism as self-conscious and self-governed. In the concluding pages of "A Poem of Pure Imagination," Warren himself states the principles of control to which his restless moving back and forth are answerable: "The first piece of evidence is the poem [or fiction] itself. And here, as I have suggested earlier, the criterion is that of internal consistency. If the elements of a poem operate together toward one end, we are entitled to interpret the poem according to that end." But "considerations [also] force on the critic the criterion of external consistency…in regard to the intellectual, the spiritual climate of the age…the over-all pattern of other artistic work by the author in question… the thought of the author as available from non-artistic sources…the facts of the author's life.…treated as conditioning factors, as factors of control in interpretation, the considerations named provide invaluable criteria."

The act of criticism does not lie in "stating discursively" what an imaginative work means; the successful imaginative work is massive in its implications, and too condensed for discursive summary without violating the richness of the imaginative object as experienced. Mere allegorical "interpretation" "does little to carry us toward the 'kernel' or 'concept' or root-attitude of the poem, which, it is true, we can never wholly frame in words but which it is the business of criticism to carry us toward." Carry us *toward*, he says: for however complex is the exploratory process, Warren always believes that he is leading a reader by criticism toward the work itself, which finally, and after however much preparation, he can only experience immediately and intuitively *for himself.*

The Burden of the Literary Mind:
Some Meditations on Robert Penn Warren
As Historian

by William C. Havard

I

The October 7, 1962, issue of the *New York Times Book Review* reported the answers of six prominent critics to the question, "Who's to take the Place of Hemingway and Faulkner?" One of the respondents, W. M. Frohock, replied, "Obviously we are thinking about novelists. Otherwise I would take Robert Penn Warren. His reputation is entrenched: superior novelist, able poet, really fine critic. But don't the novels go down hill after 'At Heaven's Gate' and 'All the King's Men'?" The reply is perhaps typical of the critical attitude toward Warren; a profound respect for the diversity of his accomplishment is compromised by a skeptical attitude about the possibility that the man can really do so many things so well. The dubious compliment to Santayana which acknowledged him to be the best poet among philosophers and the ablest philosopher among poets is implicitly applied to Warren in this reluctance to accept him as a master in any single literary genre. The reluctance to give Warren full marks is not, however, due solely to doubts about his omnicompetence. It derives in part from the accepted fact that Warren is a *philosophical* novelist. It is not sufficient for some commentators to assess the extent to which Warren's philosophical interests are intrusive and thereby tend to impair the quality of his fiction; a number of critics impugn the philosophical activity itself in the name of a purity which sparsely disguises a behavioral substitute for philosophy.

When Warren published his *Legacy of the Civil War,* in 1961, with the appropriate subtitle "Meditations on the Centennial," it soon became apparent that to his dimensions as a poet, novelist, and critic would have to be added his measure as a historian or philosopher of history. On the whole the historians have accepted his incursion with less equivocation than the literary critics. T. Harry Williams notes, for example, that "It is...a most valuable book, because these are the meditations or conclusions not only of a man who knows American history but of a sensitive literary artist who knows life. Mr. Warren has said more meaningful things about the central event in our national record than many an author has managed in thrice that spread."[1] And C. Vann Woodward, who of all contemporary American historians has the closest affinity with Warren in terms of intellectual concerns, obligations arising from the conditions attached to being a southerner, and felicity of prose style, has received him graciously, and on Warren's own terms, into the professional guild. Woodward reminds us that

> Warren was a historian before he was a poet or a novelist. His first book was a biography of John Brown. All of his novels and much of his poetry have dealt with historical themes or with characters and events in historical context. One of his major professional problems has been to define the relationship between history and poetry, to defend his use of both, and to reconcile the sorts of truth they seek and the kinds of sense they make.[2]

In assessing any philosopher's contribution a critical commentator will find it necessary to deal with his work as a whole, because philosophy is precisely the effort to synthesize diverse experiences and specialized knowledge at the highest level of generality. And so it must be with a philosophical novelist and quondam historian like Warren. This statement should not be taken, however, to imply either that there is no development in his work or that Warren is a self-consciously systematic philosopher. The first of these problems may be left to the literary critics. The second question—whether Warren is systematic in his philosophy—may not for our purposes be so easily dismissed. Of course Warren is not a systematic philosopher in the strict meaning of the term. In choosing the literary forms of poetry and fiction as the media for his philosophical inquiry, he implicitly spurns systematization because the special demands of these forms must take precedence over the traditional forms of philosophy. Even so, the choice is in itself related to the substance of his philosophical endeavor because it reveals a point often made explicit in his work—the interconnectedness of all things. In fine, certain philosophical truths, and these perhaps the quintessential ones for Warren, can only be realized and communicated

[1] In a review in the Baton Rouge *Morning Advocate,* September 17, 1961.
[2] C. Vann Woodward, "Reflections on a Centennial: The American Civil War," *The Yale Review,* L (1961), 483.

through forms originating in the imaginative experiences of the poet or novelist. Richard Rovere has identified the specific obligation which attaches to the artist who approaches reality in this way: "In Warren's view, it is man's thorny lot in life to pick up the tangled skein of good and evil and untangle it as best he can. Warren also believes, or writes as if he believes, that it is art's responsibility to lend man, the untangler, a helping hand."[3]

Warren's uses of history bear a similar relation to the whole. He is not a historical novelist who is also a philosophical novelist; he is rather a novelist who accepts historical experience as fundamental to philosophical understanding as that understanding is unfolded through the creative imagination. Robert Heilman has stated this proposition more clearly in the following comment on *World Enough and Time:* "Warren sticks to the central method of his other three novels, digging up a pretty well preserved skeleton of action from recent history, covering it with the flesh of imaginatively conceived story, and giving it the life of human (supra-historical) meaning."[4]

By giving to history full human—or supra-historical—meaning through the philosophical unification of different modes of experience, Warren avoids the charge of historicism. It is possible to infer from Warren's repeated pessimistic treatment of man's public life an acceptance of the idea that all collective action eventuates in historically predetermined failure. The general feeling aroused by the novels that the introspective awareness of individual freedom of will is a delusion soon dissipated by contact with the intractable conditions of the world is often made explicit by one or another of the fictional characters who are protagonists in the philosophical dialogue. In the...novel, *Wilderness,* for example, Aaron Blaustein represents this view. He defines himself as a worshiper of history, since all you can fall back on is history if you stop worshiping God. He then goes on to ask, "Do you know what History is?... It is the agony people have to go through...so that things will turn out as they would have turned out anyway."

Although Blaustein is clearly symbolic of the negative or pessimistic form of historicism—a *reductio ad absurdum* of Hegel and Marx—his is not the final word. That is left to the hero of the story, Adam Rosenzweig, the crippled Bavarian Jew who had come to America to fight in the Civil War for an ideal of freedom in the name of all mankind, who had been disillusioned at every point of contact with historical reality, and who yet maintained the core of his faith and his will to action, even though his choice of means and his ultimate expectations were modified by the wisdom of experience. Moreover, Adam does not emerge with a baseless exis-

[3]Richard H. Rovere, "Salute to Robert Penn Warren," *Harper's Magazine,* CCI (1950), 103.
[4]Robert B. Heilman, "Tangled Web," *Sewanee Review,* LIX (1951), 107.

tentialist conviction that man must simply endure. The hope survives, sustained by a glimmer of rationality, that meaning may be grasped. In Adam's words, *"you have to know if there is a truth in the world."* And in the affirmation that "others have been permitted" to know that truth, he wonders whether it will be vouchsafed to him. It is not Warren's contention here that if the contingencies of existence and of knowledge are such that man cannot fully conquer history through an act of will based on understanding, man's nature is so ordered that it will not allow history to conquer life?

II

This interpretation of Warren's escape from historicism anticipates conclusions that are related to the wholeness of his endeavor. When indicating something of his philosophical unity in brief space, the temptation to take refuge in digression is great because Warren's fictional materials are extraordinarily rich, complex, and fraught with the tortuousness of life itself. As Heilman puts it: "the total effect is one of a manically exhaustive ripping apart of excuses, justifications, defenses, ruses, consolations; of a furious burrowing into ever deeper layers of self-understanding until almost every clarity becomes a puzzle and every dependability a delusion."[5]

The following remarks run a risk of oversimplification because in the context no satisfactory attempt can be made to examine the methods of the literary artistry through which Warren embodies and embellishes his philosophical themes. What is offered is an abstraction of the basic problems with which he comes to grips, the logical connection of these problems, and some suggestions about the way in which he tentatively resolves them.

The striking feature of Warren's effort is the tremendous scope of his quest; for his concern is nothing less than the perennial problems of philosophy. If, because of his intense application to the fundamental questions of being, good and evil, knowledge, and justice, Warren sometimes fails, in Jamesian terms, to make the most of his *donnée* as a novelist, it is a noble failure.

The central problem—the core of Warren's burden—is the self-understanding or self-identity of the individual. The theme does not just hover around the action in the novels; practically every central character and many of the supporting ones raise it specifically to themselves or to others in the form of the direct question, "Who or what am I?" Nor is the problem of being raised in the abstract. The issue invariably arises in the mind of the sensitive, introspective hero or heroine as a result of a dramatic moral confrontation. The problem of being is brought to the surface of conscious-

[5]P. 109.

ness by the direct experience of evil; the awareness of one's own participation in evil forces the demand for self-recognition in the search for the good. The beginning of wisdom is the rational perception of the internal conflict between good and evil. The irony in Warren's novels arises because the confrontation so often occurs after it is too late to rectify the damages that have been done to one's self and to others. The understanding which results is that the individual must assume responsibility for his actions even when they were taken without awareness of either the moral issues involved or the practical consequences that these issues entailed. Only when this understanding is reached is it possible to perceive the limitations of both human action and human knowledge; and these limits, inherent in the nature of an imperfect world, define the rational bounds within which the means to human ends should be confined.

The historic implications are inseparable from these individual themes. The moral confrontation which motivates the inquiry into self-identity is contact with the world. Initial contact with the world does not ordinarily set off self-inquiry, although it may produce a self-interpretation or primitive mythic self-projection. All of us live in a world peopled by other human beings possessed by passions, moved by wills, and handicapped by the limitations of knowledge. Warren's highly differentiated characters are seldom merely allegorical figures, but it may be helpful to outline the broad range of moral types in his novels and suggest something of their relation to the world of evil and potential good.

At the bottom of the list are those characters so dominated by pride that they appear to be altogether lacking in moral sensitivity. These amoralists are the real villains in Warren's dramatic structures, or as some allege, in some of his lapses into melodrama. The prominent examples are Bogan Murdock, in *At Heaven's Gate,* and Jeremiah Beaumont's friend Wilkie Barron, in *World Enough and Time.* In their unalloyed egotism they have so completely embraced the corruption of the world that they have foreclosed the possibility of regenerative self-understanding. Devoid of all sense of responsibility and incapable of any love other than projected self-love, they either justify or even do not feel the need to justify their most capricious actions and the evils produced by the calculated means to their ends. Even in these cases the world exacts a justice that Warren leaves as devoid of explanation in human terms as Murdock and Barron are barren of internal life; Murdock's anticipated ruin and Barron's suicide are simply facts corresponding to the abstract inevitabilities of the world.

A second moral dimension is revealed in characters such as Percy Munn, in *Night Rider;* Willie Stark, in *All the King's Men;* and Jeremiah Beaumont, in *World Enough and Time.* These are characters who are made forcibly aware of external evil and the injustices of the world. Their common moral defect, presumably the one which afflicts most of mankind, is failure to grasp the relation between the evils of the world and the inner conflict between good and evil in the individual. Self-identification, or mythical self-projection, takes the form of the avenger or rectifier of perceiver wrongs. Starting with the erroneous conviction noted in *World Enough and Time* that "the idea in and of itself might redeem the world..." such a character moves to a second error expressed in the notion that "the world must redeem the idea." An act of will based on this moral necessity thrusts him into the use of "the means of the natural world, and its dark ways, to gain that end he names holy by the idea, and ah! the terror of that, the terror of that."

In the act of rebellion against the evils of the world, the moral type obsessed with the ideal cf total human justice or perfection loses the possibility of a true sense of self-identification. In this loss he connives at the corruption of his own ends through the unselective adoption of the world's means, and he contributes to his personal corruption and eventual destruction through the identification of himself with the idea to an extent which permits him to act entirely outside any moral restraints. He identifies his individual will with the absolute; in his angry virtue he excuses and justifies all. With Willie Stark the actions which result are not wholly destructive; the evils that he sees are real and he does not overly romanticize trivial or uncertain injustices in the manner of Jeremiah Beaumont. Stark's motives are not initially corrupt and his capacity for political action is not without potentiality for good. This potentiality rapidly dissipates, however, in the self-delusion which deadens the awareness of an internal personal conflict between good and evil.

The third type may be identified as Warren's modest version of the Aristotelian *spoudaios,* the morally mature man whose excellence introduces order into society. In Warren's treatment this is the prototypical character who has gone beyond the easy naturalistic openness to good and evil, has had some experience of the obsession with the "idea," and has confronted, without accompanying delusion or external projection, the dilemmas of existence, the universal tension between evil and good, the limits of human understanding, and the awesome burden of responsibility. The response to the moral confrontation in this type is a correct one with neither a turning to the "blank cup of nature" in search of innocence nor an act of willful rebellion against the evil of the world. Finally, the attainment of the limited wisdom open to man does not force a retreat from the world, but demands that the life of action continue. Warren's affirmation of objective good, even though only limitedly attainable in the world, is the variously reiterated injunction against fleeing inward "into the ironies of history and knowledge, into that wisdom which is resignation." If the idea cannot redeem the world or the world the idea, neither can the attempt to realize some relation between the two be abandoned.

In *The Cave* Warren makes a dramatic adaptation of the famous Platonic parable. Plato used the symbol of the cave to illustrate the limited vision of reality open to most of humanity and the self-closure against the potentiality of a larger vision represented by the person who had been permitted to turn from the cave toward the light. Warren reverses this use of the cave symbol. In the novel, Jasper Harrick, a young backwoods Tennessee war hero, a "cave-crawler" to get away from the world and establish self-identity, is trapped in a cave. The ordeal of the attempted rescue culminates in the creation of a heroic myth whose effect on a variety of characters is developed in contrapuntal form. The heroic qualities of the myth, while founded on a falsehood contrived for worldly benefit, touch the core of reality. And through the common trauma of participation in the myth, each of the central characters, except for the doomed Isaac Sumpter, is brought to the recognition of his hitherto sublimated moral conflict, and from this recognition comes an enlarged capacity for fulfilling his obligations to himself and to the limited circle directly affected by his actions. *The Cave* is Warren's most ambitious attempt to explore the essentially private implications of the moral dilemma in its multifold variations.

If *The Cave* is an exploration of the private aspect of the unfolding of fully developed moral character, *All the King's Men* is the definitive examination of the political implications of the search for self-understanding, obligation, and justice. Jack Burden, uneasy in the limited possibilities offered by his southern elite social heritage, becomes involved in Willie Stark's rebellion against the historical accretion of power symbolized by Burden's Landing. The combination of Stark's example as a political activist and Burden's participation in Stark's activities leads to personal tragedy which forces Burden to look inward for meaning to achieve the identity he has been seeking. The problem of action is resolved neither by naturalism nor by a genteel resignation which repudiates the world. Instead a morally mature Burden prepares to return to politics with the broader perspective and the more limited aspiration of his experience with history and a recognition of the unforeseen consequences of a blind striking out for the idea of justice.

III

But what is the relation of Warren the historian to all of this? *The Legacy of the Civil War* in a sense brings Warren full circle. The biography of John Brown launched him into the imaginative exploration of certain basic themes in Brown's character and actions, within the historical circumstances which influenced Brown and were reciprocally influenced by him. These include practically all of the philosophical elements of the novels:

the lonely search for self-identity, the compromise with the world, the commitment to the idea which justifies great evil in the name of the absolute elimination of evil, the irony of history whereby man sometimes reaches heroic proportions in a frame of action that is nonsensical, and the creation out of historical incidents of myths by which men live and die, myths whose components range over the whole scale of good and evil, of truth and falsehood, of reality and delusion. The novels explore these problems from the standpoint of universal man, mainly through the application to historical incidents of the intuitive insights and dramatic skills of the novelist, for well-handled fiction can evoke the sense of personal participation in event and plausibility of internal cause in a manner that is beyond the limits of the historian's materials and function. In *The Legacy of the Civil War*, Warren turns back to a commentary on history from the standpoint of philosophical understanding matured through the incarnation of individual and historical motivation in novel form. This little book is a summing up of Warren's reflection on man's universal problems within the particular context of American history. The themes are familiar to readers of the novels; now they are stated with the incisiveness of the thinker who has used all of his skills to master his materials through painstaking investigation and analysis.

With his opening sentence, *"The Civil War* is, for the American imagination, the greatest single event in our history,"* Warren joins the issue. In his view, "The Civil War is our only felt history— history lived in the national imagination"; before the war there was no American history in the "deepest and most inward sense." Apart from the important external facts of saving the South for the Union, freeing the slaves, and setting the nation on the new course of industrialism, what were its effects?

The first effect is the contribution of the war to the pragmatic bias of the nation. At first sight it may appear strange that Warren should embrace so morally neutral a doctrine as pragmatism. However, a reading in context reveals that this pragmatism is related less to a total relativity of existence than to the factors which limit the means to human ends, a theme much in evidence in the novels. Warren quotes with obvious approval the characterizations of Lincoln's pragmatism by T. Harry Williams and Sidney Hook. The former notes that "His [Lincoln's] personal or inner opinions were based on principle; his public or outer opinions were tempered by empiricism," while Hook indicates that Lincoln's course of action consisted in being "principled without being fanatical, and flexible without being opportunistic. ..."

American pragmatism, fostered by the Civil War, is a response to the two absolutes whose collision was an essential factor in the coming of the war, the "higher law" and "legalism." These designations apply respectively to puritan, fanatical abolitionism, and to the rigid adherence of the slaveholders to the minor logic of legal instruments in defiance of all major logic. The "higher law" men, with their corner on truth by reason of divine revelation, end by denying the very concept of society in the name of absolute idea. If these men completely repudiated society in the name of an individual purity of conscience which rejected all responsibility, the legalists of the South denied the concept of life in the society which they sought to vindicate by refusing to allow, "through the inductive scrutiny of fact, for change, for the working of the life process through history." The transcendentalists repudiated social institutions; the South repudiated criticism. Both absolutes were accompanied by compromises with the world, by hypocrisies, and by self-justifications and internal contradictions.

As a result of the head-on conflict of the ideologies, and the eventual catastrophe that their rigidities promoted, Americans learned the political lesson that "logical parties may lead logically to logical shooting, and they had had enough of that." Through violent experience they learned respect for the non-logical arrangement of political parties and politics. Warren conveys the idea that politics is best conceived as the application of common sense to issues which arise within a working political tradition with the rationality of experience behind it. No one is absolutely satisfied with the settlement, but no one is committed to the destruction of the system through which the settlement was reached. Here is a pragmatism of political means without a total rejection of objective standards.

If the war brought certain benefits to the psychology of Americans, it also levied some psychological costs. Warren notes that these costs were different for the two sides and sums up these differences in two labels which he attaches to the respective attitudes. For the South the war produced the "Great Alibi," and to the North it gave the "Treasury of Virtue." "By the Great Alibi the South explains, condones and transmutes everything.... By the Great Alibi pellagra, hookworms, and illiteracy are all explained.... Laziness becomes the aesthetic sense, blood-lust rising from a matrix of boredom and resentful misery becomes a high sense of honor, and ignorance becomes divine revelation.... By the Great Alibi the Southerner makes his big medicine. He turns defeat into victory, defects into virtues."

The Great Alibi has broadest application to the race issue. Seeing the situation as one in which history has trapped him, the southerner is powerless to confront the internal conflict that arises from his treatment of the Negro as something other than human. This moral quandary is the focus of Warren's earlier short book on *Segregation*, appropriately subtitled "The Inner Conflict in the South." *Segregation* is Warren's interview with the people of the South in an attempt to bring the conflict to the level of consciousness and to achieve a rational self-identity which may free the South from the mental and moral paralysis induced by the ironies of history and the uses of self-justification to which these ironies may be put. In the delineation of the Great Alibi he returns to the problem of the debasement of the noble and courageous elements in southern history by the obscene parody on that history reflected in contemporary racial incidents. Warren asks, "Can the man howling in the mob imagine General R. E. Lee, CSA, shaking hands with Orval Faubus, Governor of Arkansas?"

If, according to the Great Alibi, the southerner is trapped by history, the northerner is automatically redeemed because history has conferred the Treasury of Virtue on him, and with it "a plenary indulgence...for all sins past, present and future." Forgotten and forgiven is the culpability that the North shares with the South for the war; excused, too, are the failures of responsibility to act on avowed principles in regard to race and the Union. The North also avoided the internal moral struggle in the puritanical acceptance of external success as a sign of monopolized virtue. Like the race issue in the South, the Treasury of Virtue continues to be a corruptor which takes the form of "moral narcissism." American illusions of national innocence and virtue have produced a self-righteousness in relation to internal and foreign policy which enables us to condemn others and suggest the means to their spiritual regeneration with no apparent awareness that our own souls may be in jeopardy.

One recognizes in this brief summary of Warren's fully developed and image-dominated presentation of the symbols of American self-interpretation the ubiquity of the problem of the refuges available to those who refuse to confront the moral difficulties of existence and the consequences which flow from evasion of responsibility. The negative function of the myth is also made more precise at this point, for Warren asserts that, even though the Great Alibi and the Treasury of Virtue both serve deep needs of human nature, in the absence of historical realism and criticism they merely help compound the "old inherited delusions which our weakness craves."

There are, on the other hand, positive functions of the symbolic myth, because the war furnishes an image of life which condenses many kinds of meanings. The first of its offerings is a

> gallery of great human images for our contemplation..., a dazzling array of figures, noble in proportion yet human, caught out of Time as in a frieze, in stances so profoundly touching or powerfully mythic that they move us in a way no mere consideration of "historical importance" ever could. ... This was our Homeric period, and the figures loom up only a little less than gods, but even so, we recognize the lineaments and passions of men, and by that recognition of common kinship share in their grandeur.

The interest and meaning go deeper, for the war revealed a starkly realistic inner conflict. Despite southern nationalism and southern preference for the "War Between the States," the Civil War was, after all, a civil war. The ambivalence of love and hate, the guilts and the self-division "within individuals becomes a series of mirrors in which the plight of the country is reflected, and the self-division of the country a great mirror in which the individual may see imaged his own deep conflicts...." The inwardness of the experience of the Civil War, both in individuals and in the nation, constitutes the drama which painfully forces self-identification and furnishes experiential possibility for acting on a different level of rationality. Here again is the central theme of the search for identity, followed by a moral confrontation forced by tragedy, and eventuating in a moral awareness which provides the potential for matured self-interpretation.

The internal divisions were present in both sectors, but the South confronted a greater moral dilemma than the North because it had to deny so many of the things it shared with the North to confirm its slaveholding identity. The South shared not only adherence to the Union, but the "universalist conception of freedom based on natural law..., Jacksonian democracy and Christian doctrine...." In this brief list Warren affirms that the American tradition embodies a measure of objective moral good. If this interpretation is correct, Warren's seemingly ambivalent emphasis of pragmatism is clarified, because the limitations of existence require acceptance of pragmatic action within the framework of a prevailing tradition which experience has confirmed as good. The attempt to transmute that good into perfection by forcibly attacking the institutions through which it is effected and the counter-attempt to repudiate the obligations that the tradition imposes are both acts of destruction. Proper action is limited to the pragmatic attempt to realize the tradition more fully as our failings and shortcomings are manifested in history. As Warren had previously made clear in *Segregation:* "Gradualism is all you'll get. History, like nature, knows no jumps. Except the jump backward, maybe."

In the larger sense neither the evitability nor the inevitability theory of the Civil War is historically important, for both can work to the same happy end of diminishing guilt. The experience itself and what we make of it is the important thing. In a phrase which recalls the full import of the novels, Warren notes that we should "seek to end the obscene gratifications of history, and try to learn what the contemplation of the past, conducted with psychological depth and humane breadth, can do for us." While history cannot give us a program for the future, it "may help us to understand, even to frame, the logic of experience to which we shall submit...; it can give us a fuller understanding of ourselves, and of our common humanity, so that we can better face the future."

The Civil War was a tragedy. "It is the story of a crime of monstrous inhumanity, into which almost innocently men stumbled...." The entanglements increased until the powers of reason and its virtues were perverted, but, ironically and redeemingly, nobility could still be discerned through the murk, and in the conclusion there is "a reconciliation by human recog-

nition." We have not, however, been adequately instructed by that "catharsis of pity and terror. ..." We have not achieved justice, created a full sense
of community, or resolved our deep dubieties or self-deceptions. "In other
words, we are sadly human, and in our contemplation of the Civil War we
see a dramatization of our humanity. ..." Beyond all of the false comfort we
may derive from the event—the satisfactions of rancor, self-righteousness,
spite, pride, armchair blood lust, and complacency—"we can yet see in the
Civil War an image of the powerful, painful, grinding process by which an
ideal emerges out of history." This should teach us humility and at the same
time draw us "to the glory of the human effort to win meaning from the
complex and confused motives of men and the blind ruck of event." So
much for the bare bone summary of Warren's moving and profound reaf-
firmation of the historical meaning conveyed by the Civil War.

IV

At the outset of this essay the question was raised whether, in uniting
philosophical concerns, fiction, and history, Warren is engaged in a valid
function. Alfred Kazin recently pinpointed the problem in a decidedly
negative review of *The Legacy of the Civil War*.[6] Kazin's treatment is el-
liptical, for the argument is by implication *ad hominem,* in the apparent
attempt to avoid direct commitment to consideration of the philosophical
problems that Warren poses. Running through the entire review—starting
with the title, "City of the Soul," a phrase Warren uses to delineate the
southern ethos—is a rebuke to Warren for being a southerner and for taking the primordial struggle of the South seriously. An answer to this form
of criticism can be offered in terms of Warren's own categories. The psychology of the "Treasury of Virtue" obviously has such a strong hold on Kazin
that in his identification with the war's outcome he has overlooked the
shoddiness that accompanies all real socially beneficial change.

Kazin petulantly complains that he cannot see anything new in the book
and expresses wonder "that Warren can take up so cursorily a subject that
requires so much detailed handling." Words cannot be minced in regard to
this statement: it is made either as part of a pattern of deliberate obscurant-
ism or is arrant nonsense. *The Legacy of the Civil War* is a lesson in the
sources pertinent to the interpretation of the war's meaning. Warren's obvious acquaintance with historical literature, his choice of quotations, the
serious attention accorded the book by professional historians, and the earlier research that went into *John Brown* are sufficient testimony to the tech-

---

[6]*The Reporter,* XXIV (June 8, 1961), 40, 42-44. For a devastating rebuttal see Louis D. Rubin,
Jr., "Theories of Human Nature: Kazin or Warren?," *The Sewanee Review,* LXIX (1961), 501.

nical competence of the author.[7] By no means a cursory handling of an enormous subject, Warren's discussion is a distillation of more than thirty years of research and soul-searching reflection on American history. His compact is a calm philosophical summing up of a system of ideas which has been mastered and refined by prodigious mental and moral effort.

Kazin's central objection is to Warren's philosophical orientation. He agrees with the emphasis on pragmatism, but he sees in Warren's sudden enthusiasm for the term "what it is about his novels and poems that so often bothers me." In his view Warren is too much concerned with *theories* of human nature to be a good novelist or poet. These theories ought not to interest a novelist so much, for "the truth is that no matter what philosophy of life a novelist may claim, no matter how astringent or realistic or 'pragmatic' he may set himself up to be, literature itself consists in saying 'Yes' to life—not just to the 'open' life that Warren praises, but to the life in every man. ...."

The naturalism which Kazin espouses in opposition to Warren's dedication to ideas may very well be the literary man's synonym for the social scientist's affinity with "behaviorism." If so, I must take my stand with Warren, who looks for meaning not solely to the external record of man but to his internal capacity for feeling, thinking, willing, and acting. The philosophical problems of existence, purpose, good and evil, truth, justice, freedom and determinism, human limits and potentiality, and their tentative resolution have been the central concerns of the philosophical and religious traditions of this civilization and of its greatest literary expressions. If history is more than an interest in antique gossip, literature more than an elegant rendition of an emotive reaction to external stimuli, and both history and literature more than the "register of the crimes, follies, and misfortunes of mankind," neither the historian nor the novelist can afford to ignore such questions.

[7]See Heilman (p. 108) for a testimonial to Warren's care in handling historical problems.

1905 Born April 24 in Guthrie, Kentucky, where he lived, in a house on the edge of the village, until the age of fifteen. The eldest son of a businessman and a schoolteacher, he learned a great deal about the Civil War and Southern history from his maternal grandfather, who had been a cavalry officer under Bedford Forrest. The grandfather, a tobacco farmer, was also fond of quoting poetry to the boy.

1921 Graduated from Clarksville, Tennessee, High School. Warren had received an appointment to Annapolis, but before he could begin his studies for a naval career, he was blinded in one eye in an accident. Instead, he entered Vanderbilt University, Nashville, Tennessee. His original plan was to study chemical engineering, but he found literature more interesting. Among his English teachers were the poets John Crowe Ransom and Donald Davidson (for whose classes Warren wrote his first poetry at college), and Allen Tate was a fellow student. Soon after he arrived, he joined the Blue Pencil, a writing club for freshmen and sophomores; later, he helped to organize the Verse Guild, a group within the writing club devoted to poetry.

1923 The Verse Guild published a small pamphlet, *Driftwood Flames,* in which five of Warren's poems appeared. Warren's first poem for *The Fugitive* included in the June, 1923 issue: called "Crusade," it consists of the recollections of a soldier serving Count Raymond of Provence, on the night following the capture of Jerusalem. Began attending the meetings of the "Fugitive" group (at which Warren tended to align himself on the "modernist" side, with Tate).

1924 First review published in *Voices* IV (November 1924), 24-25, on Ransom's *Chills and Fever.* Warren later said of Ransom's first volume, *Poems About God* (1919), that it "opened my eyes to the fact of poetry in, even, the literal world."

1925 Graduated *summa cum laude* from Vanderbilt. Began graduate study, as a teaching fellow in English, at the University of California, Berkeley. Studied primarily Elizabethan tragedy and sixteenth- and seventeenth-century poetry. Became engaged to Emma Brescia of San Francisco.

1927   Received master's degree from the University of California. Began graduate work at Yale University. Tate helped Warren obtain a contract for a book on John Brown, and, through Tate, Warren met Katherine Anne Porter, Ford Madox Ford, and Caroline Gordon, with whom he had his first detailed talks about the craft of fiction.

1928   Entered Oxford University as a Rhodes Scholar (B. Litt., 1930).

1929   *John Brown: The Making of a Martyr* published.

1930   Contributed an essay (written while at Oxford), "The Briar Patch" to *"I'll Take My Stand: The South and the Agrarian Tradition* by "Twelve Southerners." Married Emma Brescia. Assistant Professor of English, Southwestern College, Memphis, Tennessee.

1931   Assistant Professor of English, Vanderbilt. "Prime Leaf," Warren's first published fiction, in *American Caravan* edited by Van Wyck Brooks, Paul Rosenfeld, and Lewis Mumford. Commissioned by Rosenfeld and written while Warren was at Oxford, it is set during the "tobacco wars" in Kentucky.

1933   Completed a novel, "God's Own Time," set in Kentucky in 1910-1914. A second, untitled novel begun, and finished in 1935, also set in Kentucky. Both novels rejected by publishers.

1934   Assistant Professor of English, Louisiana State University.

1935   *Thirty-Six Poems.* Founded *Southern Review* with Cleanth Brooks, Charles W. Pipkin, and Albert Erskine (late vice-president of Random House, Inc., and Warren's editor for thirty years).

1936   *An Approach to Literature* (edited, with Cleanth Brooks and John T. Purser). Awarded a Houghton Mifflin Literary Fellowship to enable him to write the book which later became *Night Rider.*

1937   *A Southern Harvest: Short Stories by Southern Writers* (edited).

1938   *Understanding Poetry* (edited, with Brooks).

1939   *Night Rider.* Awarded first Guggenheim Fellowship, which enabled him to spend the academic year 1939-1940 in Italy. Wrote verse play, "Proud Flesh," about a Southern dictator,

Governor Talos, the prototype of Willie Stark in *All the King's Men*. Unpublished. First performance, 1946. Withdrawn, after a large number of performances by little theaters and university theaters, because of general corruption of text.

1942   *Eleven Poems on the Same Theme.* Professor of English at the University of Minnesota.

1943   *At Heaven's Gate. Understanding Fiction* (edited, with Brooks).

1944   *Selected Poems 1923-1943.* Consultant in Poetry, Library of Congress, 1944-1945. While there, Katherine Anne Porter showed him material dealing with the 1826 murder trial of Jeroboam Beauchamp, which was to become the basis of *World Enough and Time.*

1946   *All the King's Men,* for which Warren was awarded the Pulitzer Prize for fiction in 1947. *Blackberry Winter.*

1947   *The Circus in the Attic, and Other Stories.* Awarded second Guggenheim Fellowship. Adapted stage play from the novel *All the King's Men.* Directed by Irwin Piscator at the President Theatre, New York, in 1948. Later translated and produced in Germany.

1949   *Modern Rhetoric, with Readings* (edited, with Brooks); published also, without readings, as *Fundamentals of Good Writing: A Handbook of Modern Rhetoric.* First honorary degree, awarded by the University of Louisville, Kentucky.

1950   *World Enough and Time: A Romantic Novel.* Professor of Playwriting, Yale Drama School.

1951   Divorced Emma Brescia.

1952   Married Eleanor Clark (by whom he has had two children, Rosanna and Gabriel). Elected to the American Philosophical Society.

1953   *Brother to Dragons: A Tale in Verse and Voices. The Southern Review* (anthology, edited with Brooks).

1954   *Short Story Masterpieces* (edited, with Albert Erskine).

1955   *Band of Angels. Six Centuries of Great Poetry* (edited, with Erskine).

1956   *Segregation: The Inner Conflict in the South* (originally in *Life* Magazine).

1957   *Promises: Poems 1954-1956*, for which Warren was awarded the Pulitzer Prize for poetry, the Edna St. Vincent Millay Prize of the Poetry Society in America, and the National Book Award in 1958. *A New Southern Harvest* (edited, with Erskine).

1958   *Selected Essays. Remember the Alamo!* (children's book).

1959   *The Cave. The Gods of Mount Olympus* (children's book). Elected to the American Academy of Arts and Letters. New version of "All the King's Men" (play) at 74th Street Theatre, New York. This version was also produced in Poland and Russia.

1960   *You, Emperors and Others: Poems 1957-1960. All the King's Men* (play). Première as "Willie Stark: His Rise and Fall."

1961   *Wilderness: A Tale of the Civil War. The Legacy of the Civil War.* Professor of English, Yale University.

1964   *Flood: A Romance of Our Time.*

1965   *Who Speaks for the Negro?* (originally in *Look* Magazine). Dramatized version of *Brother to Dragons* produced in Seattle and at the American Place Theatre, New York, and then, after revisions, elsewhere in the United States.

1966   *Selected Poems: New and Old 1923-1966*, for which Warren was awarded the Bollingen Prize in Poetry in 1967. *Faulkner: A Collection of Critical Essays* (edited).

1968   *Incarnations: Poems 1966-1968.* Grant from the National Endowment for the Arts.

1969   *Audubon: A Vision*, for which Warren was awarded the Van Wyck Brooks Award in 1970.

1970   *Selected Poems of Herman Melville* (edited). National Medal for Literature, in recognition of Warren's total contribution to the world of letters.

1971   *Meet Me in the Green Glen. Homage to Theodore Dreiser on the Centennial of His Birth. John Greenleaf Whittier: An Appraisal and a Selection* (edited).

1973   *American Literature: The Makers and the Making* (edited, with Brooks and R.W.B. Lewis). Professor Emeritus, Yale University.

1974   *Or Else: Poem/Poems 1968-1974.* Chosen by the National Endowment for the Humanities to deliver the third Annual Jefferson Lecture in the Humanities.

1975   *Democracy and Poetry* (Jefferson Lecture). Elected to the American Academy of Arts and Sciences and received from it the Emerson-Thoreau Award.

1976   *Selected Poems: 1923-1975.* Copernicus Award from the Academy of American Poets, in recognition of Warren's general achievement but with special reference to *Or Else*.

1977   *A Place to Come To.*

1978   *Now and Then: Poems 1976-1978.*

1979   *Brother to Dragons: A Tale in Verse and Voices* (rewritten version of the poem).

Notes on the Editor and Authors

RICHARD GRAY, the editor of this volume, is Senior Lecturer in the Department of Literature at the University of Essex, England. He has edited two anthologies, *American Verse of the Nineteenth Century* and *American Poetry of the Twentieth Century*, and is the author of *The Literature of Memory: Modern Writers of the American South.*

ROBERT BERNER, Associate Professor of English at the University of Wisconsin, has written articles for *Western American Literature, The Explicator, Books Abroad,* and *Southern Quarterly.* At present, he is completing a study of the works-grace distinction of the New England covenant theology as a persistent theme in American literature.

CLEANTH BROOKS, Gray Professor of Rhetoric Emeritus at Yale University, has collaborated with Warren on a number of books, including *Understanding Poetry* and *Understanding Fiction.* Among his other works are *Modern Poetry and the Tradition, The Well Wrought Urn, William Faulkner: The Yoknapatawpha Country,* and *William Faulkner: Toward Yoknapatawpha and Beyond.*

LEONARD CASPER, Professor of American Studies and creative writing at Boston College, is author of *Robert Penn Warren: The Dark and Bloody Ground* as well as recent essays on Warren, Flannery O'Connor, and Tennessee Williams. A collection of his stories, *A Lion Unannounced,* was a National Council on the Arts selection.

BARNETT GUTTENBERG is Associate Professor of English at the University of Miami. He is editor of *Faulkner Studies* and author of *Web of Being: The Novels of Robert Penn Warren.* He has also written articles on Joseph Conrad, Sylvia Plath, and James Dickey.

WILLIAM C. HAVARD, Professor and Dean of the College of Arts and Sciences at Virginia Polytechnic Institute and State University, is editor of the *Journal of Politics.* His books include *The Government and Politics of the United States* and *Institutions and Politics of American Government.*

JOHN HICKS retired in 1975 as Professor Emeritus at Southern Methodist University and Dean Emeritus of the University College. For eight years, he was chairman of the Division of Comparative Arts in Meadows School of Arts, and at the time his essay on Warren was prepared he was national Executive Director of the College English Association.

JAMES H. JUSTUS, Professor of English at the University of Indiana, is in the process of completing a book on Warren. He has also written essays on Kate Chopin, Stark Young, and John Crowe Ransom.

FREDERICK P.W. McDOWELL is Professor of English at the University of Iowa. He is the author of *Ellen Glasgow and the Ironic Art of Fiction,* as well as books on Elizabeth Madox Roberts, Caroline Gordon, and E.M. Forster. He has also written extensively on George Bernard Shaw and Virginia Woolf.

ARTHUR MIZENER is Mellon Professor of Humanities Emeritus at Cornell University. His books include *The Far Side of Paradise: A Biography of F. Scott Fitzgerald, The Sense of Life in the Modern Novel, The Saddest Story: A Critical Biography of Ford Madox Ford,* and *Scott Fitzgerald and His World.*

STANLEY PLUMLY teaches at Columbia University. His last book of poems, *Out-of-the-Body Travel,* was nominated for a National Book Critics Circle Award. At present, he is working on a new book of poems, and a book of prose entitled *Chapter and Verse.*

ALVAN S. RYAN is Professor Emeritus at the University of Massachusetts. In addition to his work on Warren, he has published essays on Orestes Brownson, Carlyle, Emerson, Newman, Hopkins, Frost, and T.S. Eliot, and has edited *The Brownson Reader.*

ALLEN SHEPHERD, Professor of English at the University of Vermont, is the author of numerous essays on Warren. He has recently written pieces on several other Southern writers, including Eudora Welty, Harry Crews, and Reynolds Price.

VICTOR STRANDBERG teaches at Duke University. In addition to his two books on Warren, he has written a number of articles on Whitman, T.S. Eliot, and Faulkner. He has just completed a study correlating some thirty American writers with the thought of William James, and he is at present preparing a book on Faulkner.

TJEBBE WESTENDORP, a former A.C.L.S. fellow and Visiting Professor at the University of North Carolina, teaches English and American literature at the University of Leiden. He has published essays on Reynolds Price, James Dickey, and the literature of war, and is now writing a book on Warren.

Selected Bibliography

Bibliographies

Grimshaw Jr., James A., *Robert Penn Warren: A Descriptive Bibliography 1917-1978*. Charlottesville: University of Virginia Press, forthcoming.

Huff, Mary N., *Robert Penn Warren: A Bibliography*. New York: David Lewis, 1968.

Strandberg, Victor, "Robert Penn Warren", in *A Bibliographical Guide to the Study of Southern Literature* edited by Louis D. Rubin Jr. Baton Rouge: Louisiana State University Press, 1969.

Also, Spiller, Robert E. and others, eds. *Literary History of the United States*, 3rd ed. New York: The Macmillan Company, 1963, with supplement, 1970; and Woodress, James, and J. Albert Robbins, eds. *American Literary Scholarship (1963-)*. Durham, N.C.: Duke University Press, 1965-

Interviews and Conversations

Ellison, Ralph, and Eugene Walter, "The Art of Fiction, XVIII: Robert Penn Warren," *Paris Review*, 4 (Spring-Summer 1957), 112-40. Reprinted in *Writers at Work: The Paris Review Interviews*, ed. Malcolm Cowley, New York: Viking Press, 1958.

Fisher, Ruth, "A Conversation with Robert Penn Warren," *Four Quarters*, 21 (Spring 1972), 3-17.

Gadp, Frank, ed. "Robert Penn Warren," in *First Person: Conversations with Novelists on Writers and Writing*. Schenectady: Union College Press, 1973.

Purdy, Rob Roy, ed., *Fugitive Reunion: Conversations at Vanderbilt*. Nashville: Vanderbilt University Press, 1959.

Sale, Richard B., "An Interview in New Haven with Robert Penn Warren," *Studies in the Novel*, 2 (1970), 325-54.

Stitt, Peter, "An Interview with Robert Penn Warren," *Sewanee Review,* 85 (Summer 1977), 467-77.

"The Uses of History in Fiction," from *Proceedings of the Thirty-Fourth Annual Meeting of the Southern Historical Association,* New Orleans, November 6, 1968.

Walker, Marshall, "Robert Penn Warren: An Interview," *Journal of American Studies,* 8 (Spring 1974), 229-45.

Special Issues

Folio (Symposium on *All The King's Men),* 15 (May 1950), 2-22.

Four Quarters (Special Robert Penn Warren Number) (Spring 1972), 3-122.

Modern Fiction Studies (Special Robert Penn Warren Number), 6 (Spring 1960), 3-88.

Ohio Review (Special Robert Penn Warren Feature) 18 (Winter 1977), 30-74.

South Atlantic Quarterly (Symposium on Robert Penn Warren), 62 (1963), 488-531.

Books and Pamphlets on Warren

Beebe, Maurice, and Leslie A. Field, eds., *"All the King's Men": A Critical Handbook,* Belmont, Calif.: Wadsworth Publishing Company, 1966.

Bohner, Charles H., *Robert Penn Warren.* Twayne United States Authors Series. New York: Twayne Publishers, 1964.

Casper, Leonard, *Robert Penn Warren: The Dark and Bloody Ground.* Seattle: University of Washington Press, 1960.

Chambers, Robert, ed., *Twentieth Century Interpretations of "All the King's Men."* Twentieth Century Interpretations Series. Englewood Cliffs, N.J.: Prentice-Hall, Inc., 1973.

Guttenberg, Barnett, *Web of Being: The Novels of Robert Penn Warren.* Nashville: Vanderbilt University Press, 1975.

Light, James F., ed., *The Merrill Studies in "All the King's Men."* Columbus, Ohio: Charles E. Merrill Publishing Company, 1971.

Longley, John L., Jr., *Robert Penn Warren.* Southwest Writers Series. Austin, Texas: Steck-Vaughn Company, 1969.

Longley, John L., Jr., ed., *Robert Penn Warren: A Collection of Critical Essays.* New York: New York University Press, 1965.

Moore, L. Hugh, Jr., *Robert Penn Warren and History: The "Big Myth We Live."* Gravenhage, The Netherlands: Mouton and Company, 1970.

Sochatoff, A. Fred and others, *"All the King's Men": A Symposium.* Carnegie Series in English. Pittsburgh: Carnegie Institute of Technology Press, 1957.

Strandberg, Victor, *A Colder Fire, The Poetry of Robert Penn Warren.* Lexington: University Press of Kentucky, 1965.

————. *The Poetic Vision of Robert Penn Warren.* Lexington; University Press of Kentucky, 1977. (Includes some material from *A Colder Fire.)*

West, Paul, *Robert Penn Warren.* Minnesota Pamphlets on American writers. Minneapolis: University of Minnesota Press, 1964.

Some General Works Containing Chapters on Warren

Baumbach, Jonathan, *The Landscape of Nightmare: Studies in the Contemporary American Novel.* New York: New York University Press, 1965.

Bradbury, John M., *The Fugitives: A Critical Account* Chapel Hill: University of North Carolina Press, 1959.

Brooks, Cleanth, *The Hidden God: Studies in Hemingway, Faulkner, Yeats, Eliot, and Warren.* New Haven: Yale University Press, 1963. (Most of the chapter on Warren is included in this volume.)

Frank, Joseph, *The Widening Gyre: Crisis and Mastery in Modern Literature.* New Brunswick, N.J.: Rutgers University Press, 1963.

Frohock, W.M., *The Novel of Violence in America,* 2nd ed., Dallas: Southern Methodist University Press, 1957.

Gossett, Louise Y., *Violence in Recent Southern Fiction.* Durham, N.C.: Duke University Press, 1965.

Gray, Richard, *The Literature of Memory: Modern Writers of the American South.* Baltimore: The Johns Hopkins University Press, 1977.

Rajan, Balachandra, ed., *Modern American Poetry.* New York: Roy Publishers, n.d. London: Dennis Dobson, 1950.

Rubin Jr., Louis D., *The Faraway Country: Writers of the Modern South.* Seattle: University of Washington Press, 1963.

_____. and Robert D. Jacobs, eds., *South: Modern Southern Literature in Its Cultural Setting*. Garden City, N.Y.: Doubleday and Co., Inc., 1961.

_____. *Southern Renascence: The Literature of the Modern South*. Baltimore: The Johns Hopkins University Press, 1953.

Stewart, John L., *The Burden of Time: The Fugitives and Agrarians*. Princeton, N.J.: Princeton University Press, 1965.

TWENTIETH CENTURY VIEWS

AMERICAN AUTHORS: PUBLISHED

EDWARD ALBEE
edited by C. W. E. Bigsby
SHERWOOD ANDERSON
edited by Walter B. Rideout
JAMES BALDWIN
edited by Keneth Kinnamon
**IMAMU AMIRI BARAKA
(LEROI JONES)**
edited by Kimberly W. Benston
SAUL BELLOW
edited by Earl Rovit
**CONTEMPORARY WOMEN
NOVELISTS**
edited by Patricia Meyer Spacks
JAMES FENIMORE COOPER
edited by Wayne Fields
E. E. CUMMINGS
edited by Norman Friedman
EMILY DICKINSON
edited by Richard B. Sewall
DOS PASSOS
edited by Andrew Hook
DREISER
edited by John Lydenberg
RALPH ELLISON
edited by John Hersey
EMERSON
edited by Milton R. Konvitz
and Stephen E. Whicher
FAULKNER
edited by Robert Penn Warren
F. SCOTT FITZGERALD
edited by Arthur Mizener
BENJAMIN FRANKLIN
edited by Brian M. Barbour
ROBERT FROST
edited by James M. Cox
HAWTHORNE
edited by A. N. Kaul
HEMINGWAY
edited by Robert P. Weeks
HENRY JAMES
edited by Leon Edel
SINCLAIR LEWIS
edited by Mark Schorer
ROBERT LOWELL
edited by Thomas Parkinson
NORMAN MAILER
edited by Leo Braudy
BERNARD MALAMUD
edited by Leslie and Joyce Field

MELVILLE
edited by Richard Chase
ARTHUR MILLER
edited by Robert W. Corrigan
**THE MODERN
AMERICAN THEATER**
edited by Alvin B. Kernan
**MODERN BLACK
NOVELISTS**
edited by M. G. Cooke
MODERN BLACK POETS
edited by Donald B. Gibson
MODERN CHICANO WRITERS
edited by Joseph Sommers
and Tomás Ybarra-Frausto
O'NEILL
edited by John Gassner
ORWELL
edited by Raymond Williams
POE
edited by Robert Regan
KATHERINE ANNE PORTER
edited by Robert Penn Warren
PYNCHON
edited by Edward Mendelson
SCIENCE FICTION
edited by Mark Rose
STEINBECK
edited by Robert Murray Davis
WALLACE STEVENS
edited by Marie Borroff
THOREAU
edited by Sherman Paul
THURBER
edited by Charles S. Holmes
MARK TWAIN
edited by Henry Nash Smith
JOHN UPDIKE
edited by David Thorburn
and Howard Eiland
NATHANAEL WEST
edited by Jay Martin
THE WESTERN
edited by James K. Folsom
EDITH WHARTON
edited by Irving Howe
WHITMAN
edited by Roy Harvey Pearce
TENNESSEE WILLIAMS
edited by Stephen S. Stanton
WILLIAM CARLOS WILLIAMS
edited by J. Hillis Miller
THOMAS WOLFE
edited by Louis D. Rubin, Jr.

TWENTIETH CENTURY VIEWS

TWENTIETH CENTURY VIEWS

European Authors: Published

AESCHYLUS
edited by Marsh H. McCall, Jr.

BAUDELAIRE
edited by Henri Peyre

SAMUEL BECKETT
edited by Martin Esslin

BRECHT
edited by Peter Demetz

CAMUS
edited by Germaine Brée

CERVANTES
edited by Lowry Nelson, Jr.

CHEKHOV
edited by Robert Louis Jackson

DANTE
edited by John Freccero

DOSTOEVSKY
edited by René Wellek

EURIPIDES
edited by Erich Segal

FLAUBERT
edited by Raymond Giraud

GENET
edited by Peter Brooks
and Joseph Halpern

GIDE
edited by David Littlejohn

GOETHE
edited by Victor Lange

HESSE
edited by Theodore Ziolkowski

HOMER
edited by George Steiner
and Robert Fagles

IBSEN
edited by Rolf Fjelde

IONESCO
edited by Rosette C. Lamont

KAFKA
edited by Ronald Gray

LORCA
edited by Manuel Duran

MALRAUX
edited by R. W. B. Lewis

THOMAS MANN
edited by Henry Hatfield

MOLIERE
edited by Jacques Guicharnaud

PASTERNAK
edited by Victor Erlich

PIRANDELLO
edited by Glauco Cambon

PROUST
edited by René Girard

SARTRE
edited by Edith Kern

SOLZHENITSYN
edited by Kathryn B. Feuer

SOPHOCLES
edited by Thomas Woodard

STENDHAL
edited by Victor Brombert

STRINDBERG
edited by Otto Reinert

TOLSTOY
edited by Ralph E. Matlaw

VIRGIL
edited by Steele Commager

VOLTAIRE
edited by William F. Bottiglia

DATE	BORROWER'S NAME	